ASIA-PACIFIC
TRADE AND INVESTMENT REPORT
2014

RECENT TRENDS AND DEVELOPMENTS

United Nations
New York, 2014

ECONOMIC AND SOCIAL COMMISSION FOR ASIA AND THE PACIFIC

ASIA-PACIFIC TRADE AND INVESTMENT REPORT 2014

Recent Trends and Developments

United Nations publication
Sales No. E.15.II.F.2

ISBN: 978-92-1-120682-1
eISBN: 978-92-1-057112-8
ISSN: 2221-500X
ST/ESCAP/2701

For further information on this publication, please contact:
Mr Ravi Ratnayake
Director
Trade and Investment Division
ESCAP, United Nations Building
Rajadamnern Nok Avenue
Bangkok 10200, Thailand
Tel: (+66-2) 288-1902
Fax: (+66-2) 288-1027, 288-3066
e-mail: escap-tid@un.org

Reference to dollars ($) are to United States dollars unless otherwise stated.

A space is used to distinguish thousands and millions.

Where the designation "country or area" appears, it covers countries, territories, cities or areas.

RECENT TRENDS AND DEVELOPMENTS

FOREWORD

Trade and investment have been indispensable driving forces of economic growth in Asia-Pacific economies for more than two decades. Growing exports and rising regional economic integration helped countries in the region to create productive employment and to more widely share the benefits of such growth.

The 2008-2009 global financial crisis, however, provided powerful illustrations of the limitations of this approach. Increased volatility and deepened uncertainties, which continue today, create strong incentives for our region to adjust its model of export-led growth to mitigate the adverse impacts of the external environment. To more fully harness opportunities and improve public welfare, there is a need to exploit newer trade frontiers. Twenty-first century trade and investment offers a renewed opportunity to support and nurture sustainable development.

This edition of ESCAP's Asia-Pacific Trade and Investment Report (APTIR) shows that, while the Asia-Pacific region remains the most dynamic pole of the global economy, growth in trade and investment has yet to return to pre-crisis levels. Regional trade growth weakened in 2013, and in the first half of 2014, and although growth in 2015 is expected to increase to 7 per cent, ongoing uncertainties in global macroeconomic prospects mean this is far from assured.

The lengthy shadows cast by the crisis highlight the need for economic rebalancing. In part, this requires refocusing on domestic value addition of exports, rather than increasing gross exports alone. Regional economies also need to diversify away from dependence on traditional sources of export-demand in Europe and the United States, developing domestic demand and better integrating with other regional economies. In this context, it is encouraging that APTIR 2014 shows consolidated intraregional trade, with more than half of regional exports now directed to other Asia-Pacific countries.

A key finding of the Report however, is that concentrations of exports and imports remain uneven across the region. East and North-East Asia alone accounted for about 60 per cent of both total regional merchandise exports and imports in 2013. In a similar vein, 65 per cent of all services exports from the Asia-Pacific region are attributable to just six economies. This implies that large gaps remain between countries in terms of their trade competitiveness and level of diversification, and that great potential remains still untapped, especially in the services sectors of many countries. The availability of competitive business and trade services, which support industrial exports, is also increasingly essential.

Asia-Pacific attracted $549 billion of foreign direct investment (FDI) in 2013, a rise of 6.6 per cent, accounting for almost 38 per cent of global inflows, yet this was still lower than the global increase and lagged behind other fast-growing regions such as Latin America. On a more positive note, the Report indicates a noticeable diversification in the destination of FDI within the region – with new locations and smaller players now attracting more foreign investors, and on a larger scale.

Intraregional FDI is also expanding in importance, with inflows through mergers and acquisitions totalling more than $153 billion, accounting for almost one third of total regional FDI inflows last year, and also flowing to a diverse range of destinations. Given the importance of foreign investment in transferring technology and generating jobs, this is a promising development and augurs well for deepening global value chains, stimulating higher returns and generating decent jobs.

APTIR 2014 underscores the importance of countries remaining open to imports, and not resorting to unnecessarily trade-restrictive measures. The Report traces a worrying trend of increasingly restrictive measures across the region, dominated by behind-the-border non-tariff measures, many of which have had unintended and detrimental consequences for the region's least developed countries, presenting particular obstacles to small and medium-sized exporters.

Trade facilitation measures can reduce trade costs and boost competitiveness. ESCAP's analysis shows numerous hurdles to trade in the form of inefficient regulations and customs procedures, but encouraging progress is being made in introducing paperless trade and other trade facilitation measures.

Policymakers should take steps to lower barriers to trade. Progress in multilateral negotiations, including effective and speedy implementation of the WTO Trade Facilitation Agreement, would help. Regional trade liberalization agreements can also boost trade and integration, especially if many of the existing agreements can be consolidated. Completion of the Trans-Pacific Partnership and the Regional Comprehensive Economic Partnership as open-ended agreements, for example, could lead to the cancelling or consolidation of as many as 54 separate preferential trade agreements, and vastly simplify the Asia-Pacific "noodle-bowl" problem, while also addressing investment and other barriers to trade.

Asia and the Pacific must lead the way in fostering multilateralism to ensure that trade supports sustainable development and helps to deliver the future of inclusive and sustainable growth we want. The data and analysis in this 2014 Asia-Pacific Trade and Investment Report are valuable inputs to the work being done to mainstream trade considerations in the post-2015 development agenda.

Shamshad Akhtar

Under-Secretary-General of the United Nations and
Executive Secretary, United Nations Economic and Social
Commission for Asia and the Pacific

ACKNOWLEDGEMENTS

The Asia-Pacific Trade and Investment Report (APTIR) 2014 was prepared under the substantive direction and guidance of Ravi Ratnayake, Director, Trade and Investment Division (TID) of the Economic and Social Commission for Asia and the Pacific (ESCAP). The core team of authors led by Mia Mikic, comprised TID staff (in alphabetical order) Witada Anukoonwattaka, Yann Duval, Adam Heal, Soo Hyun Kim, Rajan Ratna, Khan Salehin, Heini Salonen and Tengfei Wang. Many research assistants from the Asia-Pacific Research and Training Network on Trade (ARTNeT) as well as ESCAP interns contributed to the report through: the compilation and tabulation of statistical data; the preparation of country and subregional trade briefs; and undertaking background research and referencing. These were (also in alphabetical order): Maria B. Borda, Panit Buranawijarn, Yisi Chen, Romain Galgani, Daniela García Santibáñez, Alin Horj, Fiona Jing Huang, Benjamin Jourdan, Diana Lee, Teodora Mladenovic, Giovanni Palmioli, Maria Romera, Chorthip Utoktham and Pei Zhao. Several interns and ARTNeT associated researchers assisted ESCAP with the translation of country and subregional trade briefs into national languages for easier and more effective dissemination. These were Sven Callebaut, Mi Jin Choi, Phouphet Kyophilavong, Yuyuan Li, Dionisius Narjoko, Puspa Sharma, Angel Versetti, Enkhbold Voroshilov, Vu Hoang Dat and Mohammad Yunus. Eric Hermouet and Krisana Boonpriroje of the ESCAP Statistics Division and Panjai Limchupong of TID collaborated on the preparation of the trade performance indicator tables available from the ESCAP online statistical database.

We acknowledge with appreciation the efforts of the following peer reviewers for ensuring the quality and relevance of APTIR 2014. Reviewers from ESCAP were: Shuvojit Banerjee, Sudip Basu, and Marko Javorsek. Reviewers from other institutions were: Florian Alburo (CATIF), Zdenek Drabek (independent consultant), Jose Duran (ECLAC), Simon Evenett (St. Gallen University), Selim Raihan (SANEM and University of Dhaka), Srirat Rastapana (Government of Thailand), Xaysomphet Norasingh (Government of the Lao People's Democratic Republic) and Martin Wermelinger (OECD).

Robert Oliver and Adam Heal provided substantive editing of the report, while Charuwan Chongsathien of TID and John Loftus of ESCAP's Editorial Unit performed final checks. The graphic concept, design and layout was originally created by Marie-Ange Sylvain-Holmgren for APTIR 2013 and was used again for this volume under the expert application of Clung Wicha Press Co., Ltd. ESCAP Strategic Communications and Advocacy Section provided support in disseminating and communicating APTIR's finding through media outlets, while Martin Dessart helped with arrangements for timely online publication, making sure APTIR 2014 is accessible by readers worldwide.

CONTENTS

CHAPTER 4 TRADE FACILITATION IN THE ASIA-PACIFIC REGION: A BRIGHT OUTLOOK

CHAPTER 5 LIBERALIZATION OR PROTECTION: TRADE POLICY AT A CROSSROADS

CHAPTER 6 PREFERENTIAL TRADE POLICIES AND AGREEMENTS

BOXES

FIGURES

TABLES

ABBREVIATIONS

AANZFTA	ASEAN-Australia-New Zealand Free Trade Agreement
ADB	Asian Development Bank
AEC	ASEAN Economic Community
AEO	authorized economic operators
APEC	Asia-Pacific Economic Cooperation
APTA	Asia-Pacific Trade Agreement
APTIAD	Asia-Pacific Trade and Investment Agreements Database
ARTNeT	Asia-Pacific Research and Training Network on Trade
ASEAN	Association of Southeast Asian Nations
BIMSTEC	Bay of Bengal Initiative for Multi-Sectoral Technical and Economic Cooperation
BPA	business process analysis
BRICS	Brazil, Russian Federation, India, China and South Africa
DFQF	duty-free quota-free
EIA	economic integration agreement
EPA	economic partnership agreement
EU	European Union
FDI	foreign direct investment
FTA	free trade agreement
GATS	General Agreement on Trade in Services
GDP	gross domestic product
GSP	Generalized System of Preferences
GTA	Global Trade Alert
GVCs	global value chains
IMF	International Monetary Fund
ISIC	International Standard Industrial Classification of All Economic Activities
M&A	mergers and acquisitions
nec	not elsewhere classified
NTFB	national trade facilitation body
NTMs	non-tariff measures
OECD	Organisation for Economic Co-operation and Development
PICTA	Pacific Island Countries Trade Agreement
PTA	preferential trade agreement
QE	quantitative easing
RCEP	Regional Comprehensive Economic Partnership
RCA	revealed comparative advantage
SAFTA	Agreement on South Asian Free Trade Area

SASEC	South Asia Subregional Economic Cooperation
SATNET	Network for Knowledge Transfer on Sustainable Agricultural Technologies and Improved Market Linkages in South and Southeast Asia
SPS	sanitary and phytosanitary
TBT	technical barriers to trade
TFA	Trade Facilitation Agreement
TFAF	WTO Trade Facilitation Agreement Facility
TIR	International Road Transport (Transports Internationaux Routiers)
TNCs	transnational corporations
TPP	Trans-Pacific Partnership
TTBs	temporary trade barriers
TTFMM	Trade and Transport Facilitation Monitoring Mechanism
UNCTAD	United Nations Conference on Trade and Development
UNNExT	United Nations Network of Experts on Paperless Trade for Asia and the Pacific
UNWTO	United Nations World Tourism Organization
WITS	World Integrated Trade Solution
WTO	World Trade Organization

EXECUTIVE SUMMARY

INTRODUCTION

Trade growth in Asia and the Pacific continued to weaken in 2013. In the final two quarters of 2013, growth rates for exports and imports in the region were below global averages for the first time in a decade. Despite this slowdown, Asia and the Pacific has become the largest trading area in the world, accounting for close to 37% of world trade. More than half the total trade in the region is with other Asia-Pacific economies. China is the second-largest merchandise exporter and third-largest merchandise importer globally.[1] More than 10 other developing economies of the region are in the global top 25 exporters and importers, alongside Japan and Australia. The overall economic performance of the region continues to outpace other parts of the world.

Although Africa is now also growing rapidly. Growth remains lower than in the pre-crisis era, but there is no doubt that rising trade and investment flows continue to be behind much of the region's relative success. Economies in the region continue, however, to re-examine the long-term viability of reliance on exports to traditional markets. The sharp collapse of world trade in 2008 and 2009 illustrated the need to reduce dependence on external sources of demand. Instead, growth strategies need to focus on identifying more diversified and stable sources of demand growth, which will include fostering domestic and regional sources of demand through deeper integration, enhanced connectivity and reform of trade policies.

The Asia-Pacific Trade and Investment Report (APTIR) 2014 analyses recent regional trends and provides an analysis of developments in: (a) intraregional trade in goods and services; (b) foreign direct investment; (c) trade facilitation measures; (d) trade policy measures; and (e) preferential trade agreements. The main findings of the report are summarized below.

A. CONTINUING SHADOW OF CRISIS HIGHLIGHTS THE ONGOING NEED FOR REBALANCING

Developments in 2013 and, so far, in 2014 show that the prolonged consequences of the 2008-2009 global financial crisis have cast a shadow over the trade prospects of Asia and the Pacific. Intraregional demand is evidently vulnerable to the ongoing global economic slowdown. It is expected that the growth of merchandise trade by developing Asia-Pacific economies will continue to be slow-paced in the remainder of 2014, compared with the pre-crisis period, with average export growth of 5% in real terms. This growth is expected to range from a low of 2% (Russian Federation) to a high of 7% (Singapore and the Philippines).

Analysis of individual country performances confirms that most otherwise dynamic trading economies in Asia and the Pacific are experiencing an export growth slowdown compared with the same period in 2013. China experienced trade stagnation during the first five months of 2014. Exports from India, the second-most populous country in the region, increased marginally by 1.9% while its imports fell by more than 13%. Nevertheless, several economies that are labour- and resource-intensive exporters, registered double digit export growth in 2013. They included Afghanistan (20%), Bangladesh (16%), Cambodia (19%), the Cook Islands (50%), Georgia (22%), Kiribati (29%), Myanmar (26.5%), Uzbekistan (13%), and Viet Nam (15%).

Intraregional trade increased in importance during the past decade, especially on the export side. The share of intraregional exports increased from 44% of total Asia-Pacific exports in 2000 to 52% in 2013. However, intraregional trade patterns are not uniform across subregions. In fact, the largest trading partner of most subregions is East and North-East Asia (see table 1.2 in chapter 1), mainly because China figures so prominently in these countries' trade. Furthermore, heavy reliance on a few trading partners yields an extreme level of intraregional trade dependence in the cases of the Asia-Pacific's least developed countries and landlocked developing countries (figure A).

The export performance of the Asia-Pacific region is expected to improve in 2015 to reach a growth rate of 7% in real terms. However, considerable uncertainties in the trade outlook remain. On the economic side, these

FIGURE A Intraregional import dependency by Asia-Pacific economies, 2012

(Percentage of total merchandise imports)

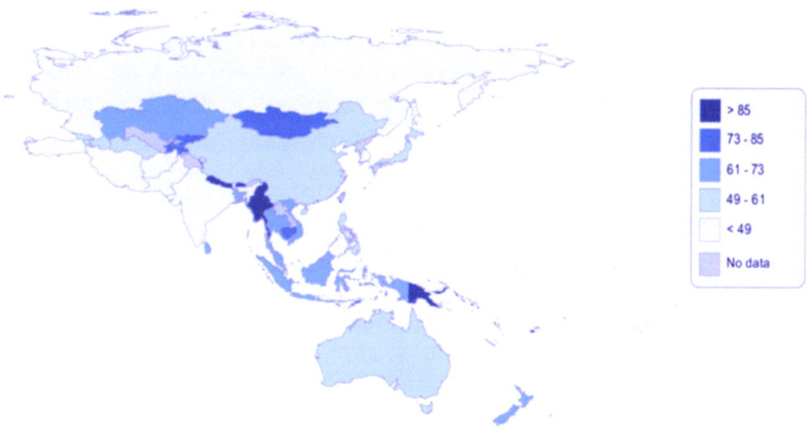

Source: Figure 1.7 in chapter 1.

stem from fluctuations in the economic recovery of the United States and the risks of a Chinese economic hard-landing. Politically, the risks of increased geopolitical tension and instability remain high with possible spillovers for trade and investment.

As the region is not immune to global economic uncertainties, the need to focus on long-term strategies for increasing competitiveness has never been greater. Policies should be adjusted to secure benefits from new and emerging forms of trade and production. These encompass growing connections between countries through participation in global value chains (GVCs). Dispersed production across many locations is fuelling both growing trade in intermediate inputs and rising demand for services related to coordination of production, such as logistics. In a world where most countries participate increasingly in GVCs, raising the value-added of exports is more important than increasing gross exports. APTIR 2014 uses a simple indicator of revealed comparative advantage to demonstrate that the value-added by domestic producers is the key to enhancing overall competitiveness and facilitating entry to international production networks or GVCs. As explained in chapter 1, failure in the world of globalized production to distinguish between gross exports and domestic value-added in exports can lead to misguided trade and industrial policies.

B. REGIONAL POTENTIAL IN SERVICES TRADE GOING UNEXPLOITED

Growth in commercial services exports from the Asia-Pacific region lagged behind the world average in 2013. This slowing of overall services export growth was driven by the diverse performances of leading regional services exporters. While China and India performed quite strongly, other exporters - especially the advanced economies - were unable to maintain their export growth momentum.

Although the divergence in export performance is discouraging, of more general concern is the uneven use of services trade opportunities in the region. The concentration of services exports and imports is extremely high, with 65% of services exports attributable to just six economies in the region: China, India, Japan, the Republic of Korea, Singapore and Hong Kong, China. This implies that a large gap exists in trade competitiveness between these leading performers and the rest of the region.

Given that the main component of regional service exports is business services, which contribute significantly to the value-added of industrial exports, the performance gap is quite alarming for the rest of the Asia-Pacific. This gap in business service exports could also indicate a bottleneck in improving the competitiveness of an economy's industrial exports. The removal of restrictions on trade in services could raise the efficiency of service industries and provide support for exports.

Travel services are also an important growth sector, particularly for small island economies and least developed countries. Through strong backward and forward linkages with domestic activities, the sector's expansion has significant consequences on employment and environmental prospects. It is encouraging that, in contrast to services trade in general, Asia-Pacific trade in travel services has continued to grow strongly during recent years. Yet there remains considerable scope for further improvements to tourism infrastructure to boost arrivals in emerging economies, especially Pacific islands countries.

While trade in commercial services amounts to only 15%-17% of total Asia-Pacific trade – less than the share globally – this measurement underrepresents the true importance of services in trade.[2] As discussed in chapter 2, services are increasingly becoming embedded in manufacturing production. The expansion of global value chains involving multiple Asia-Pacific economies has contributed to the increasing importance of business, communications and transportation services as critical components that link and facilitate these international production networks for industrial exports. While the role of services value-added in industrial exports has been increasing, detailed evaluations are still very limited because of a lack of data. Chapter 2 uses the most recent OECD-WTO Trade in Value Added (TiVA) database, launched in May 2013, to shed further light on the extent of this so-called "servicification."

According to the trade value-added data, services contributed 29% to the value of global industrial output in 2009. Exports by industrial sectors included services content of more than 30% by value (figure 2.6 in chapter 2). Exports from high-tech industrial sectors participating in global value chains, especially transport equipment, tend to have higher services content (37%) than other sectors. In contrast, gross exports by traditional industrial sectors typically contain a lower value of embodied services at not more than 30% of total value. For example, in the case of mining and quarrying, the exports services share was only 10%, while in agriculture, forestry, hunting and fishing it was 24%, and in textiles, textile products, leather and footwear it was 25%.

Although domestically-provided services dominate the service content in manufacturing exports, it is expected that imported services will supply an increasing share among those industries that are characterized by international product fragmentation. Available data, although still limited at present, appear to support this conjecture. Overall, domestic services content accounts for about 19% of the value of industrial exports while foreign content accounts for about 10%. Foreign services content appears to be relatively higher than average in those industrial sectors perceived to be part of fragmented international production networks, including electrical and optical equipment and transport equipment. The foreign services content in exports from those two sectors was 15% and 13%, respectively.

C. NEW LOCATIONS AND SECTORS CAPTURE GROWING INTEREST FROM ASIA-PACIFIC INVESTORS

In 2013, global foreign direct investment (FDI) showed signs of recovery from the weaker performance recorded in 2012, reaching a total value of $1.46 trillion. Developing economies, in particular, continued to attract an increased share of global FDI and were recipients of more than a half of global FDI inflows. The Asia-Pacific region experienced a 7% increase of FDI inflows – lower than the 9% global increase. Although the Asia-Pacific region remained attractive to investors, accounting for 38% of total global FDI, growth in FDI lagged behind the performance of recent years and was lower than in other fast-growing regions such as Latin America.

Whether this represents a longer-term slowdown in regional investment or is a temporary trend remains uncertain. Nonetheless, there does appear to be a shift in the destination of FDI within the region, traditional major recipients are expectedly seeing slower growth with smaller players now attract more foreign investors and on a larger scale. As a result, investments across the region are characterized by increasing diversification in locations and sectors.

Government policies that encourage or hinder FDI play an important role in explaining performance in attracting investment. Indeed, FDI inflows varied greatly among different subregions and countries. The East and North-

East Asia subregion experienced the biggest growth of FDI inflows, attracting 36% more compared with 2012. However, the South-East Asia subregion has proved to be the most resilient, experiencing undisrupted growth in FDI inflows since 2009.

Many Asia-Pacific economies are also significant external investors. In terms of FDI outflows, in 2013 the Asia-Pacific region experienced a significant increase of 15.1%. The region accounted for a 38% share of global FDI outflows. China is undoubtedly one of the most important players in the region, not only as an investment destination but also as a source of investment. China's outward FDI flows have risen continuously during the past decade, encouraged by explicit government support for businesses to internationalize. Investment from Japan also rose by 33% in 2013.

The usage of different modes of investment is also changing. Traditionally, within the Asia-Pacific region, greenfield FDI was the most significant mode of entry for investors. However, since 2008 there has been a decline in the relative importance of greenfield FDI and an increase in mergers and acquisitions (M&A). Between 2011 and 2013, intraregional greenfield FDI inflows in the region dropped by 43% with the downward trend visible in most major destination countries.

Intraregional FDI continues to be shaped by global macroeconomic changes. Reflecting the shift in the global centre of economic gravity towards the Asia-Pacific region, intraregional FDI investors are increasingly replacing investors from European countries and the United States – traditionally the top investors in the region. Intraregional M&A deals accounted for a significant share of total FDI inflows in several major markets. Although global FDI inflows through M&A to the Asia-Pacific region decreased in both 2012 and 2013, intraregional FDI inflows through M&A remained substantial at a total of $153.8 billion, accounting for almost one third of total FDI inflows and a much higher share in certain economies, for example, in China (71.5%), Hong Kong, China (66%), and the Republic of Korea, (45.1%).

Intraregional FDI investors are also investing in a broader range of industries – diversifying away from natural resource-heavy industries to more knowledge-based industries and services. FDI increased in industries such as health care, pharmaceuticals and biotechnology, building and construction, consumer products and business services.

Looking ahead, a number of the "mega-regional" trade agreements under negotiation (see below) also include discussions on investment. These treaties, if agreed, could further improve the investment climate and support more open trade and investment regimes, thereby improving future economic prospects in the region.

D. INEFFICIENT REGULATIONS DRIVE UP TRADE COSTS

The WTO Trade Facilitation Agreement (TFA), concluded at the ninth WTO Ministerial Conference in December 2013, is the first major global trade agreement to be concluded since the establishment of WTO in 1995. Although implementation of the TFA remains uncertain, the Agreement provides evidence of a global consensus on the importance of trade facilitation for sustainable economic development, as well as a narrow, but concrete framework through which countries may simplify and enhance the transparency of their trade procedures.

At the regional level, progress is being made towards a regional arrangement on the facilitation of cross-border paperless trade, since the adoption by ESCAP member States in May 2012 of a resolution on enabling the cross-border recognition of electronic data and documents for inclusive and sustainable intraregional trade facilitation. This also suggests that the region is committed to make significant progress in this area in the coming years.

Chapter 4 provides a preliminary regional assessment of the implementation of trade facilitation measures included in the TFA as well as the development of trade services and systems for paperless trade facilitation based on surveys carried out by the ESCAP secretariat since 2012. Because of the great importance of the agricultural sector for inclusive trade and development on the one hand and the fact that agricultural trade costs on the other are typically twice as high as those for manufacturing goods,[3] this year's APTIR presents findings from country- and product-specific agricultural trade process analyses. It reveals significant and persistent barriers to trade. For example, in Myanmar, no less than 20 actors are involved in the export of rice (see table 4.1 in chapter 4). In the Lao People's Democratic Republic, visits are required by three agencies to the premises of the animal feed importers to provide three separate reports for verifying the request for import. In Nepal, local administration still charges an export fee even though there is a national policy of not imposing such fees. Furthermore, in Bangladesh and Thailand it can take up to 17.5 days and 14 days , respectively, to obtain the sanitary and phytosanitary (SPS) certificate, including laboratory tests, necessary for exporting shrimp (see figure B). This accounts for more than half of the total time required to complete export procedures within these two countries. In Cambodia, it takes between five to seven days to complete the same procedure. In Nepal, Cambodia, Myanmar and Sri Lanka, it takes only one day to obtain the SPS certificate.

FIGURE B Days required for export of agricultural products

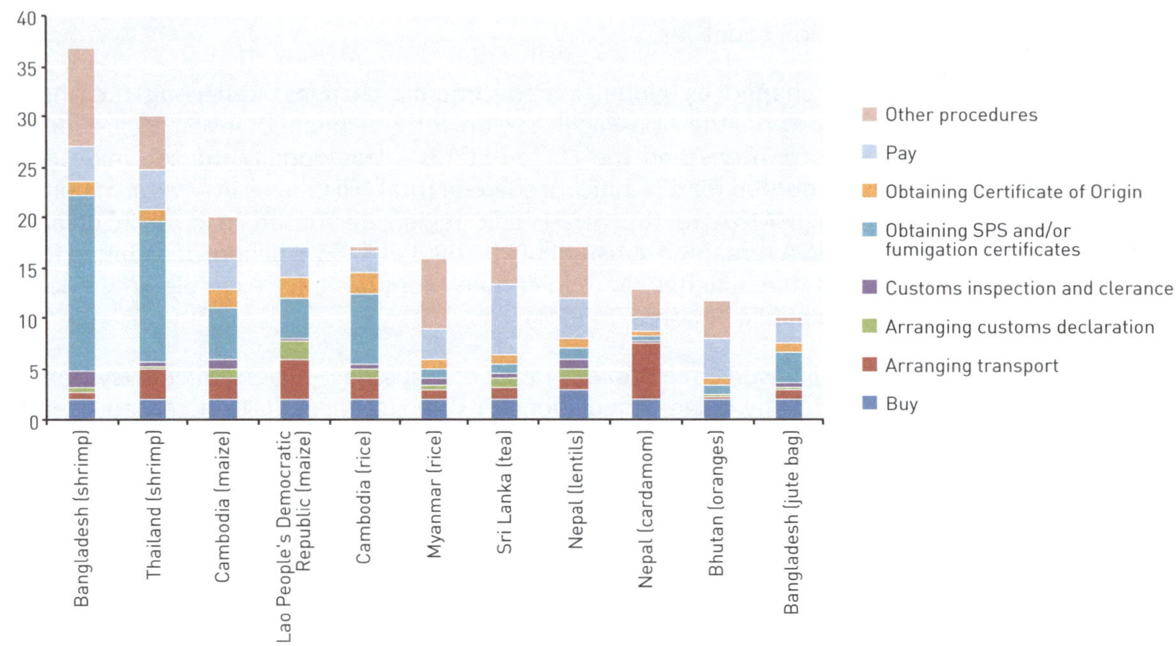

Source: Figure 4.6 in chapter 4.

These findings have important implications for policymakers and other stakeholders involved in trade facilitation. First, they confirm that many agricultural trade procedures are not only complex but also specific to the sector or product, suggesting the need for trade facilitation support programmes dedicated to agriculture and food products.

Second and more generally, the trade process analysis studies suggest that a whole-supply-chain approach is essential to making significant progress in reducing trade transaction costs and improving competitiveness. This is because the most important bottlenecks may not be at the border and may also relate to inefficient services by the private sector rather than by government agencies. Accordingly, this requires policymakers to monitor the performance along the entire supply chain and to identify solutions to streamline trade process continuously, as proposed in previous issues of APTIR. The chapter also proposes some concrete actions as a way forward for countries and the region in three areas of immediate importance: (a) implementation of the TFA measures; (b) development of cross-border paperless trade; and (c) establishment of sustainable trade facilitation monitoring mechanisms.

E. DANGEROUS DRIFT AWAY FROM OPENNESS NEEDS TO BE REVERSED

Trade policies in the Asia-Pacific economies show signs of both protectionist and liberalizing tendencies with the overall outlook remaining uncertain. The latter half of 2013 and the first half of 2014 have seen some positive signs of renewed interest in liberalization, suggesting that post-2008 crisis pressures for protection of domestic producers may be weakening. In the major G20 economies, the pace of introducing new trade-restrictive measures recorded by WTO had at least plateaued in the six months up to May 2014.

However, regional trade policy continues to show worrying signs of a drift away from openness. While Asia-Pacific countries adopted both liberalizing and trade-restrictive measures, from October 2012 to November 2013 the balance tipped further towards trade-restrictive measures, when 72 new trade-restrictive measures were recorded compared with 37 liberalizing measures. Overall, tariff increases were the most common trade-restrictive measure (see table 5.1 in chapter 5); the period saw 106 tariff increases globally, 28 of these in the Asia-Pacific region (of which all but three were in the region's developing countries).

Usage of trade remedies is also increasing barriers to trade; during the above period 70 new measures were introduced in the Asia-Pacific region. This was greater than the number of terminations meaning that the overall number of barriers to trade increased, although this trend may be turning (see box 5.1 in chapter 5). Anti-dumping initiations were by far the most common form of action, with India being the largest initiator. China was the country most targeted by trade remedies.

New energy is needed to reverse this trend and seize opportunities to boost trade, growth and prosperity. In the near-term, many temporary trade barriers introduced in the immediate aftermath of the global financial crisis are approaching their "sunset clauses". By choosing not to renew these trade restrictive measures, Governments could send a strong signal in favour of openness. In the longer-term, real progress is needed both through the negotiation of effective regional trade agreements and through a commitment to implement the WTO "Bali Package" as a first step towards further multilateral liberalization.

Likewise, securing greater market access for least developed countries' products and ensuring that they do not suffer impacts unduly from trade restrictive measures should be a high priority for regional policymakers. The total number of new less-transparent measures having an impact on at least one Asia-Pacific least developed country was at its highest in 2009 immediately after the financial crisis as many countries took measures to protect domestic industries. Worryingly, despite a fall in new measures in 2010 and 2011, there has been a recent rebound in trade-restrictive measures that have had an impact on Asia-Pacific least developed countries (see figure 5.6 in chapter 5). In 2013, the total number of measures introduced was more than 60% higher than in 2011. New measures in 2013 were dominated by behind-the-border non-tariff measures, which present particular obstacles for small and medium-sized exporters from the least developed countries.

It is important that least developed countries gain meaningful market access to not only to developed country markets but also to large, growing emerging markets. For example, more could be done in the "BRICS" economies (Brazil, the Russian Federation, India, China and South Africa) to remove barriers to least developed countries' products. While trade volumes have grown substantially between these groups of economies, there is scope for increasing trade further by lowering tariff and non-tariff barriers on both sides, reducing tariff escalation, extending preferential access for least developed country exports, and making rules of origin more liberal in the existing preference schemes. For example, China and India have introduced duty-free quota-free access for many products from least developed countries; however, while this is to be welcomed, coverage could be extended further.

In addition to greater commitment to tackling the most significant tariff and non-tariff barriers through international coordination, scaled-up technical assistance - for example, through Aid for Trade - can also help least developed countries realize their trade and development potential.

F. MEGA-REGIONAL DEALS CAN HELP UNTANGLE THE "NOODLE BOWL"

The proliferation of preferential trade agreements (PTAs) continues, although there is evidence of a plateau being reached, especially with regard to the involvement of Asia-Pacific economies. Whether this is due to positive movement in the WTO Bali Ministerial Conference or to the fact that most of the countries have already concluded PTAs with their most desired trading partners, is undetermined.

However, some economies may be expected to revisit existing agreements and to negotiate deeper integration as well as expanding coverage. This could follow the trend in recent PTAs, of including additional issues such as competition, government procurement and investments – which were dropped from the Doha agenda. There are already a number of examples of current members repeatedly expanding bilateral commitments (for example, China and Hong Kong, China and Macao, China, respectively; Australia and New Zealand; and the plurilateral agreements moving towards creating economic communities such as the ASEAN Economic Community and the Euro-Asian Economic Community). Efforts appear to be underway to forge a consensus for including these WTO-plus areas in future multilateral discussions by first building a critical mass of PTAs that incorporate such provisions.

The Asia-Pacific region has been the nexus of PTA activity; of a total of 253 global physical trade agreements in force, 150 agreements involve regional economies. Many agreements are between developing economies, thus establishing a foundation for stronger South-South trade. The economies in the North and Central Asian subregion were the major contributors to Asia-Pacific PTAs in the 1990s. However, success in reformulating of some of the arrangements in that subregion into ambitious customs unions - for example, the one between Belarus, Kazakhstan and the Russian Federation - and plans to move towards an economic community might re-energize the drive by those countries towards regional integration.[4] Since the early 2000s, South-East Asia, through ASEAN, has played a dynamic role in expanding the web of PTAs.

Almost as many Asia-Pacific PTAs involve partners outside the region as countries within within the region - 72 of the total 150 agreements are with external countries. Judging from the total number, it appears that the agreements in the region are mostly bilateral in nature; however, but most subregions also have significant initiatives with multiple members, with the exception of East and North-East Asian economies.

The Asia-Pacific region suffers from a multiplicity of PTAs with complex and overlapping rules – a problem known as the "noodle bowl". Regional economies therefore need to start reducing the complexity of terms negotiated in PTAs and to try to consolidate their numerous PTAs. This will simplify trade transactions and reduce costs for exporters. At present, the usage of PTAs by businesses is often low because of excessive complexity. A few such efforts in the Asia-Pacific region appear to be under way.[5] The Asia-Pacific Trade Agreement (APTA) is expanding its membership and provides an open-ended agreement that any developing member State of ESCAP can join. It remains to be seen if the agreement can also be opened to the three developed countries in the region and if, at the same time, it can be converted into a more progressive type of free trade agreement covering more areas.

Other agreements that are emerging as strong alternatives are the Regional Comprehensive Economic Partnership (RCEP), which involves 16 Asia-Pacific economies, and the Trans-Pacific Partnership (TPP) between 12 economies from Asia and the Pacific Rim. It is important to note that there are seven economies opting for membership between both mega-blocs (figure 6.5 in chapter 6). It is not certain whether, after the implementation of RCEP and TPP agreements, the ASEAN+1 agreements and other existing agreements (more than 50 in total) will be nullified or not. Only when RCEP and TPP become open-ended agreements and replace all other existing bilateral agreements between their members can a true consolidation be achieved that will genuinely address the "noodle bowl" problem.

ENDNOTES

1 When excluding intra-European Union trade and when the European Union is not treated as a single entity, China becomes the largest trader when measured by the sum of merchandise exports and imports.

2 Economic and Social Commission for Asia and the Pacific, *Asia-Pacific Trade and Investment Report 2013 - Turning the Tide: Towards Inclusive Trade and Investment*. Sales No. E.14.II.F.2. Available from www.unescap.org/resources/asia-pacific-trade-and-investment-report-2013-turning-tide-towards-inclusive-trade-and.

3 Ibid.

4 This process might be complicated in the near future due to political problems that deepened in some parts of the subregion during 2014.

5 The most recent example is the one among those members of the ASEAN-Australia-New Zealand FTA (AANZFTA) that signed the First Protocol to Amend the Agreement Establishing the AANZFTA on 27 August 2014. The Protocol will provide for improved administrative efficiency by customs authorities as well as encourage business utilization of AANZFTA.

1 MERCHANDISE TRADE REMAINS SUBDUED

This chapter provides an analysis of recent trends in trade in goods of the Asia-Pacific region which is now the largest trading region in the world. With a 38% share of world exports and 37% of world imports.[1] Recent developments reveal that growth in merchandise trade in the Asia-Pacific region continued to slow down in 2013 and pressures are mounting on trade prospects for the Asia-Pacific region. As the region is not immune to global economic uncertainties, the need to focus on long-term strategies for securing benefits from new and emerging forms of trade and production has never been greater. From the analysis, which is based on newly available data on trade in value-added, this chapter highlights the fact that in order to enhance the competitiveness position of a country in the world of globalized production focus needs to be placed on raising domestic value-added rather than just increasing gross exports. Failure to distinguish between gross exports and domestic value-added in exports can lead to misguided trade and industrial policies.

> ***The Asia-Pacific region as a whole is now the largest trading region in the world, with a 38% share of world exports, and 37% of world imports.***

A. ASIA AND THE PACIFIC CONTINUES TO EXPERIENCE LACKLUSTRE PERFORMANCE IN MERCHANDISE TRADE

Slower export growth in the Asia-Pacific region translated into a reduced trade surplus with the rest of the world, amounting to $75 billion in 2013.

Although the world economy looks to be in better shape than in recent years, a fully-fledged recovery from the consequences of the 2008 global financial crisis is still not visible. In 2013 the United States registered modest growth, whereas the Eurozone economies continued to struggle with internal and external shocks. China, the world's third major growth pole, is also adjusting to lower economic growth; total merchandise export growth remained at less than 8% since 2012 as compared with 20% in 2011, reflecting both domestic restructuring and weakness in external demand. Nevertheless, the country still performed considerably better than other Asia-Pacific trading economies.

It is thus not surprising to find that, on average, growth in merchandise trade in the Asia-Pacific region continued to slow down in 2013. Total exports and imports from the region grew by only 2% in 2013 (figure 1.1). The developing countries of the Asia-Pacific region, including China, performed twice as well as the regional total; their exports and imports each grew at around 4%. However, when exports by China, which account for about 30% of the Asia-Pacific total, are excluded the growth rate of exports from other Asia-Pacific developing countries was just 2%. This slower export growth translated into a substantially reduced Asia- Pacific merchandise trade surplus with the rest of the world; the surplus fell from a peak of slightly more than $480 billion in 2007 to only $75 billion in 2013.[2]

FIGURE 1.1 Annual merchandise trade growth of Asia-Pacific developing economies, 2007-2013

(Year-on-year percentage change)

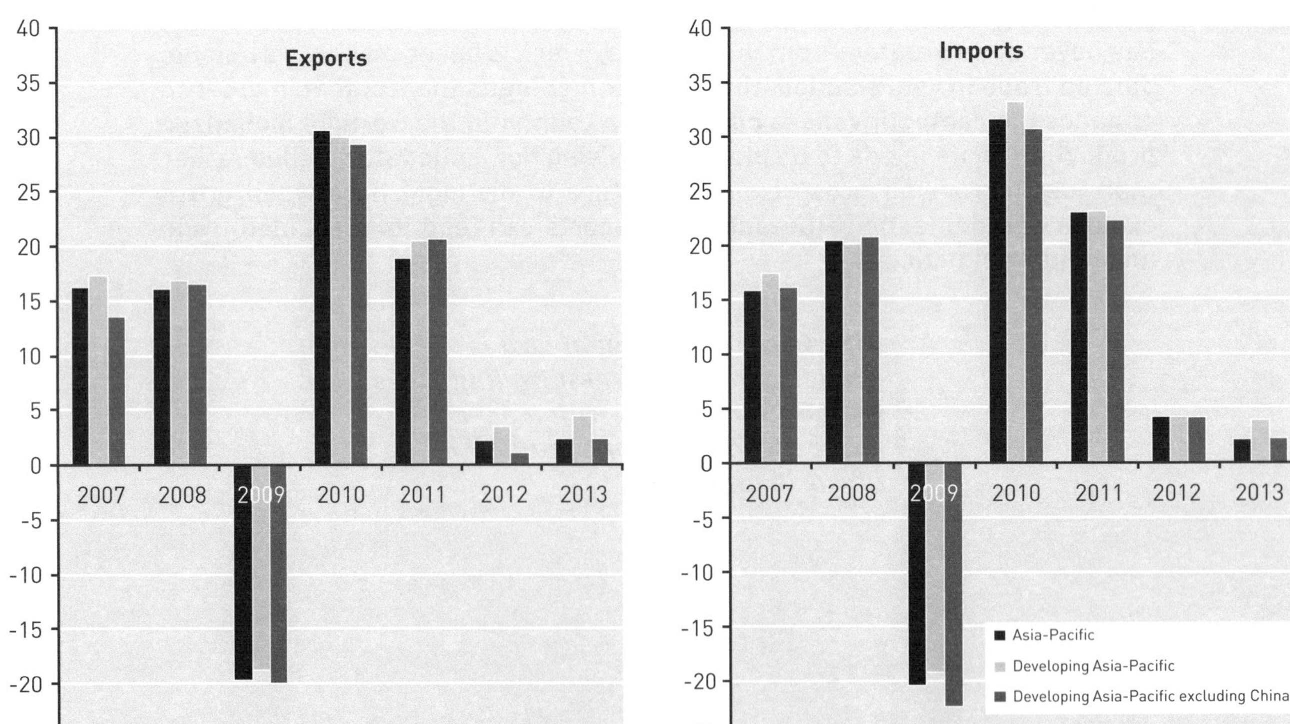

Source: ESCAP calculation, based on country data from the World Trade Organization, International Trade Statistics Database (accessed September 2014). Country data are available from the ESCAP online statistical database.

The above-mentioned improvement in the global economy has been associated with an investment boom in the energy sector of the United States of America. It is, however, unclear when and to what extent this will benefit exports from Asia and the Pacific. Judging by the recent trade statistics, there are few encouraging signs. In fact, the year-on-year export growth of Asia and the Pacific was particularly weak in the first quarter of 2014 (figure 1.2). This means that a global growth that is relying more on capital investment in the energy sector than on the consumer consumption might not be doing much for export-led Asia-Pacific economies. Exports from "the factory of Asia" thus may not fully benefit from the recovery in the United States, at least not in the near future (see box 1.1).

To make matters worse, the slowing of growth in the Chinese economy and its trade is posing risks to export prospects for the rest of the Asia-Pacific region, since 15% of their total exports are to China.[3] On the other hand, China is also

FIGURE 1.2

Quarterly growth of Asia-Pacific merchandise trade

(Year-on-year percentage change)

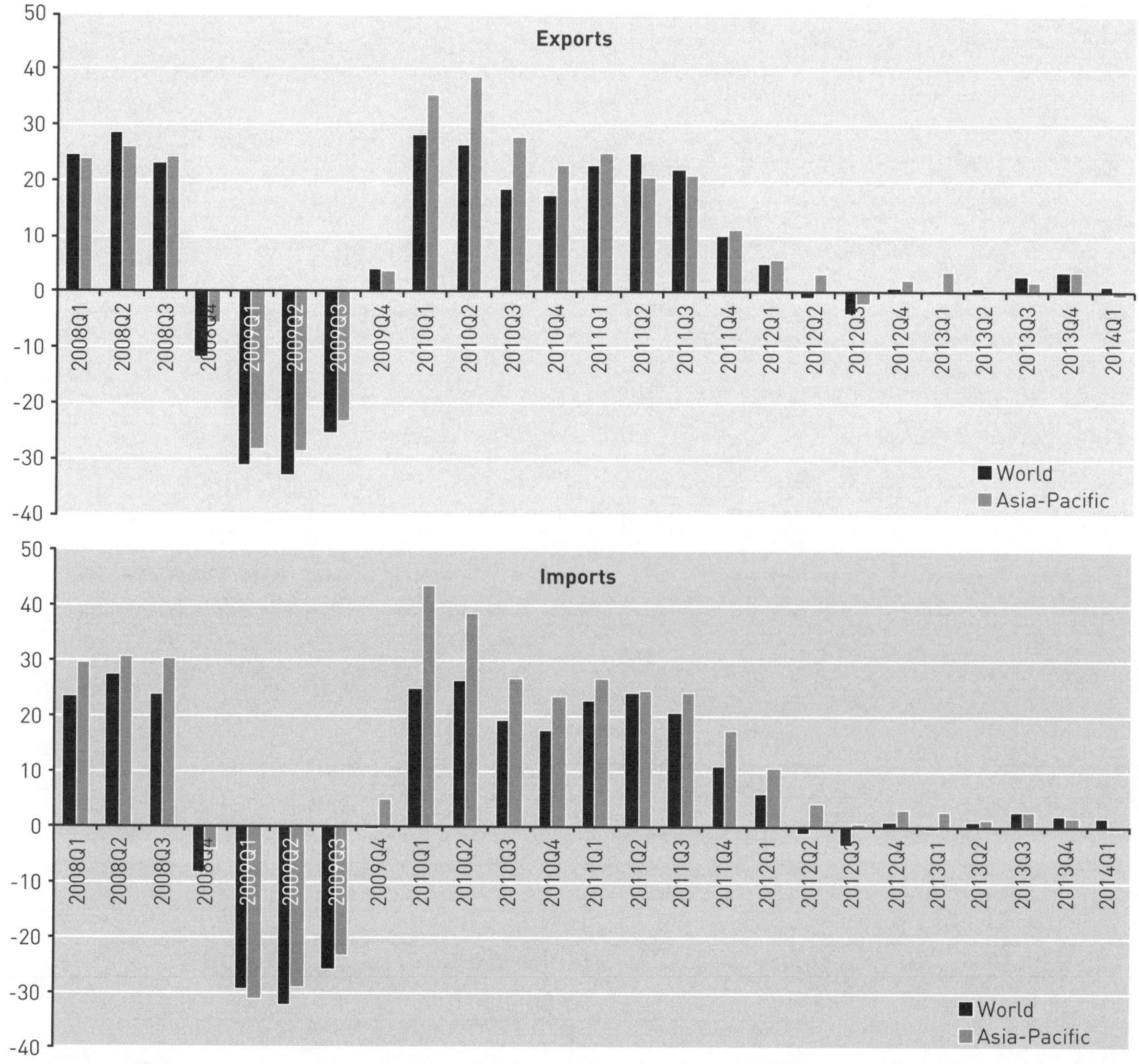

Source: ESCAP calculation, based on country data from World Trade Organization online short-term merchandise trade statistics (accessed July 2014).

Box 1.1 Dynamics of global economic recovery and implications for Asia-Pacific trade prospects

Signs of a modest economic recovery in the United States in the second half of 2013 have perhaps prematurely relieved the fears of a long-term global recession given the performance of the world's largest economy in the first quarter of 2014. Nevertheless, investment expansion in the energy sector and other economic activities in the United States appear to be picking up, at least according to indicators of employment, industrial production, manufacturing shipment and the stock market index. This acceleration is in stark contrast with developments in Japan and the Eurozone where the risks of economic recession remain at the fore with weak domestic consumption, deflation and high unemployment, especially in the Euro area.

Despite some improved prospects, downside risks remain for developing economies in Asia and the Pacific. The risks come from both the continued uncertainties in advanced economies and a rising threat from the economic slowdown of China. With regard to external uncertainties, it is disappointing that, despite the strengthening economic activities in the United States, robust demand for exports from developing Asia-Pacific region has not yet emerged. In fact, imports by the United States continue to decline (International Monetary Fund, 2014). There are several possible reasons for this. One explanation points out that the current recovery is driven by capital investment in areas such as oil and gas exploration, which is not an import-intensive sector. Second, the role of weakened consumer spending growth cannot be ignored as American households have hit their debt ceiling.

Furthermore, the tapering of "quantitative easing" (QE), which had been a source of global liquidity in recent years, is increasing the risks of economic volatility for developing economies. In the light of the economic recovery, the crisis-related measures have been progressively removed (hence the term "QE tapering") since 1 January 2014.[a] The tightening of monetary policy implies tighter financial conditions and pressure to move towards currency depreciation for emerging and developing economies that were the major recipients of capital inflows during the QE measures.[b] Although the trend towards currency depreciation might be welcomed by exporters, concerns are more about the increasing currency volatility, especially for those countries that have limited foreign currency reserves.

A rising threat from within the Asia-Pacific region is emerging from the continuing Chinese economic slowdown. It is clear that the era of double-digit economic growth for the Chinese economy is over, and economic growth of 7% to 8% will be a "new normal" (ESCAP, 2014; p.36). Chinese President Xi Jinping has made it clear that the nation needs to adapt to the slower pace of economic growth as the Government is reluctant to roll out large stimuli that would support higher growth (Bloomberg, 2014). The Government of China has so far limited its support for tax breaks as well as speeding up infrastructure and social housing investment. The Government of China is making efforts to curb a credit boom that threatens to undermine the financial system.

China is also suffering from relatively slower export growth. Merchandise exports grew by only 7.2% in 2013. As observed from the data on Chinese trade during the first five months

Figure A Economic recovery of the United States: selected economic indicators

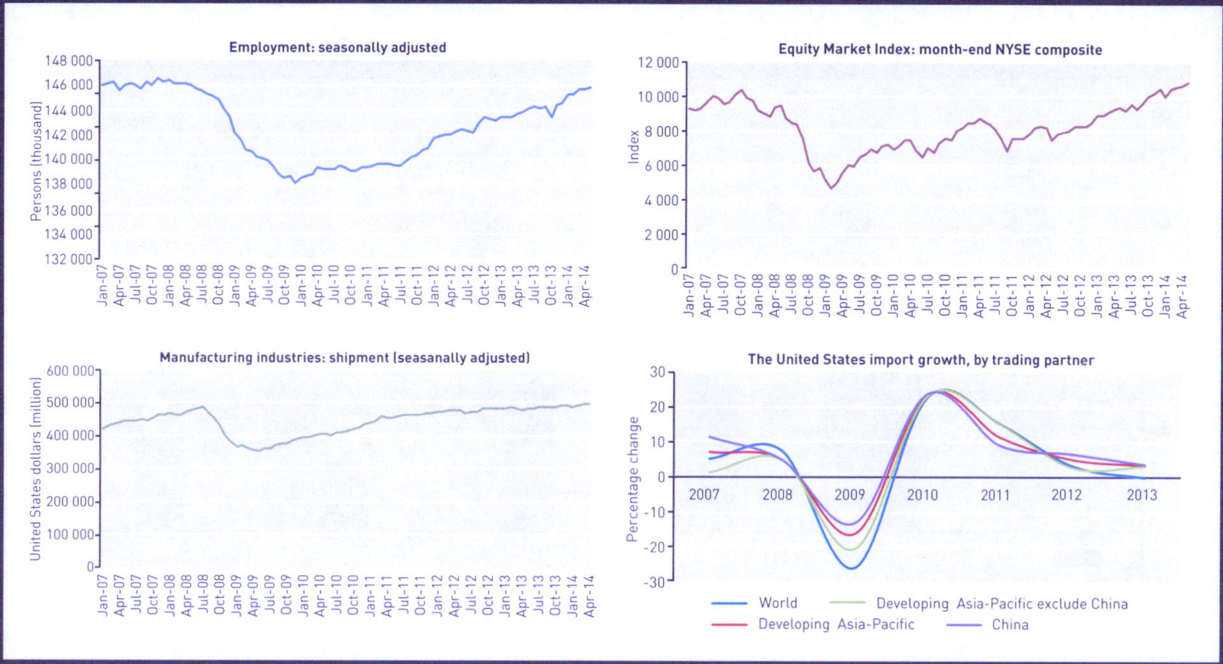

Source: ESCAP calculation based on data from CEIC and United Nations Comtrade (accessed June 2014).

of 2014, the country's recent trade performance has been particularly weak. Chinese exports during the first five months of 2014 dropped by 0.3% on a year-on-year basis, and its imports grew by just 0.9%. Given the current global economic environment, exports are not going to be the strong engine driving the Chinese economy in the foreseeable future.

Economic rebalancing by China may also have a significant impact on the recovery path of the rest of the region. The increasing correlation between Chinese industrial production and exports by Asia-Pacific countries is evident in figure B. Taking the 1997-2004 period, when several Asia-Pacific countries were facing the adjustment process from the negative impact of Asian financial crisis as a cut-off, it can clearly be seen that the correlation between Chinese industrial output and exports by selected countries increased remarkably in the recent period except in the case of Bangladesh.

Overall, the prospects for Asia-Pacific trade during the remainder of 2014 and in 2015 will be dominated by the downside risks. The major concern is that the threat from the economic slowdown of China already exists while the economic recovery of advanced economies remains fragile. Given the growing trade and production linkages within the region during the past decade, emerging and developing Asia-Pacific countries will be vulnerable.

Figure B Correlation coefficients between Chinese industrial output and exports by selected countries during different time periods

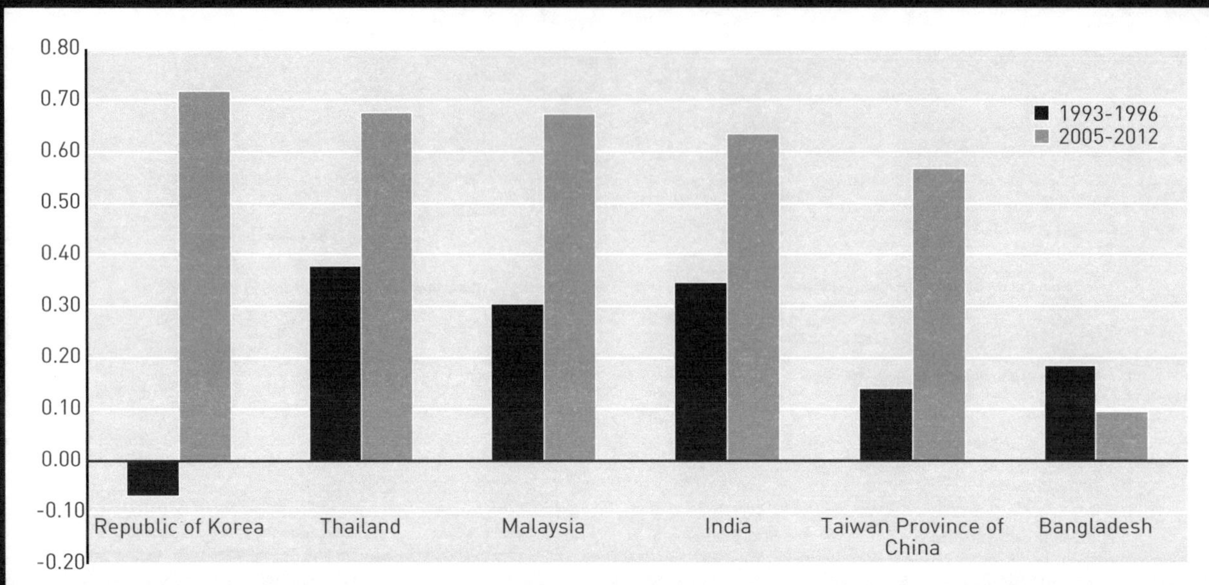

Source: ESCAP calculation, using national sources from CEIC (accessed June 2014).

[a] The Federal Reserve reduced its monthly purchase of treasury bonds worth $45 billion and $40 billion in mortgage-backed securities to $40 billion and $35 billion, respectively, effective 1 January 2014. This was followed by cutting purchases to $35 billion of treasury bonds and $30 billion of mortgage-backed securities from February 2014 onwards.

[b] The adverse impact on economic growth in emerging economies is likely to be mostly temporary as it is a part of the normalization process. According to an estimate made by Moody's (2014), emerging economies could face a cumulative 2013-2016 GDP growth loss of between 2.8% and 3.1% due to QE tapering. However, other commentators suggest there are medium to long-term impact too (other than volatility aspect) because countries will have greater difficulty raising foreign financing once interest rate differentials with the United States decline.

the major supplier of goods to the rest of Asia and the Pacific; around 16% of their imports are sourced from China. The downward move from double-digit rates of growth to a much slower pace is a source of concern for the rest of Asia and the Pacific as, in the short term, they cannot substitute for the Chinese market with other external markets or their own domestic demand.

> ***So far, in 2014 most dynamic traders in the Asia-Pacific region are experiencing an export growth slowdown.***

Analysis of individual country performances confirms that most otherwise dynamic trading economies in developing Asia-Pacific region are experiencing an export growth slowdown compared with the same period in 2013. China experienced trade stagnation during the first five months of 2014. Exports from the Republic of Korea grew less than 3% during the same period. Export growth of other countries in the region has also been sluggish, falling to the lowest levels during the past two years (figure 1.3). In contrast, several small economies, including least developed and landlocked developing countries that are labour- and resource-intensive exporters, registered double digit export growth in 2013. They included Afghanistan (20%), Bangladesh (16%), Cambodia (19%), the Cook Islands (50%), Georgia (22%), Kiribati (29%), Myanmar (26.5%), Uzbekistan (13%) and Viet Nam (15%).

> ***Economies with labour- and resource-intensive exports registered double-digit export growth.***

Near-term prospects

Overall, global uncertainties especially those from China's economic and export slowdown remain a threat to trade growth in 2014. The expectations of flat export growth for China in 2014 will undermine the prospects for countries supplying intermediate inputs to China for further processing and then export including some domestic value-added. Likewise, countries exporting mineral resources, raw materials, and machinery to China will not be able to rely

FIGURE 1.3 Quarterly growth of merchandise trade in selected Asian economies

(Year-on-year percentage change)

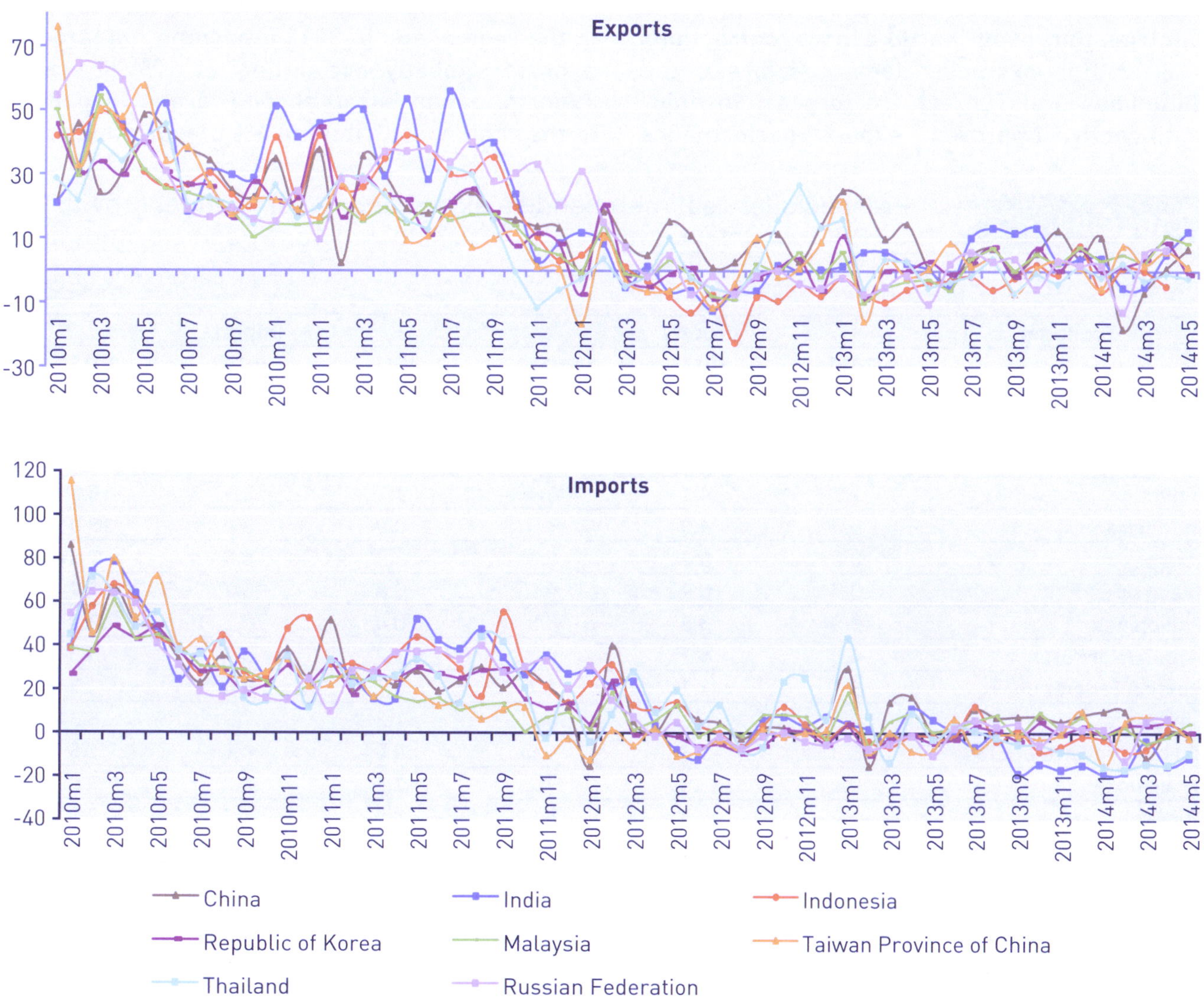

Source: ESCAP calculation, based on World Trade Organization online short-term statistics (accessed July 2014).

on Chinese import demand as they did in the past. Total Chinese demand from infrastructure investment, domestic consumption and the services sectors will be insufficient to sustain the earlier high rates of economic growth.

In 2014, Asia-Pacific economies will see an average export growth of around 4.8% and import growth of 3.7%.

Taking all these factors into account, it is expected that the growth of merchandise trade by developing Asia-Pacific economies will continue to be slow for the remainder of 2014, with average growth of 4.8% for exports and 3.7% for imports (table 1.1). Nevertheless, as the recovery of the United States is expected to strengthen in late 2014 (IMF, 2014), some countries that experienced export contractions in 2013 (for example, Japan, Malaysia, the Philippines and Turkey) are forecast to enjoy significantly improved export performance (from their low-base levels). Still, it will not be until 2015 that the Asia-Pacific region will see the return of more buoyant trade growth. In that year, economic recovery in the United States through stronger consumption growth should support improved export prospects for developing Asia-Pacific exports and imports, when they are forecast to expand by 6.8 % and 7.3%, respectively, in real terms.

B. SUBREGIONAL PERFORMANCE

The region's dominance in world trade is driven by the large economies in East and North-East Asia (figure 1.4), which contributed 23% of world exports and 22% of world imports in 2013. Since 2004, China has been the largest exporter in the region, and in 2013 it became the largest exporter globally, accounting for 12% of world exports. Japan is the second largest exporter in the region, contributing 4% of world exports,

TABLE 1.1 Prospects for real merchandise export and import annual growth for selected Asia-Pacific economies[a]

(Annual percentage growth)

Economy	Exports			Imports		
	2013	2014[b]	2015[b]	2013	2014[b]	2015[b]
Australia	6.8	8.0	6.6	-3.7	1.1	5.2
China	5.8	5.6	8.1	6.4	5.9	9.2
Hong Kong, China	8.8	4.2	7.9	10.3	4.6	7.9
India	7.7	4.1	6.4	-1.7	2.5	6.0
Indonesia	5.0	4.0	13.5	0.9	3.0	15.0
Japan	-0.6	6.3	6.0	3.3	6.6	2.6
Malaysia	-0.7	6.4	4.6	0.8	6.2	4.7
Philippines	-3.8	6.8	6.5	-0.4	10.2	12.2
Republic of Korea	4.5	4.7	6.3	1.2	3.7	6.5
Russian Federation	3.1	1.7	1.7	0.1	-4.4	1.3
Singapore	3.6	6.8	6.2	1.2	7.7	5.3
Taiwan Province of China	3.3	3.3	5.8	4.0	4.8	7.5
Thailand	0.2	3.0	4.2	1.8	-6.8	3.0
Turkey	-1.2	7.3	5.6	8.5	1.4	7.3
Asia and the Pacific[c]	**4.1**	**5.1**	**6.7**	**3.4**	**4.3**	**6.7**
Developing Asia-Pacific[c]	**4.6**	**4.8**	**6.8**	**3.7**	**3.7**	**7.3**

Source: ESCAP estimates based on projections at country level from Oxford Economic global model as of July 2014 , except for the Russian Federation as of September 2014.

[a] The growth rates are estimated based on constant prices and exchange rates.

[b] Projections.

[c] Regional trade growth is the trade-weighted average growth rates.

slightly higher than the Republic of Korea and Hong Kong, China, whose exports accounted for about 3% of world exports in 2013. South-East Asia's share of world exports in 2013 was about 7%, comprised mostly exports by five ASEAN member States: Singapore (2.2%); Malaysia and Thailand (1.2% each); Indonesia (1%); and Viet Nam (0.7%). On the import side, their shares showed similar results. North and Central Asia captured about 4% of world exports and 3% of world imports, with about three quarters of that share attributable to the Russian Federation. South and South-West Asia has not yet increased its share in world exports above 3.2%, but its share in world imports is now more than 4%. The largest contribution has been by India with the share of more than 55% of the exports by the South and South-West Asian subregion. The Pacific subregion represents only 1.6% of world exports and imports, with Australia and New Zealand accounting for 94% of that trade.

C. INTRAREGIONAL TRADE

The share of intraregional trade increased during the past decade, especially on the export side. The share of intraregional exports increased from 44% of total Asia-Pacific exports in 2000 to 52% in 2013 (figure 1.5). The increase was driven by exports to developing Asia-Pacific countries whose share increased from 33% to 44% during the same period. At the same time, the share of exports going to developed markets – principally the United States, the European Union and developed Asia-Pacific countries – declined from 51% to 36%.

FIGURE 1.4 Asia-Pacific subregions' share in the world merchandise trade, 2000-2013

(Percentage of world exports and imports)

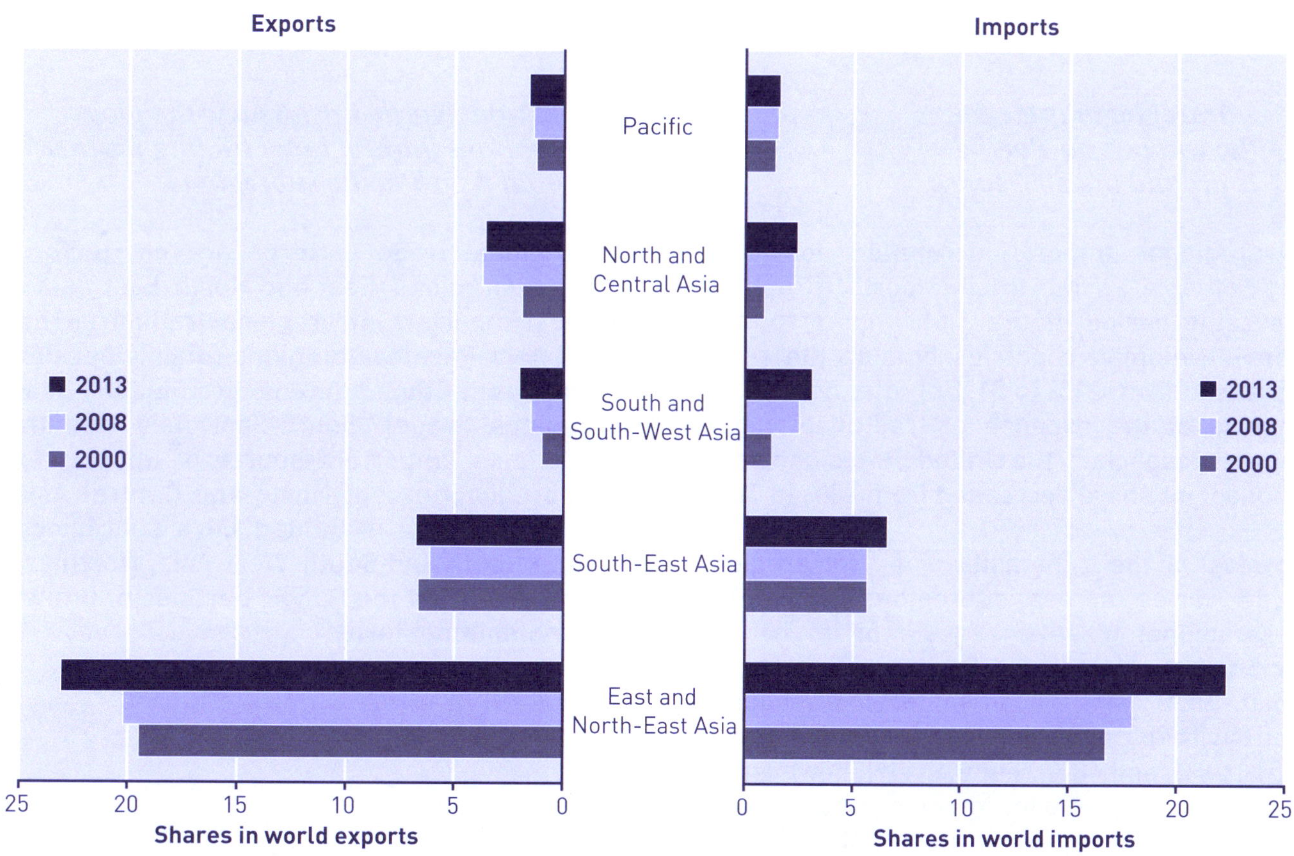

Source: ESCAP calculation, based on country data from the World Trade Organization International Trade statistics database (accessed June 2014).

FIGURE 1.5 Destinations of merchandise exports from Asia and the Pacific, 2013

(Percentage of total merchandise exports)

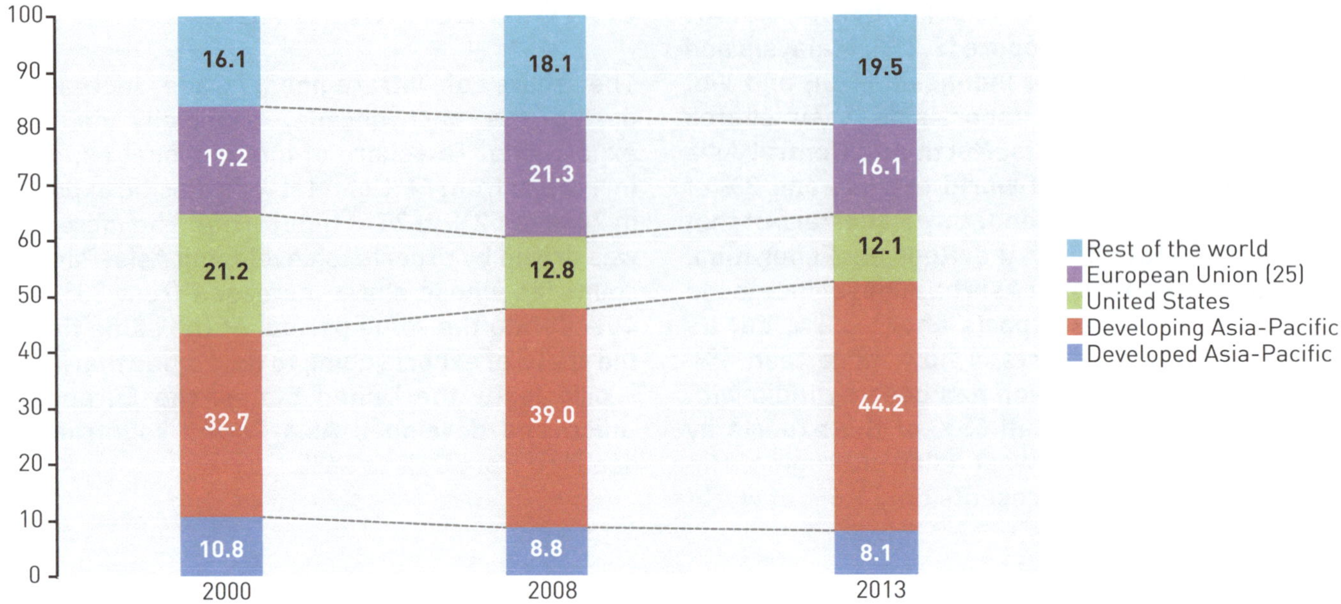

Source: ESCAP calculation, based on United Nations Comtrade data accessed through the World Bank, World Integrated Trade Solution (WITS) Database (accessed July 2014).

Intraregional trade for the whole Asia-Pacific is around the 50% mark.

Intraregional imports accounted for about 50% of Asia-Pacific total imports throughout the same period (figure 1.6). Import sourcing from developing countries outside the region increased from 21% to 31% of total Asia-Pacific imports at the expense of traditional import sources, especially the United States and Japan whose joint share decreased from 28% to 18%.

However, the intensity of intraregional trade varies across subregions (table 1.2). Intraregional trade linkages tend to be high for South-East Asia, the Pacific, and North and North-East Asia, whose imports are sourced from within the region at a significant level (60%, 58%, and 48%, respectively); however, the shares of intraregional imports were relatively small in the cases of North and Central Asia, and South and South-West Asia (39% and 35%, respectively).

East and North-East Asia is the most important intraregional trading partner for all Asia-Pacific subregions.

Intraregional trade patterns are not uniform across subregions. East and North-East Asia is the most important intraregional trading partner for all Asia-Pacific subregions (mainly because imports from China figure so prominently in all subregions' trade). South-East Asia was the second most important source of imports for all subregions except North and Central Asia. At present, there is limited intra-subregional trade in South and South-West Asia, North and Central Asia, and the Pacific because of limited trade complementarity.

FIGURE 1.6

Sources of Asia-Pacific merchandise imports, 2013

(Percentage of total merchandise imports)

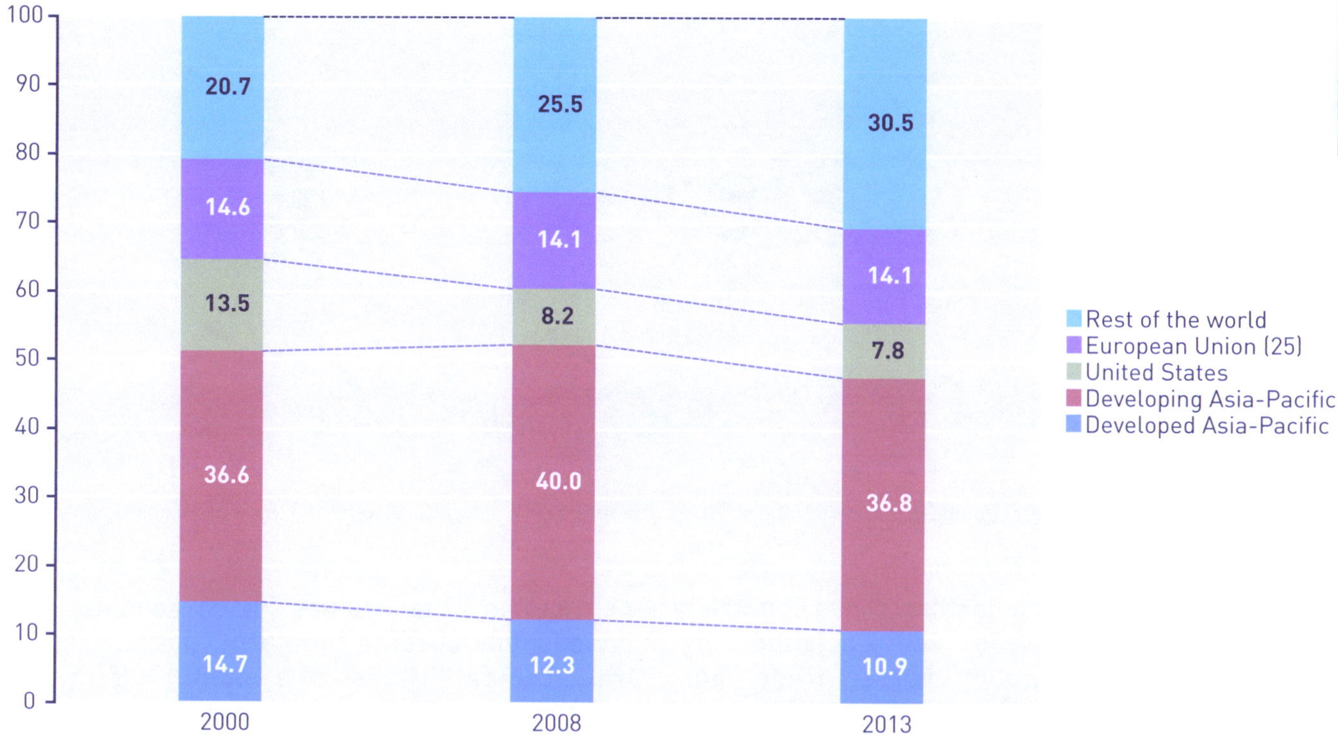

Source: ESCAP calculation, based on United Nations Comtrade data accessed through WITS (accessed July 2014).

> ***All Asia-Pacific subregions trade more intensively with East and North-East Asia, than within themselves.***

Although the intraregional trade shares indicate a relatively high level of regional integration as a whole, further diversification of export and import markets is still important. The heavy reliance on a few trading partners yields an extreme level of intraregional trade dependence in the cases of Asia-Pacific least developed countries and landlocked developing countries (figure 1.7). As a result of high trade costs due to

TABLE 1.2

Intraregional merchandise imports, by Asia-Pacific subregion, 2013

(Percentage of total merchandise imports)

Importers	Exporters					
	ENEA	SEA	SSWA	NCA	Pacific	Asia-Pacific
East and North-East Asia (ENEA)	23.3	11.8	2.6	3.3	5.9	47.0
South-East Asia (SEA)	30.6	22.7	2.5	1.6	2.4	59.7
South and South-West Asia (SSWA)	16.8	7.4	4.8	4.5	1.8	35.2
North and Central Asia (NCA)	23.4	2.6	4.5	8.4	0.3	39.2
Pacific	31.0	18.3	1.6	0.6	6.1	57.5
Asia-Pacific	24.2	13.0	2.9	3.4	4.3	47.8

Source: ESCAP calculation, based on United Nations Comtrade data accessed through WITS (accessed August 2014). Country data are available from the ESCAP online statistics database.

FIGURE 1.7 Intraregional import dependency by Asia-Pacific economies, 2012

(Intraregional import as percentage of total merchandise imports)

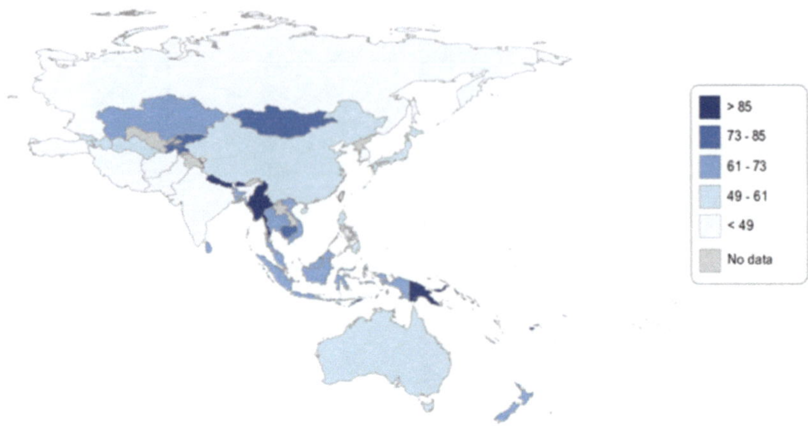

Source: ESCAP online statistical database (accessed August 2014). The interactive map is available from www.unescap.org/stat/data/visual/sp-countries/StatPlanet.html .

natural and man-made factors, those countries rely heavily on trade with neighbouring countries, partly through border trade. For example, exports to China, India and Thailand represented more than 70% of total exports by Myanmar in 2012, while exports to India accounted for 50% of total exports by Nepal.

D. ASSESSING TRADE COMPETITIVENESS BY USING DOMESTIC VALUE-ADDED OF EXPORTS

Trade competitiveness has been an important policy issue. Losing trade competitiveness is viewed as one of the factors causing trade deficits and, consequently, more aggressive protectionist measures. Improving competitiveness and enhancing trade, then, can lead to a growth recovery. This is confirmed by the 2014 policy agenda for growth and resilience of the G20 countries, which emphasizes the role of trade in achieving the target of raising the level of their output by at least 2% in a five-year period (G20, 2014).

To get a real picture of a country's competitiveness, one has to look at its domestic value-added in its exports.

As joining the global value chains has increasingly become the norm, the analysis of trade competitiveness of a country has to take into account the linkages and contributions of countries in their export production. The question is whether or not a standard approach to measuring the competitiveness based on gross exports will provide full information in the modern trade environment where global supply chains proliferate, and where countries use more and more of imported intermediate inputs to produce exports. For example, the use of official trade statistics demonstrates that China holds a leading position in hi-tech exports. This is misleading because the value of final-product exports contains a substantive share of imported intermediate products, so that the value-added by China in those exports is only a small fraction of the gross product value.[4]

The revealed comparative advantage (RCA) index is one of the most commonly used trade performance indices for shedding light on a country's relative trade competitiveness.[5] The RCA index is seen as representing relative trade competitiveness. A value of the index greater than one indicates that the country in focus has a competitive advantage in the respective sector vis-à-vis rest of the world. It is based on the assumption that the pattern of trade reflects the intercountry differences in relative production costs or advantages (Balassa, 1965 and 1989). The RCA is calculated as a product or a sector share in that country's total exports divided by that product or sector share in world total exports. In simple words, it is a ratio of a country and world export concentration at a product or a sector level. As gross export values include values of imported components, RCA indices calculated by using gross values may not accurately represent the characteristics of a nation's production costs. With the globalization of production becoming common, a more accurate measurement of RCA should be based on domestic value-added embodied in gross exports.[6]

Using the Trade in Value Added (TiVA) Database of OECD, figure 1.8 presents the RCA indices based on gross exports (RCA_{ij}) and domestic value-added embodied in gross exports (RCA_DVA_{ij}) in 2009 for electrical and optical equipment, transport and equipment, machinery and equipment, textiles and textile products, and leather and footwear. These indices show that analysing the comparative advantage through the lens of value-added trade might change the perceptions of Asia-Pacific manufacturing competitiveness. The economies are separated into two groups. One group includes the economies whose RCA indices based on gross-export values are higher than those calculated based on value-added and these are shown in the left-hand side in figure 1.8. The second group comprises economies whose gross-export value based RCA indices are lower than the domestic value-added based RCA indices.

FIGURE 1.8 Revealed comparative advantage indices based on gross- and value-added exports of selected sectors, 2009

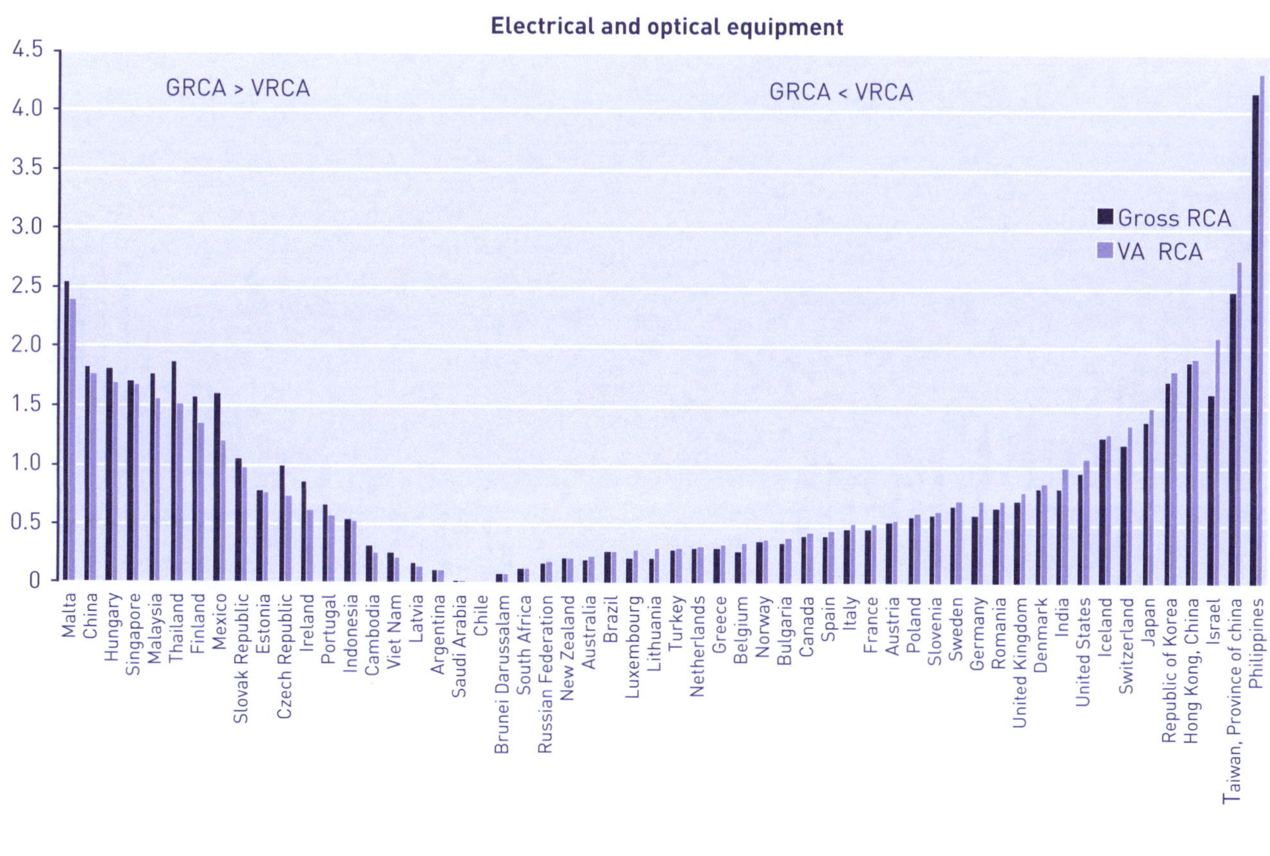

FIGURE 1.8 (continued)

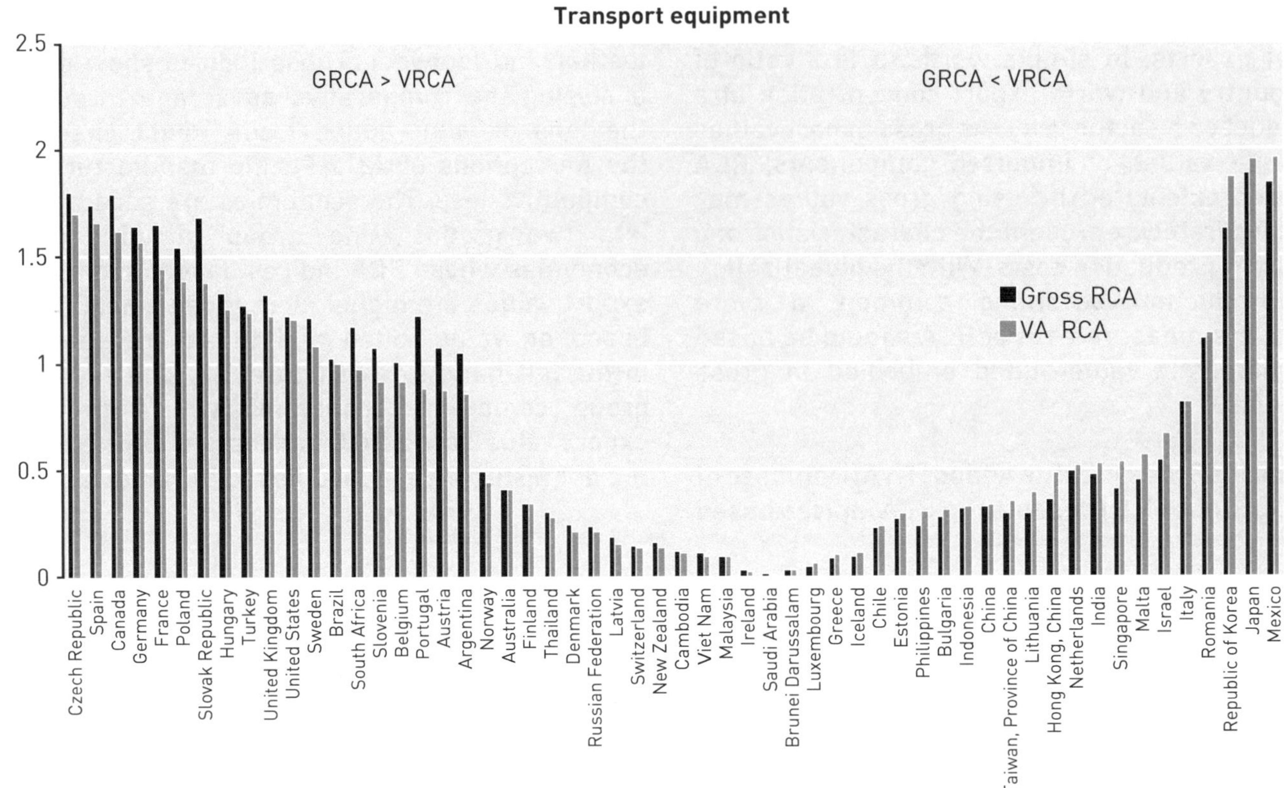

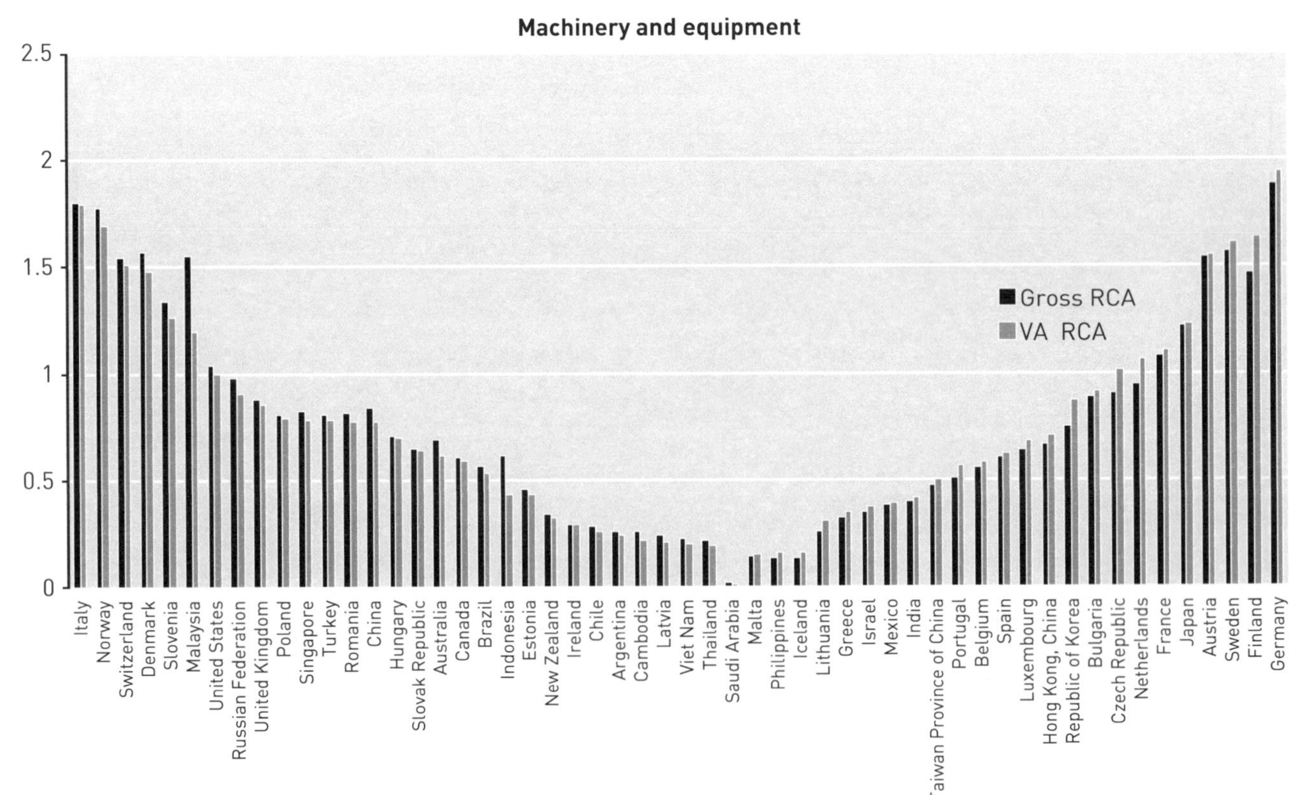

FIGURE 1.8

(continued)

Textiles, textile products, leather and footwear

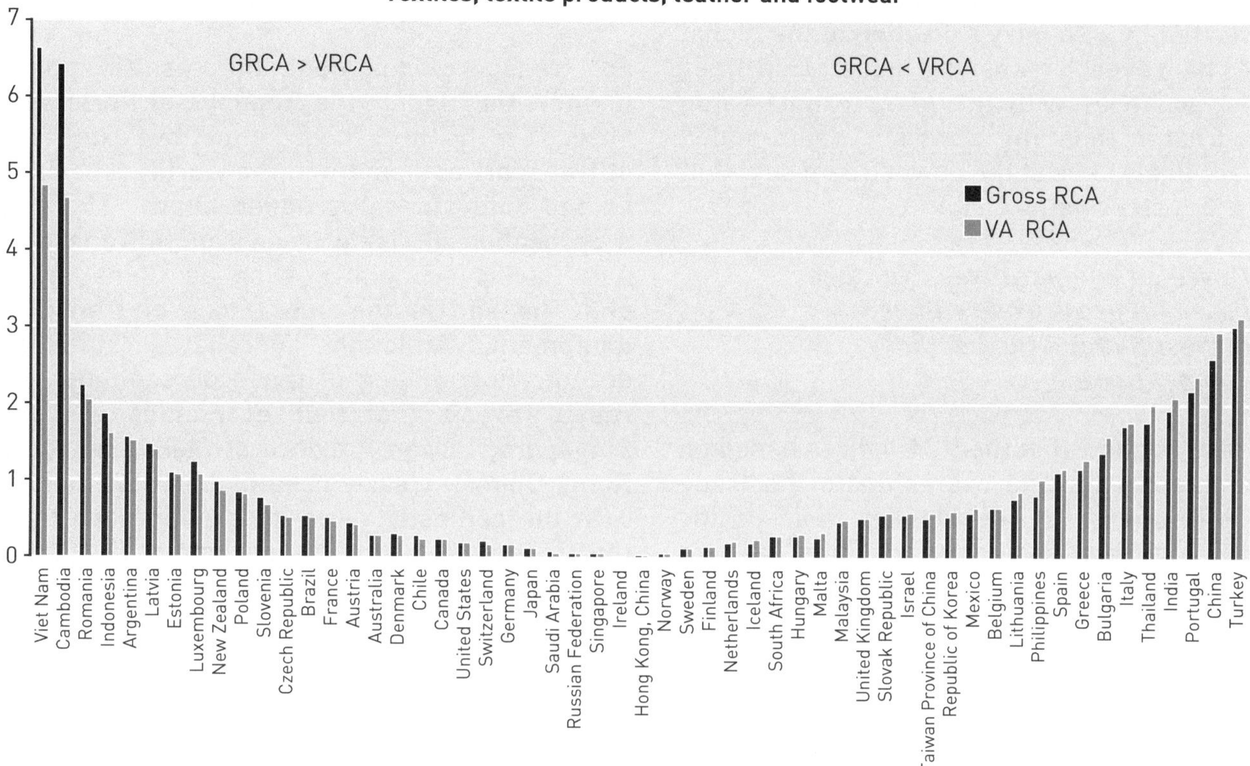

Food products, beverages and tobacco

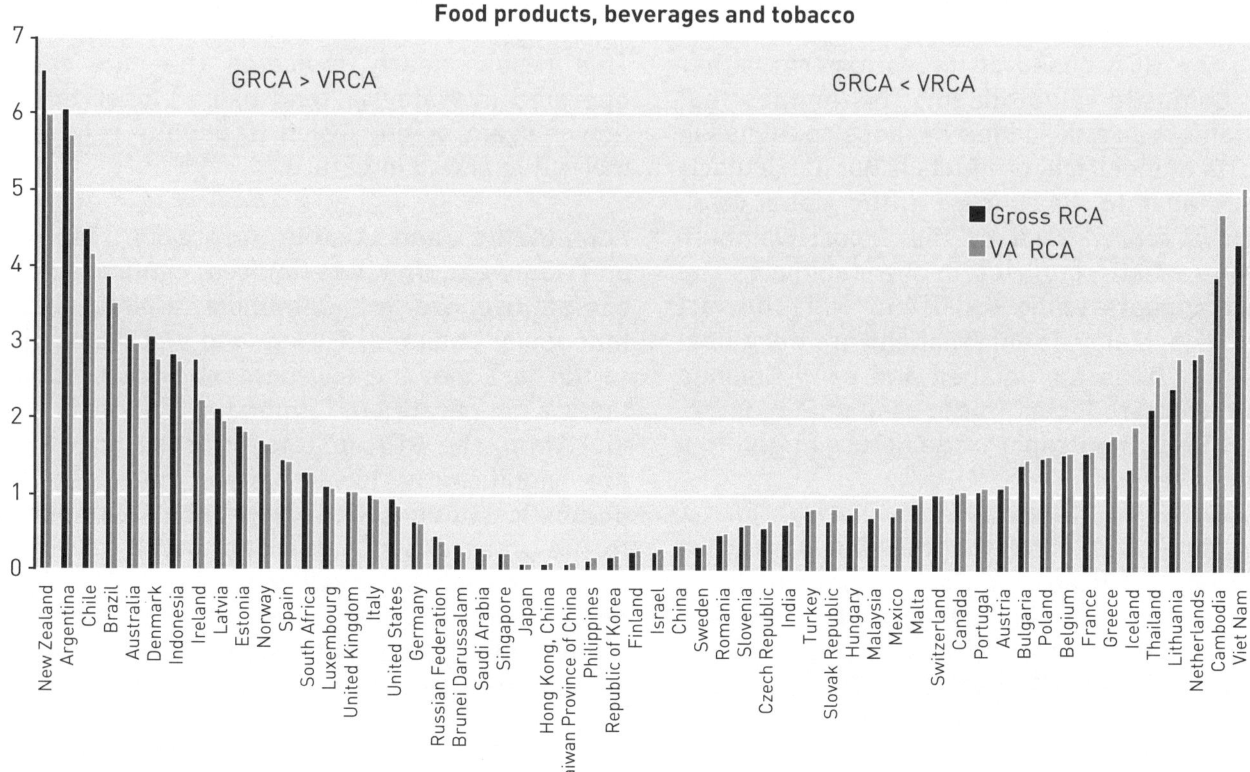

Source: Based on data from the OECD-WTO TiVA database.

The difference in the values of RCA indices based on the two approaches reveals biases generated by the gross-export value based RCA indices. The direction of the difference tends to be affected by a country's position in the global value chain of each respective industry.[7] In other words, countries with the gross export value RCA greater than the domestic value-added RCA are likely to be at the downstream segment of the industry's value chain.

> *Revealed comparative advantage based on gross trade values overestimates Asia-Pacific competitive edge.*

The results show that the RCA indices based on gross exports tend to overestimate the trade competitiveness of developing Asia-Pacific countries where assembly activities tend to be located. In the case of the electrical and optical equipment sectors, both approaches demonstrate that eight Asia-Pacific economies have competitive advantage, i.e. China; Japan; Malaysia; the Philippines; Singapore; Thailand; Hong Kong, China; and Taiwan Province of China. Among those economies, the competitive advantages of China, Malaysia, Singapore and Thailand appear to be overestimated when using the RCA based on gross exports rather than domestic value-added.[8] This implies that the domestic value-added by those countries in exports of electrical products is not particularly high relative to the average at the global level, which is represented by the export-weighted average of all countries in the database. The result appears to be consistent with the fact that China, Malaysia and Thailand are the global assembly hubs for finished and semi-finished electronics products.[9] In the case of Singapore, that country's entrepôt trade nature might be a possible reason.

It should also be noted that the two approaches sometimes indicate a different competiveness position. For example, India appears to have no trade competitiveness in electrical equipment sector based on the traditional RCA. However, that country's position improves slightly when measured by domestic content. A possible interpretation of this result is that the country has not yet become a competitive exporter of electrical equipment, but that its existing production activities are not low-value added tasks relative to the average at the global level.[10]

For transport equipment, the results appear to show that Japan, the Republic of Korea and Mexico are the three most competitive exporters of transport equipment in the world, especially on the domestic-value added basis. There is a perception of rising trade competiveness of Asia-Pacific economies such as China, India and Thailand in the subsectors of transport equipment. Although aggregated statistics do not allow testing of those perceptions, the result reveals that four economies – India, Singapore, Taiwan Province of China and Hong Kong, China – clearly have higher RCA indices with the domestic value-added approach than the gross export value measurement. The result reflects the fact that the production activities in those economies tend to include a considerable content of value-added by domestic labour as well as producers parts and components.

For the machinery and equipment sector, only Malaysia and Japan appear to be competitive. Malaysia's competiveness is significantly lower when using domestic value-added measures. This result clearly indicates that the tasks operated in Malaysia tend to be closer to the downstream stage, which is usually relatively low-value added in nature.

For textile and textile products, leather and footwear, the two indices confirm trade competitiveness for Cambodia, China, India, Indonesia, Thailand, Turkey and Viet Nam. Due to the fact that the low-domestic value-added tasks are operated in Cambodia, Indonesia and Viet Nam, the RCA indices of those countries are significantly lower when measured by domestic value-added approach (compared to the gross-export value approach). It should also be noted that measuring the RCA indices on domestic value-added improves the position of the Philippines in these sectors from not competitive closer to being competitive.

For the food, beverages and tobacco sector, the trade strength of Australia, Cambodia,

Indonesia, New Zealand, Thailand and Viet Nam are confirmed by both measures. The results show that the competitiveness of those Asia-Pacific economies, with the exception of Indonesia, is significantly underestimated if gross export values are used.

Overall, the comparisons of the two RCA measures indicate the importance of the linkages and contributions of countries in the global value chains when evaluating trade competitiveness. The competitive strength of a country should be measured from a domestic value-added content in exports, not from a gross-export value. Also, formulating trade policy and policy measures in the new trade environment needs to take into account the imported content in other countries' exports. Ignoring the rising imported component in such exports could lead to misguided trade and industrial policies. For example, trade restrictions imposed on imports of smartphones by the United States will reduce that country's imports of smartphones from China; at the same time, however, the software firms in the United States that supply information technology applications to the smartphone producers in China will also be hurt by falling overseas demand for their software, which is unlikely to be fully compensated by rising demand by local smartphone producers at higher domestic prices.

CONCLUSION

The developments in 2013 and, so far, in 2014 continue to show that the prolonged consequence of the global 2008 financial crisis is still posing risks to the trade prospects of Asia and the Pacific. Intraregional demand is evidently vulnerable to the global economic slowdown. It is expected that the growth of merchandise trade by developing Asia-Pacific economies will continue to be slow-paced in the remainder of 2014, with average export growth of 5% in real terms. This growth is expected to range from a low of 2% (Russian Federation) to a high of 7% (Singapore and the Philippines).

Despite significant uncertainties, it is expected that buoyant Asia-Pacific exports will improve in 2015 to reach a growth rate of 7% in real terms. The risks stem from the fluctuations in the economic recovery of the United States and the risks of a Chinese economic hard landing, and can also easily be worsened by the increasing number of political and military conflicts in the region and globally.

As the region is evidently not immune to the global economic uncertainties, the need to focus on long-term strategies to increase competitiveness has never been greater. However, the new form of trade and production encompassing trade in intermediate inputs as well as the growing demand for services to co-ordinate dispersed production locations highlights the risks of policies that ignore the interconnection of production between countries participation in global value chains (GVCs). In a world where the participation of a country in the GVCs has become the norm, raising the value of gross exports or the unit value of exports should not be the only focus. It is actually the value-added by domestic producers that matters. To strengthen competitiveness for countries with international production linkages, a key is strengthening productive capacity in order to raise domestic value-added of exports, not just to increase gross exports. In the globalization of production, failure to distinguish between gross exports and domestic value-added in exports can lead to misguided trade and industrial policies.

ENDNOTES

1 This includes intraregional trade flows and flows with the rest of the world.

2 These numbers are estimates by the ESCAP secretariat, based on WTO data at the time of preparing this report. More recent revisions of trade data by WTO may result in a different trade balance value. In addition, the use of other sources of trade data may also produce different amounts. The total value for Asia-Pacific trade includes the trade of Taiwan Province of China.

3 A portion of that amount is used in further processing, which is then exported as final products to the rest of the world.

4 For example, in 2009 China exported 25.7 million iPhone units valued at $4.6 billion. The decomposition of the global value chain of the iPhone reveals that, a merely $0.17 billion or about 3.6%, was the actual

value added by Chinese workers (Xing, 2011).

5 RCA of country i in industry j based on gross exports is defined as $RCA_{ij} = \frac{(X_{ij} / \sum_i X_{ij})}{(\sum_j X_{ij} / \sum_{i,j} X_{ij})}$, where X_{ij} is exports of sector j by country i, $\sum_i X_{ij}$ is world exports of commodity j, $\sum_i X_{ij}$ is total exports of country i, and $\sum_{(i,j)} X_{ij}$ is total world exports. A value of RCA_{ij} greater than one indicates that country i is more specialized in exports of sector j than the world on a whole, which is interpreted as country i holding a comparative advantage in that sector.

6 The TiVA database provides the RCA of country i based on domestic value-added embodied in gross exports of industry j (RCA_DVA_{ij}). The formulation is similar to the RCA based on gross export values, but uses domestic value-added embodied in gross exports ($XDVA_{ij}$) of industry j by country i instead of using gross export values:

$$RCA\_DVA_{ij} = \frac{XDVA_{ij} / \sum_i XDVA_{ij}}{\sum_j XDVA_{ij} / \sum_{(i,j)} XDVA_{ij}}.$$

7 One possible reason for this is the high level of aggregation used in this calculation. Such aggregation causes a significant loss of insight from subsectors that typically participate in global value chains but have to be grouped in one broad sector. For example, the highly aggregated index cannot reveal the facts of the electronic subsector where many developing countries' exports are actually small if measured by domestic value-added embodied in gross exports. In the TiVA database, 31 industries at 2-digit ISIC Revision 3 classification are aggregated into nine broad industrial sectors. While the high level of aggregation is necessary to maximize cross-country comparability, such aggregation can create substantial biases.

8 In contrast, those Asia-Pacific economies exporting parts and components – including India, Japan, the Republic of Korea, the Philippines, Taiwan Province of China and Hong Kong, China – tend to have higher RCA indices based on domestic value-added than the gross export ones.

9 An example of semi-finished products is a hard-disk drive. In general, its production process includes assembling imported parts and components, and the products need further processing before becoming a finished good.

10 It should also be noted that a calculation of the RCA index for the United States based on the gross export value, which shows no comparative advantage in the electrical and optical equipment sector, should be taken as a grain of salt. The result indicates that the United States tends to have advantages in the high value-added parts of the sector.

REFERENCES

Balassa, B.A. (1965). Trade liberalization and "revealed" comparative advantage. *The Manchester School*, vol. 33, No. 2, pp. 99-123.

_____ (1989). "Revealed" comparative advantage revisited. In *Comparative Advantage, Trade Policy and Economic Development*. B.A. Ballasa, ed., pp. 63-79. New York: New York University Press.

Bloomberg (2014). Xi says China must adapt to new normal' of slower growth. *Bloomberg News*, 12 May. Available from www.bloomberg.com/news/2014-05-11/xi-says-china-must-adapt-to-new-normal-of-slower-growth.html .

Economic and Social Commission for Asia and the Pacific (2014). *Economic and Social Survey of Asia and the Pacific 2014: Regional Connectivity for Shared Prosperity*. Sales No. E.14.II.F.4. Available from www.unescap.org/resources/economic-and-social-survey-asia-and-pacific-2014 .

G20 (2014). A G20 agenda for growth and resilience 2014. Policy Note, July 2014. Available from https://www.g20.org/sites/default/files/g20_resources/library/Policy%20Note%20-%20Growth%20and%20Resillence.pdf .

International Monetary Fund (2014). World Economic Outlook Update: July 2014. Washington, D.C. Available from www.imf.org/external/pubs/ft/weo/2014/update/02/pdf/0714.pdf .

Manova, Kalina, and Zhihong Yu (2012). Firms and credit constraints along the global value chain: processing trade in China. NBER Working Paper No.18561. Cambridge, M.A.: National Bureau of Economic Research. Available from www.nber.org/papers/w18561 .

Moody's (2014). QE tapering: impact differs amongst emerging markets. Moody's Investor Service, 6 February. Available from https://www.moodys.com/researchdocumentcontentpage.aspx?docid=PBC_163755 .

Xing, Yuquing (2012). The People's Republic of China's high-tech exports: myth and reality. ADBI Working Paper No. 357. Tokyo: Asian Development bank Institute. Available from www.adbi.org/files/2012.04.25.wp357.prc.high.tech.exports.myth.reality.pdf .

Online databases

CEIC Database. Available from ceicdata.securities.com/cdmWeb/ .

Economic and Social Commission for Asia and the Pacific. ESCAP online statistical database. Available from www.unescap.org/stat/data/statdb/DataExplorer.aspx .

International Monetary Fund. World Economic Outlook database. Accessed April 2011. Available from www.imf.org/external/data.htm .

Oxford Economics Database. Available from www.oxford economics.com/OE_FA_IntMac.asp .

OECD-WTO. Trade in Value Added (TiVA). Available from http://stats.oecd.org/Index.aspx?DataSetCode= TIVA_OECD_WTO .

United Nations, Statistics Division, Department of Economic and Social Affairs. United Nations Comtrade database. Available from www.comtrade.un.org (accessed October 2010).

World Bank. World Integrated Trade Solution (WITS) database. Available from http://wits.worldbank.org/ .

World Trade Organization. Short-term merchandise trade statistics. Available from www.wto.org/english/res_e/statis_e/quarterly_world_exp_e.htm .

2 TRENDS AND DEVELOPMENTS IN COMMERCIAL SERVICES TRADE[1]

A. ASIA-PACIFIC EXPORTS OF COMMERCIAL SERVICES CONTINUE TO SLOW

A slow-down of merchandise exports by Asia-Pacific economies during 2013 was also accompanied by continued stagnation of its commercial services exports in contrast to a modest worldwide recovery in services exports.[2] For the first time since 2004 with the exception of 2009 (figure 2.1), the Asian and Pacific region's growth in trade of commercial services lagged behind global growth. World export growth jumped from 2.4% in 2012 to 5.6% in 2013, increasing the export value to more than $4,600 billion, led by the recovery of European Union exports, which accounted for almost one half of world services exports.

FIGURE 2.1 Annual growth in commercial services trade: Asia-Pacific region and the world

(Year-on-year percentage change)

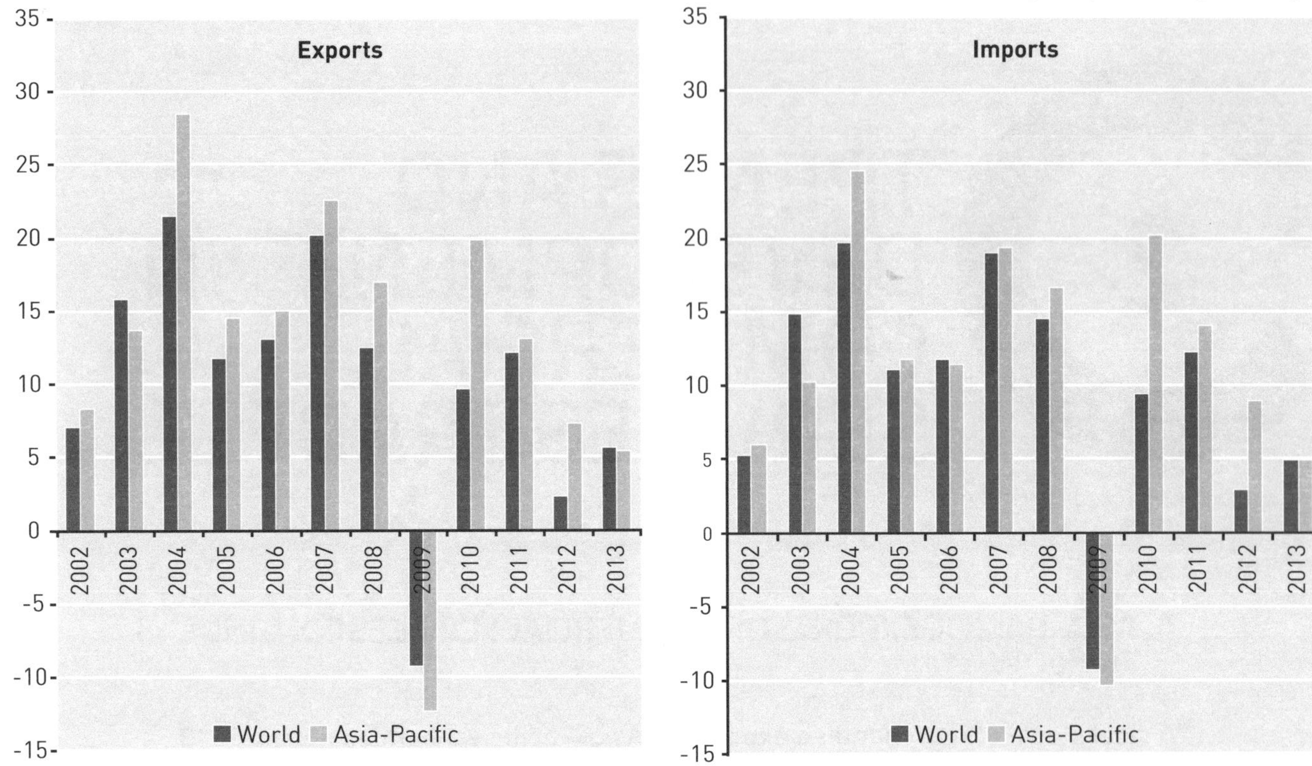

Source: ESCAP calculation, based on data from the WTO International Trade Statistics Database (accessed September 2014).

In contrast, major exporters in Asia and the Pacific, such as China, India, the Republic of Korea and Singapore experienced slower growth of services exports. Indeed, the average growth for the region decreased from 7.4% in 2012 to 5.4% in 2013. The growth of services imports decelerated significantly from 8.4% to 5% in 2013. As a result, the growth performance of commercial services trade by the Asia-Pacific region became closer to the rest of the world (figure 2.1). Nevertheless, in terms of export value the Asian and Pacific economies together surpassed the extra-European Union and the United States exports which were $891 billion and $662 billion, respectively, in 2013.

The region's growth of commercial services trade lagged behind global growth in 2013.

Asia-Pacific as a whole accounts for 29% of world exports of commercial services, but 65% of that share comes from just six economies.

With a recorded export value of $1,338 billion in 2013 (figure 2.2),[3] the Asia-Pacific region accounted for about 29% of world exports of commercial services.[4] Six economies contributed more than 65% of the exports: China (15%); India (11%); Japan (11%); Hong Kong, China (10%); Singapore (9%); and the Republic of Korea (8%). Other important exporters also include the Russian Federation (5%), Thailand (4.4%), Australia, Macao, China and Taiwan Province of China (4% each), Turkey (3.5%) and Malaysia (3%).

Major exporting countries displayed a diverse performance in 2013. While relatively advanced countries, including Australia, Japan and the Republic of Korea, saw their marginal export

FIGURE 2.2 Value of trade in commercial services between the Asia-Pacific region and the world, 2000-2013

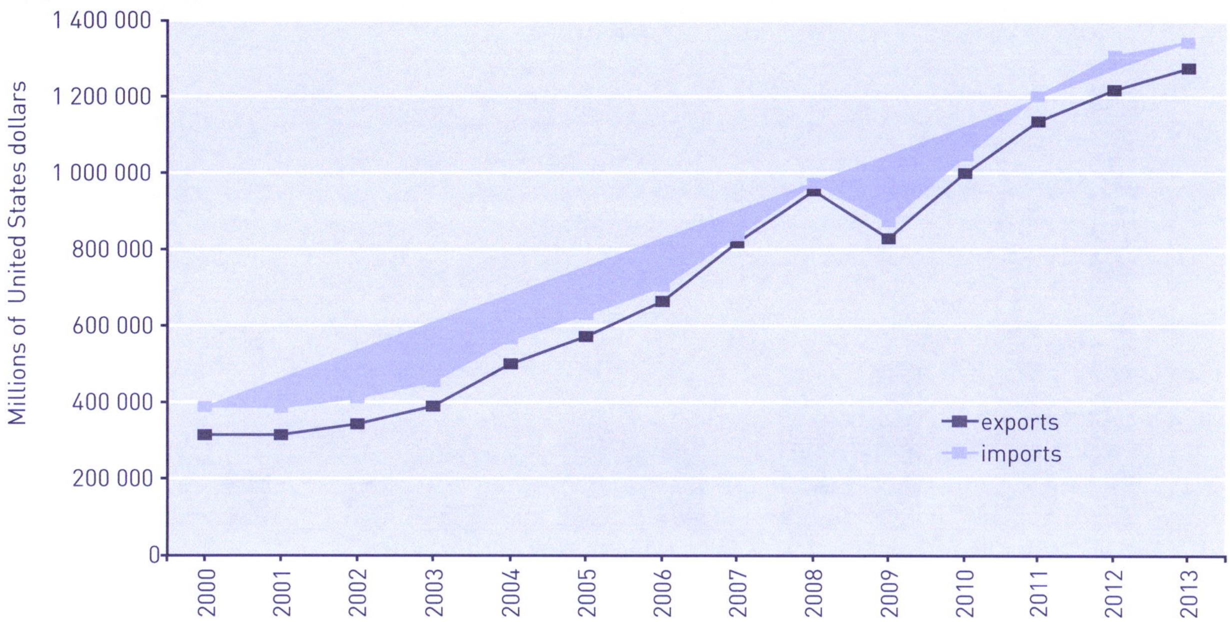

Source: ESCAP calculation, based on data from the WTO International Trade Statistics Database (accessed September 2014).

growth, China maintained its export growth at 7.5% due to a 52% jump in its financial services exports and strong growth of other business services exports, making it the fourth-largest exporter in that category. India performed moderately with export growth of 4% (which was mainly driven by the expansion of computer and information services).

The region is a net importer of commercial services; in 2013, its imports was $1,398 billion, accounting for 32% of world imports.[5] Major importing countries included: China (24%); Japan (12%); India (9%); the Russian Federation (9%); the Republic of Korea (9%); and Singapore (8%). Except for China and the Russian Federation, whose imports grew by more than 18%, other major importing countries experienced an import slowdown in 2013 as a result of moderation of domestic demand combined with the downturn in goods exports which in turn caused an expected a reduction in intermediate service imports due to "servicification" phenomenon (see section D for more details).

B. DIVERSE PERFORMANCE BY THE SUBREGIONS

Figure 2.3 provides a geographical breakdown of the Asian and Pacific commercial services trade from 1999 to 2013. The East and North-East Asian subregion was the largest contributor to the region's services trade. This subregion accounted for 53% of Asian and the Pacific commercial services exports to the world and 51% of imports from the world in 2013. The remaining trade is split between the other four subregions of Asia and the Pacific in the following way. South-East Asia took one fifth of the services trade followed by South and South-West Asia, which accounted for 15% of exports and 12% of imports. North and Central Asia, despite recording the fastest growth in exports in 2013, still accounted for only 6% while imports were almost double at 11%. The Pacific subregion came last with a share of 5% both in exports and in imports of the total Asia-Pacific region. The Pacific subregion's trade is dominated by Australia and New Zealand as those two countries account for more than 95% of exports and imports by that subregion. During the observed period, North and Central Asia as well as South and South-West Asia

FIGURE 2.3 Commercial services trade by subregion as a share of total Asia-Pacific trade in commercial services

(Percentage of Asia-Pacific exports and imports)

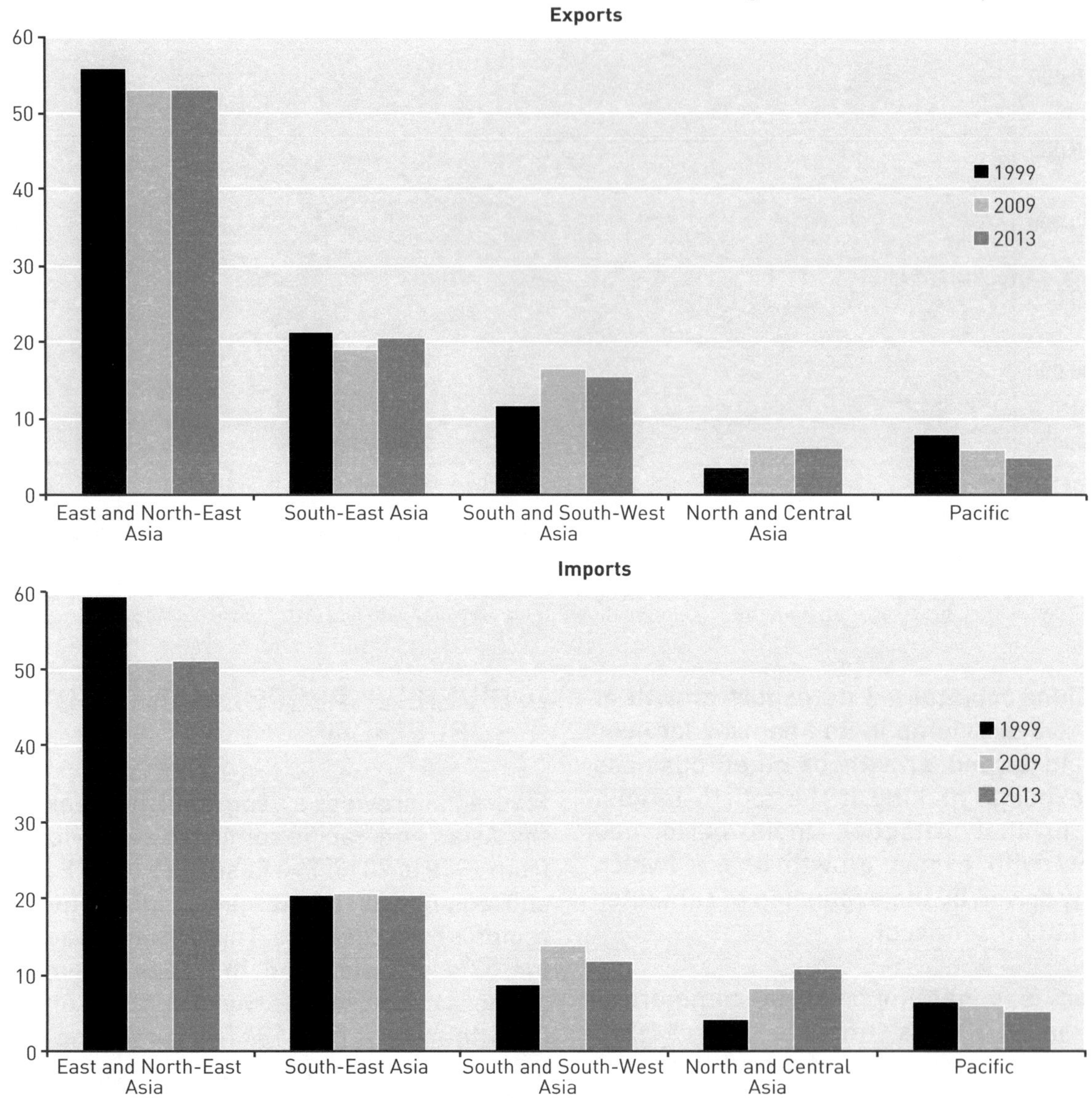

Source: ESCAP calculation, based on the WTO International Trade Statistics Database (accessed July 2014).

significantly increased their shares of the Asia-Pacific services trade at the expense of East and North-East Asia and the Pacific whose shares have declined.

> *Robust export growth has made China and India gaining the shares in Asia-Pacific exports at the expense of relatively advanced economies in the region.*

Focusing on individual economies reveals some significant changes in country shares as well as export and import dynamics during the period studied. India more than doubled its share to reach 11% of the exports by the region (amounting to 3% of global exports). Similarly, China increased its share from 9% to 15% (equivalent to 4.4% of global exports). Japan's share, on the other hand, dropped from 21% to 11% during the same period, and it is now only the third-ranked exporter in the region.

C. SECTORAL BREAKDOWN

Commercial services trade statistics comprise three broad categories: (a) transportation; (b)

FIGURE 2.4 Exports of Asia-Pacific commercial services, by sector, 2001 and 2013

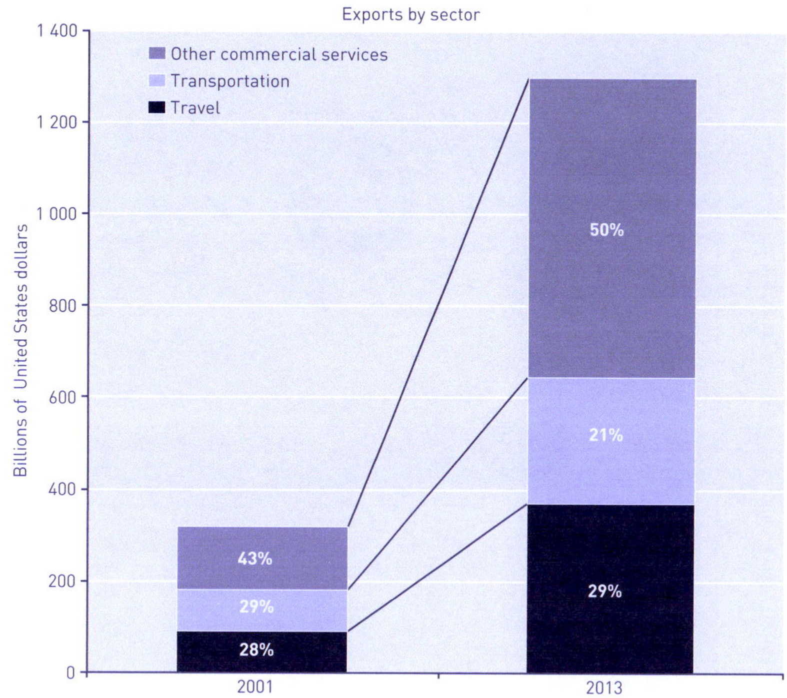

Source: ESCAP calculation, based on the WTO International Trade Statistics Database, commercial services (accessed July 2014).

travel; and (c) other commercial services.[6] The category of other commercial services typically dominates the total commercial services exports.[7] From 2001 to 2013, other commercial services exports increased more rapidly than exports from the other sectors. As a result, the share of other commercial services in total exports increased from 43% to 50% at the expense of transportation services, the share of which dropped from 29% to 21%. Despite a decreasing share, export value of transportation services increased from $92 billion to $275.5 billion during the same period (figure 2.4)

Other business services subsector accounts for more than 50% of total services exports by the region.

From 2001 to 2013, exports of other commercial services, travel and transportation grew annually by 14%, 12.5% and 9.6%, respectively (vertical axis of figure 2.4). Those rates were higher than the growth of global exports by those categories, i.e. 11.5% for other commercial services, 8.5% for transportation services and 8% for travel services (horizontal axis of figure 2.5).

As stated above, the Asian and Pacific region succeeded in capturing an increased share of the global exports of commercial services, up from 21% in 2001 to 29% in 2013. The largest increase in the Asia-Pacific share in exports of travel services, where the expansion of intraregional demand from China supported an expansion of the tourism sector (see box 2.1 for more details). During the same period, the share of exports of transportation services moved up marginally from 27% to 31%. Asia-Pacific exports of other commercial services registered an increase in the share of global exports, up from 20% to 26%.

The breakdown of the export of other commercial services into its eight subcategories is shown in table 2.1. From 2001 to 2013, exports of other commercial services increased almost fourfold from $136 billion to $652 billion. Around 57% of the other commercial services exports were in the broad subcategory of "other business services". The remaining share was spread across the other seven subcategories, some of which recorded marked increases in their shares. Computer and information services, in particular, increased their share from 7%

FIGURE 2.5 Growth of Asia-Pacific commercial services exports, 2001-2013

(Percentage per annum)

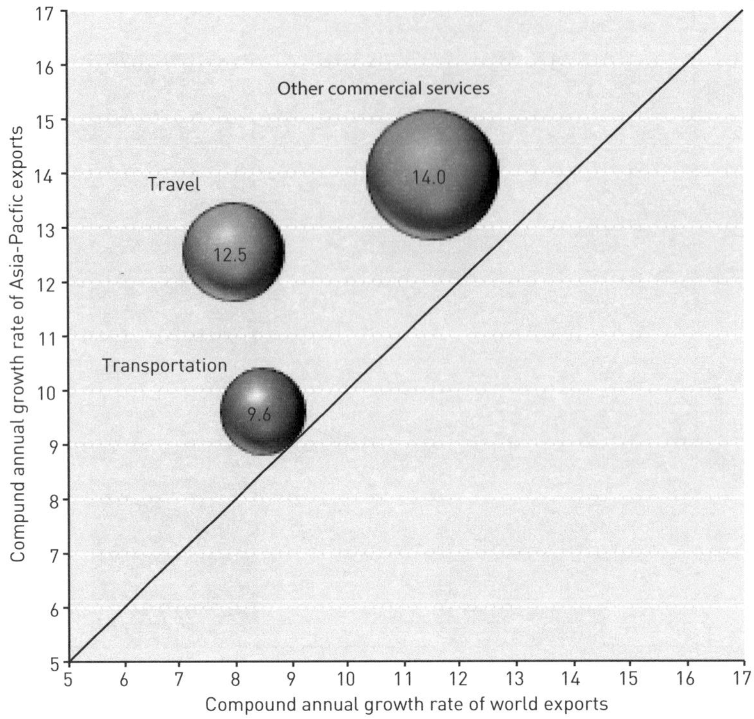

Source: ESCAP calculation, based on the WTO International Trade Statistics Database (accessed July 2014).

Note: The size of the bubbles represents export value of a respective service sector.

to 13% of Asia-Pacific exports during the same period. Indeed, the share of Asia-Pacific exports in the world market increased in most of the subcategories, except in the cases of communication services, and royalties and licence fees (table 2.1). In particular, the Asia-Pacific region's share in the world exports increased dramatically in exports of construction services, computer and information services, and personal and recreational services.

TABLE 2.1 Other commercial services exports breakdown – comparison between 2001 and 2013

(Value in billions of United States dollars and percentage share)

Service sector	Export value		Shares in Asia-Pacific exports		Asia-Pacific shares in world exports	
	2001	2013	2001	2013	2001	2013
Other commercial services	135.8	652.1	100	100	19.8	25.6
Communications services	6.1	17.9	4.5	2.7	16.9	15.7
Computer and information services	9.7	82.6	7.1	12.7	18.2	28.9
Construction	9.3	52.6	6.9	8.1	29.4	50.6
Financial services	12.2	58.7	9.0	9.0	13.0	17.7
Insurance services	3.3	14.8	2.5	2.3	11.2	13.1
Other business services	81.0	374.2	59.6	57.4	24.0	30.1
Personal, cultural and recreational services	1.1	7.0	0.8	1.1	8.2	16.7
Royalties and license fees	12.9	42.3	9.5	6.5	14.3	13.6

Source: ESCAP calculation, based on the WTO International Trade Statistics Database (accessed July 2014).

Box 2.1 International tourism in the Asia-Pacific region[a]

For international tourism, 2013 proved to be another strong year, with 1.1 billion international tourist arrivals registered globally, according to the United Nations World Tourism Organization (UNWTO, 2014c).[b] The Asia-Pacific region was the most dynamic actor, leading the growth of world tourism with particularly strong first and third quarters (see figure below). The international arrivals to Asia and the Pacific grew 6% in 2013. This made Asia-Pacific tourism sector performing marginally better than the one in Europe and Africa where the growth rate was 5%[c] The outlook for 2014 is promising; the UNWTO forecast expects growth in international arrivals to destinations in Asia and the Pacific to remain steady at 5% to 6% in 2014. However, the gap between tourism growth in the Asia-Pacific region and the world is decreasing as tourism is picking up pace in the rest of the world (see table).

> ***Increasing tourist arrivals in other regions are closing the gap with the dynamic Asia-Pacific sector***

In 2013, Asia and the Pacific captured almost 23% of international tourist arrivals; almost half of whom were arrivals in East and North-East Asia (11.7% of global international tourist arrivals), with South-East Asia following closely behind (8.5%). The share of arrivals in North and Central Asia, Oceaniad and South Asia remained low at 1.7%, 1.2% and 1.4%, respectively.

Overall, East and North-East Asia remained the most popular subregion within Asia and the Pacific, with 51.2% of all tourist arrivals in the region, but recording a relatively slow growth rate of 3.5% in 2013. China remained the most popular destination with a 43.8% share. South-East Asia received 37.5% of total international tourist arrivals but was the fastest growing subregion with an increase of 10% in 2013 on the back of growing intraregional demand from China. Major destinations were Thailand and Malaysia, which attracted 28.5% and 27.6%, respectively, of international tourist arrivals within the subregion. North and Central Asian countries also registered strong growth of 10%, mainly driven by international arrivals in the Russian Federation, which accounted for 65% of all arrivals to the subregion.[e]

South and South-West Asia showed solid growth of 6.1% in 2013; the subregion's most popular destination was India, which accounted for 44.2% of all visitors to the subregion in that year. The Pacific subregion saw an increase of 4.4% in tourist arrivals in 2013, with the top destination being Australia with a 51.1% share of international tourists and a growth rate of 5.8%.[f] Although the small base value of international arrival in the Pacific island countries makes the annual growth swing significant, there was an impressive average growth of 6% per year from 2000 to 2012 (Chen and others, 2014).

At the country level, the most dynamic growth rates in international tourist arrivals in 2013 were recorded by Myanmar (44.9%), Kiribati (38.5%), Timor-Leste (29.2%) and Sri Lanka (26.7%). Japan also made a strong recovery in the growth of tourist arrivals by 24% in 2013.

Box 2.1 (continued)

The features of the tourist arrivals in Asia and the Pacific are also similarly reflected in international tourism receipts. East and North-East Asia and South-East Asia received the largest shares of tourism receipts (51.5% and 29.9%, respectively, of a total $358 billion in 2013). In South-East Asia, Thailand received the largest share of international tourism receipts and experienced the highest growth rate. The country captured 39.2% of receipts in the subregion based on a growth rate of 23.1% compared with 2012. In East and North-East Asia, the receipt from tourism was spread more evenly compared with South-East Asia. Other large tourism-income recipients in 2013 were China (28%), Hong Kong, China (21.1%) and Macao, China (28%). On the other hand, in terms of growth, Japan experienced the highest rate in 2013, with receipts increasing by 25.3%; this growth is projected to continue into 2014 for which the first quarter statistics indicate a 35.2% increase compared with the previous year.

Rising intraregional tourism has become the global trend. Intraregional tourism tends to grow faster than travel across regions. In 2013, intraregional air passenger arrivals grew by 3.6%, while total arrivals globally grew by 3.3%. In Asia and the Pacific, intraregional arrivals increased by 2.4% in 2013; September to December, in particular, saw exceptionally strong growth of 5.8%. This trend is expected to continue. Based on flight reservations data, from January to April 2014 intraregional travel grew by about 8.2% compared with the same period in 2013. Japan, in particular, benefitted from this intraregional growth in 2013 with some 78.3% of arrivals originating from the Asian region, including China (10.9%), the Republic of Korea (30.6%), Taiwan Province of China (32%) and Hong Kong, China (11%).[g]

Signs of modest recovery in advanced economies as well as a robust trend in outbound flow from China make the outlook positive for 2014. Based on comments from tourism experts, Chinese demand for outbound travel is still strong (UNWTO, 2014a). In South-East Asia, the annual performance of Thailand, the major tourist destination of South-East Asia, might show some weakening due to the political unrest during the first half of 2014. However, the subregion as a whole still has strong potential.

The ASEAN Economic Community (AEC), which will be fully implemented by the end of 2015, should enhance intra-ASEAN travel. Following the establishment of visa-free travel for ASEAN nationals – together the ASEAN business travel card that allows frequent business travellers from ASEAN countries to stay for months at a time in other ASEAN countries without the need to obtain a visa – ASEAN countries are also working with relevant agencies on the development of a common visa for non-ASEAN nationals. A common ASEAN visa will make ASEAN destinations more attractive as they will allow easier and cheaper access for non-ASEAN tourists.

Intraregional tourism is also an important source of income for the Pacific island countries where it holds a considerable share of gross domestic product. According to Chen and others (2014), the main sources of tourist arrivals in most Pacific island countries are – in addition to Australia, New Zealand and the United States – Asian economies, especially Japan, the Republic of Korea and Taiwan Province of China. It should be noted that for the Pacific island countries, the tourism industry is the main driver of their gross domestic product, both directly and indirectly.[h]

Box 2.1 (continued)

As stated by the United Nations Conference on Trade and Development (2013, p. 7), tourism is not only needed for its crucial contribution to the balance of payments and macroeconomic stability, but also as a sector with strong and diverse backward and forward linkages that "catalyse a multiplier effect that can generate broad-based economic benefits at the national level as well as employment opportunities and poverty reduction at the local level". In terms of growth potential, the gravity model analysis carried out by Chen and others (2014) showed that, given their geographical and cultural natures, the Pacific island countries offer more favourable conditions for tourism exports than goods exports.

Rising export growth opportunities emerge from the rapid expansion of tourist arrivals from Asia, in particular from China. However, investment to improve tourist infrastructure and services as well as marketing and information dissemination is necessary for the islands to be able to exploit their export potential.

FIGURE Year-on-year percentage growth in international tourist arrivals

(Percentage)

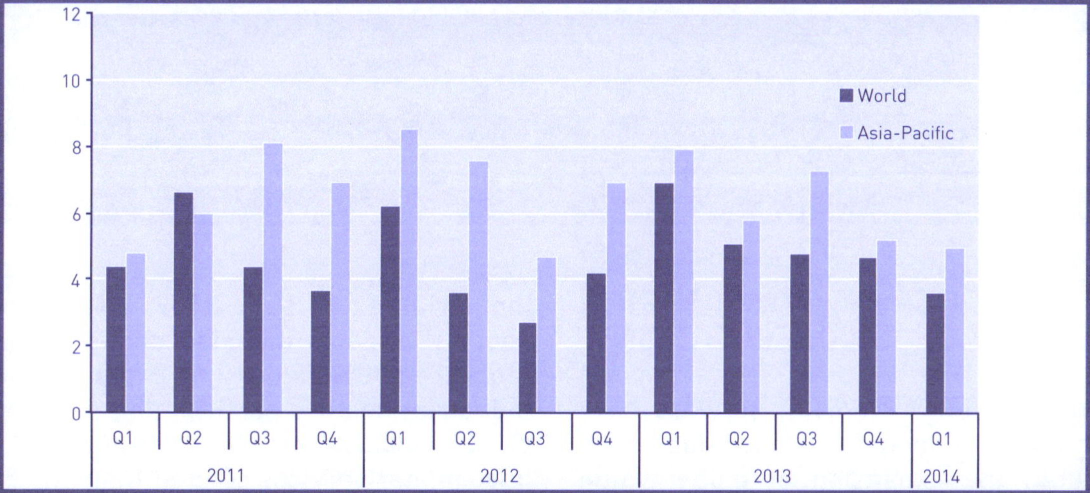

Source: UNWTO (2014b).

TABLE Tourist arrivals: annual growth rates for 2010-2013 and 2014 projections

(Percentage)

Region	2010	2011	2012	2013	2014 Projection
World	6.5	4.9	4.1	5.0	4.0-4.5
Europe	3.1	6.4	3.6	5.4	3.0-4.0
Asia and the Pacific	13.2	6.6	6.9	6.2	5.0-6.0
Americas	6.6	3.6	4.5	3.6	3.0-4.0
Africa	9.3	-0.6	6.6	5.4	4.0-6.0
Middle East	11.5	-6.1	-5.4	-0.2	0.0-5.0*

Source: UNWTO, 2014b.

* The wide range of the UNWTO projection is due to the high uncertainty of the political and security situation in the Middle East.

Box 2.1 (continued)

[a] International tourism is one of the 12 sectors covered by the WTO General Agreement on Trade in Services (GATS), and it is also often included in preferential trade agreements. However, it does not feature as a self-standing service activity in trade statistics; rather, it is subsumed under travel services. In national accounts it does not often appear as a well-defined category, even though it is an important source of income and employment for many developing and least developed countries, especially in Asia and the Pacific.

[b] UNWTO, 2014b.

[c] The Asian and Pacific region in the WTO definition comprises the following economies: Australia; Bhutan; Cambodia; China; Cook Islands; Guam; Fiji; French Polynesia; Hong Kong, China; India; Indonesia; Japan; Kiribati; Macao, China; Maldives; Malaysia; Marshall Islands; Myanmar; Nepal; New Caledonia; New Zealand; Niue; Northern Mariana Islands; Pakistan; Palau; Papua New Guinea; Republic of Korea; Samoa; Singapore; Solomon Islands; Sri Lanka; Taiwan Province of China; Thailand; Tonga; Vanuatu; and Viet Nam. Countries in North and Central Asia are included as a part of Europe under the WTO definition.

[d] "Oceania" as a region in the UNWTO statistics covers in addition to countries of "Pacific" under ESCAP's subregions Heard and McDonald Islands; Norfolk Island; Pitcairn; Tokelau; and Wallis and Futuna Islands.

[e] North and Central Asian countries are included as a part of Central and Eastern Europe according to the UNWTO definition. Data are not available for Turkmenistan and Uzbekistan.

[f] Statistics for New Zealand were unavailable at the time of preparation of this report (July 2014).

[g] ESCAP calculation based on data from www.tourism.jp/en/statistics/ (accessed 23 April 2014).

[h] According to Chen and others (2014), tourism accounts for more than 50% and 30% of the GDP of Palau and Vanuatu, respectively.

D. FURTHER PROGRESS IN MEASURING THE EXTENT OF "SERVICIFICATION"

As discussed in ESCAP (2013), services have been increasingly embedded in manufacturing. In particular, the expansion of global value chains involving several Asia-Pacific economies has contributed to services such as business services, communication and transportation becoming a critical component linking and facilitating international production networks for industrial exports. While the role of services value-added in industrial exports has been increasing, detailed evaluation is still unavailable to many economies due to limited availability and reliability of data. This section utilizes the best available data to contribute to this topic. The calculation in this section is based on the OECD-WTO Trade in Value Added (TiVA) database launched in May 2013.[8]

According to the trade value-added data, services contributed 29% to the global industrial exports in 2009.[9] Many industrial sectors' exports included services content of more than 30% (figure 2.6). Exports of high-tech industrial sectors participating in global value chains, especially transport equipment, tend to have higher services content than other sectors (37%). In contrast, the traditional industrial sectors' gross exports typically contain a smaller value of services (not more than 30%). For example, in the case of mining and quarrying, the export services' share was only 10% while in agriculture, forestry, hunting and fishing it was 24%, and in textiles, textile products, leather and footwear it was 25%.

Although domestically-provided services dominate the services content in manufacturing exports, it is expected that imported services will be supplying an increasing share in those industries that are characterized by international product fragmentation. The data, however limited they are at present, appear to support this conjecture. Overall, domestic services content accounts for about 19% of industrial exports while foreign content accounts for about 10%. Foreign services content seems to be relatively higher than the average for those industrial sectors perceived to be part of international fragmentation of production, including the electrical and optical equipment and the transport equipment sectors. The foreign services content in exports from those two sectors was 15% and 13%, respectively.

> ***Rising international fragmentation of production has made a growing component of services content in industrial exports, especially services sourced from foreign countries.***

The share of total services value in industrial exports has increased over time, especially in the transport sector (a rise of almost 7 percentage points from 1995 to 2009) as illustrated in figure 2.7. The exception was the mining and quarrying sector in which the share of services in exports decreased by almost 4 percentage points during the same period. The significant increases of foreign services content compared with domestic services content reflects a rapid pace of international "servicification", especially in capital and technologically-intensive sectors such as basic metal and fabricated metal products, chemical and non-metallic mineral products, electrical and optical equipment, machinery and equipment, manufacturing (nec), and recycling and transport equipment.

FIGURE 2.6 Services content in gross exports, by industrial sector, 2009

(Percentage of global export value)

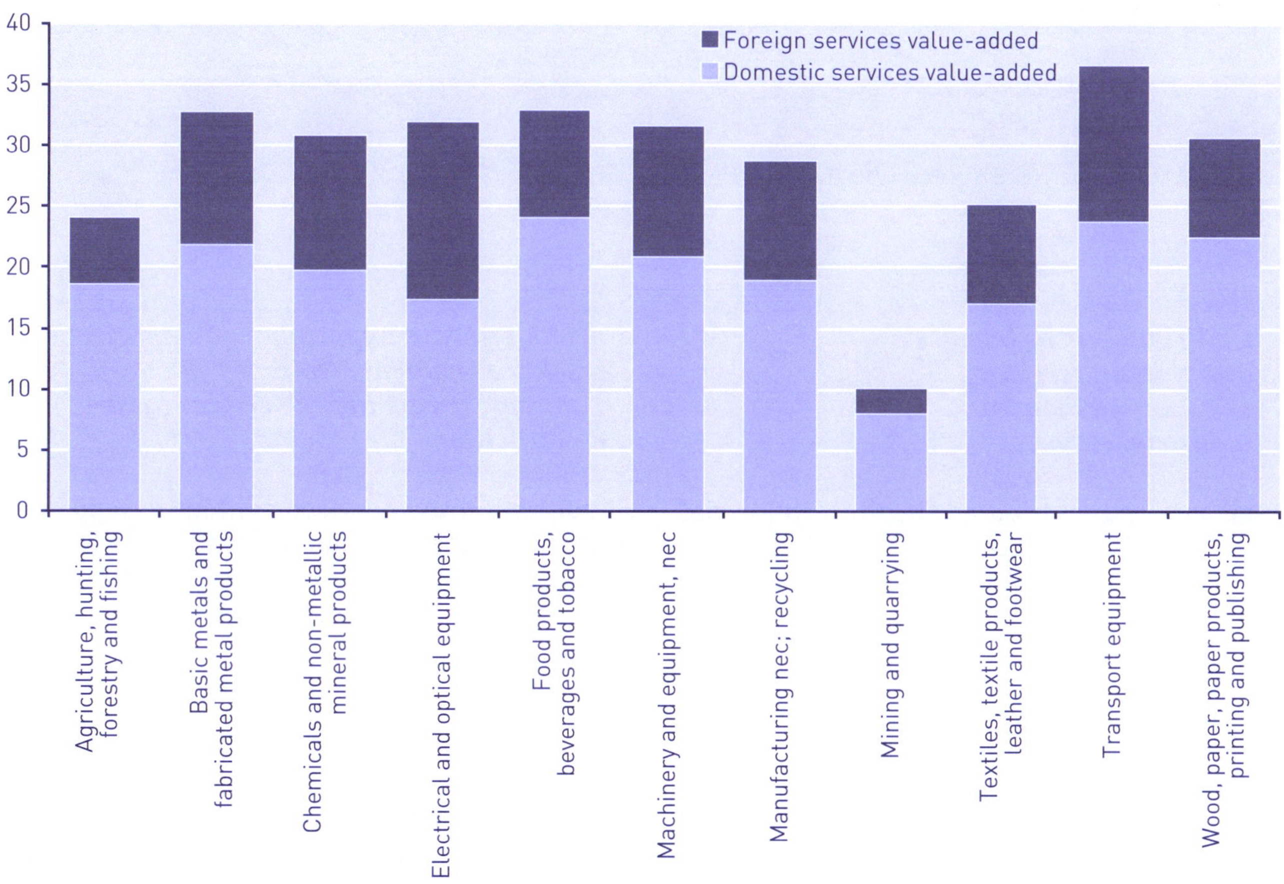

Source: ESCAP calculation based on OECD-WTO TiVA database (2013).

FIGURE 2.7 Changes in the shares of services value-added in gross industrial exports, 1995-2009

(Percentage points)

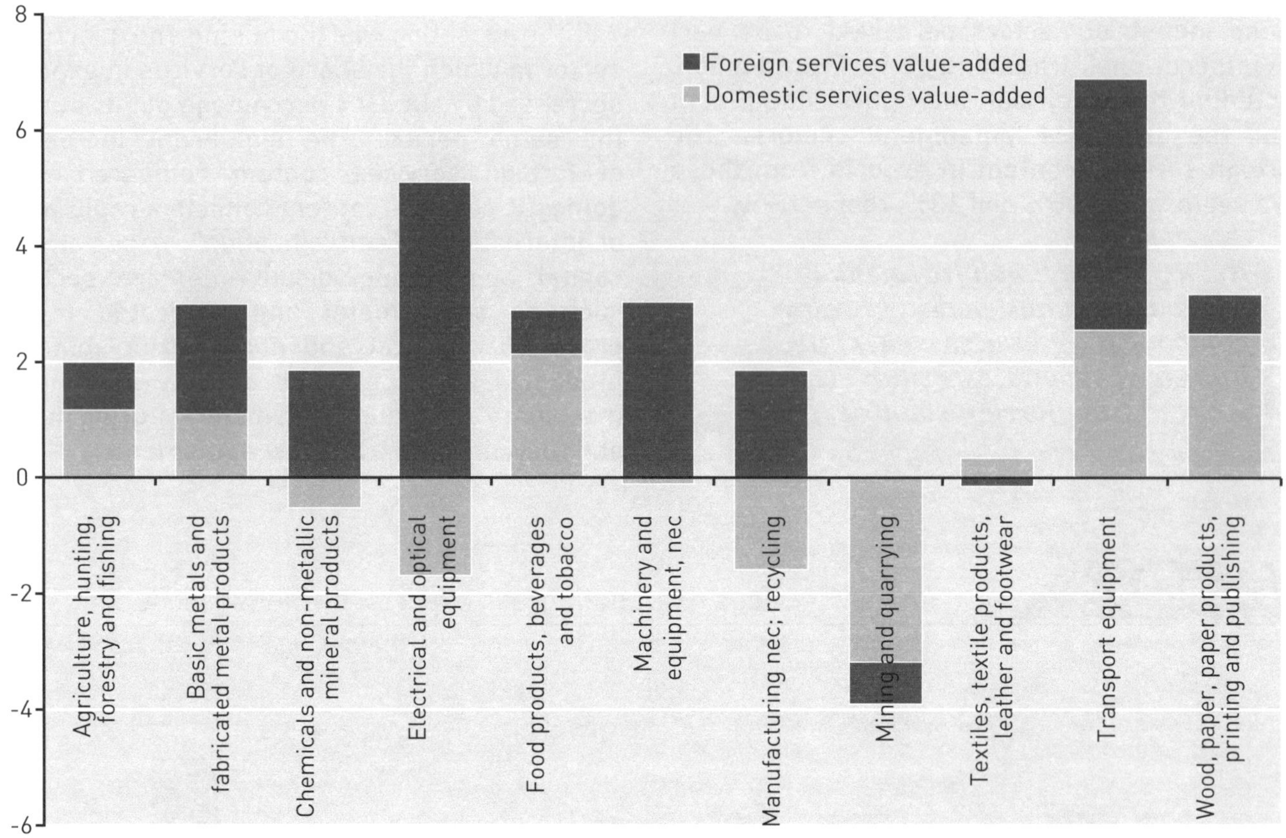

Source: ESCAP calculation based on OECD-WTO TiVA database (2013).

Contributions by business and trading services are a key element of industrial exports.

Not all services contributed equally to industrial sector exports. Available data reveal that the major contributor was business services, followed by wholesale and retail trade, and hotels and restaurants (figure 2.8). Around two thirds of the inputs from services are sourced domestically, although there is some variation across service sectors. Logistics-related services, including transport, storage, post and telecommunications, hold a higher share of imported services (38%), while imported services feature less in public utility services including electricity, gas and water supply (28%).

The growing importance of imported services content also imply the need to remove remaining services trade restrictions.

About half of the services content in industrial exports is accounted for by business services, wholesale and retail trade, and hotels and restaurants. This pattern did not change much during 1995-2009, but there was a clear shift from domestically-supplied to foreign-supplied services – 85% of the increases in the share of business services in industrial exports came from foreign services input (figure 2.9). While shares of imports of services of all types grew during 1995-2009, the share of domestically-provided services decreased in several sectors including logistics-related services, utility services and financial services.

FIGURE 2.8

Services inputs to gross industrial exports, 2009

(Percentage of gross industrial exports)

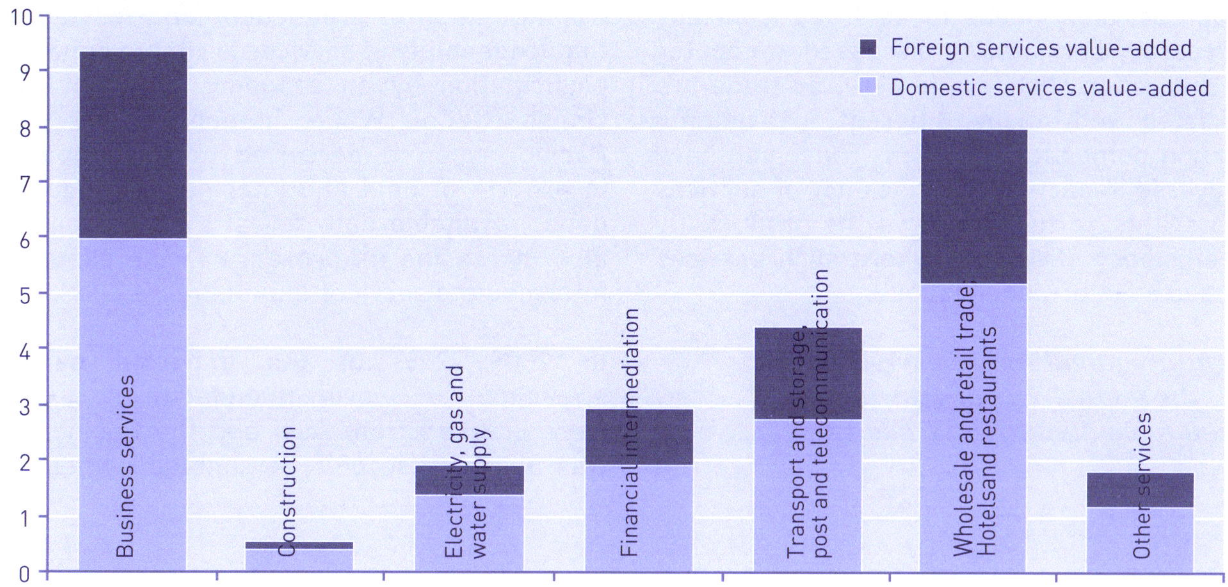

Source: ESCAP calculation based on OECD-WTO TiVA database (2013).

FIGURE 2.9

Changes in services value-added in gross industrial exports, by source, 1995-2009

(Percentage points)

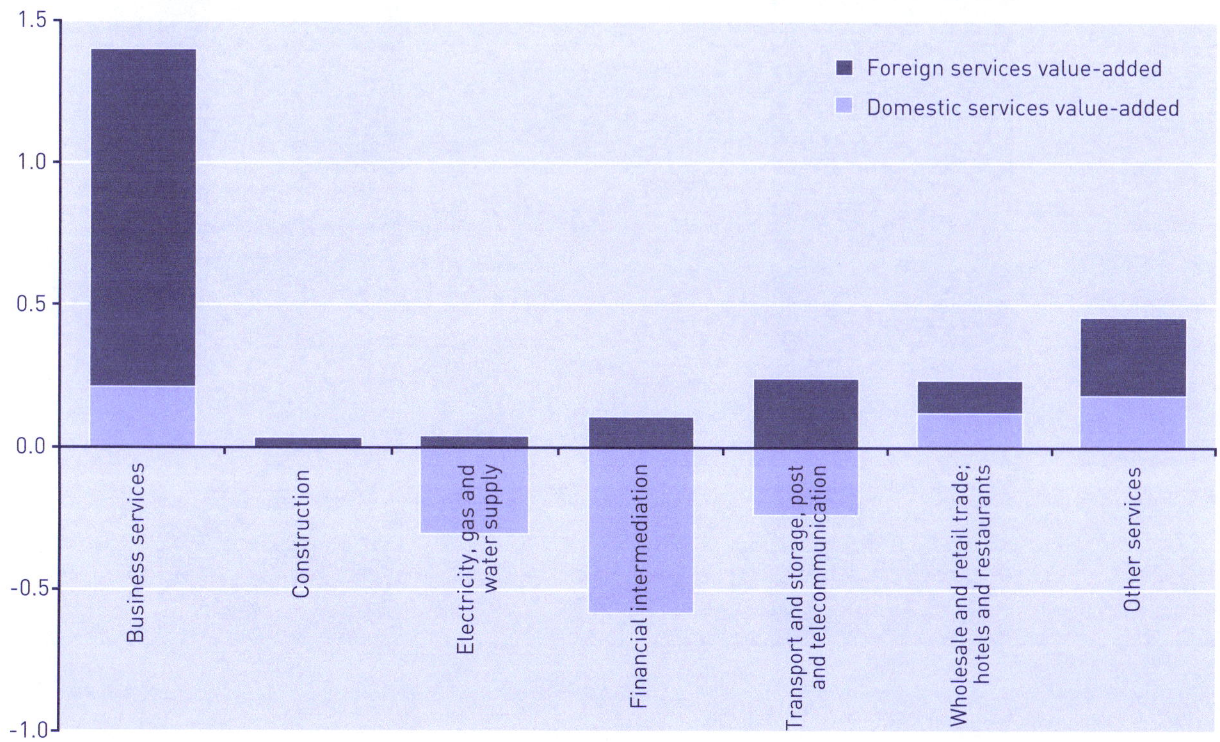

Source: ESCAP calculation based on OECD-WTO TiVA database (2013).

The increasing trend in services' content as intermediate inputs, especially those services that are foreign supplied, means that access to such services needs to be freed from any unnecessary barriers. As discussed in chapter 5 of this report, barriers to services trade are associated with many different instruments including domestic regulation. These can have an adverse impact on the efficiency of services sectors; this, in turn, reduces the productivity and efficiency of sectors where such services are used as intermediate inputs.

Intraregional trade in services is the main driver of growing intermediate services trade.

The increasing content of foreign-supplied services in manufacturing exports of sectors that are characterized by international fragmentation of production confirms the fact that tradeability of services is vital to enhancing participation by an economy in global value chains (GVCs). While, in general, the Asia-Pacific region is perceived to be competitive in exports of final and intermediate industrial goods, available data reveal that the region is also increasing its presence in the exports of intermediate services inputs (figure 2.10).

In 2009, 29% of the imported services embedded in world manufacturing exports were sourced from Asia and the Pacific. This was an increase of 5 percentage points from

FIGURE 2.10 Flows of imported services inputs contained in gross industrial exports, 2000 and 2009

(Percentage of imported services inputs of industrial exports)

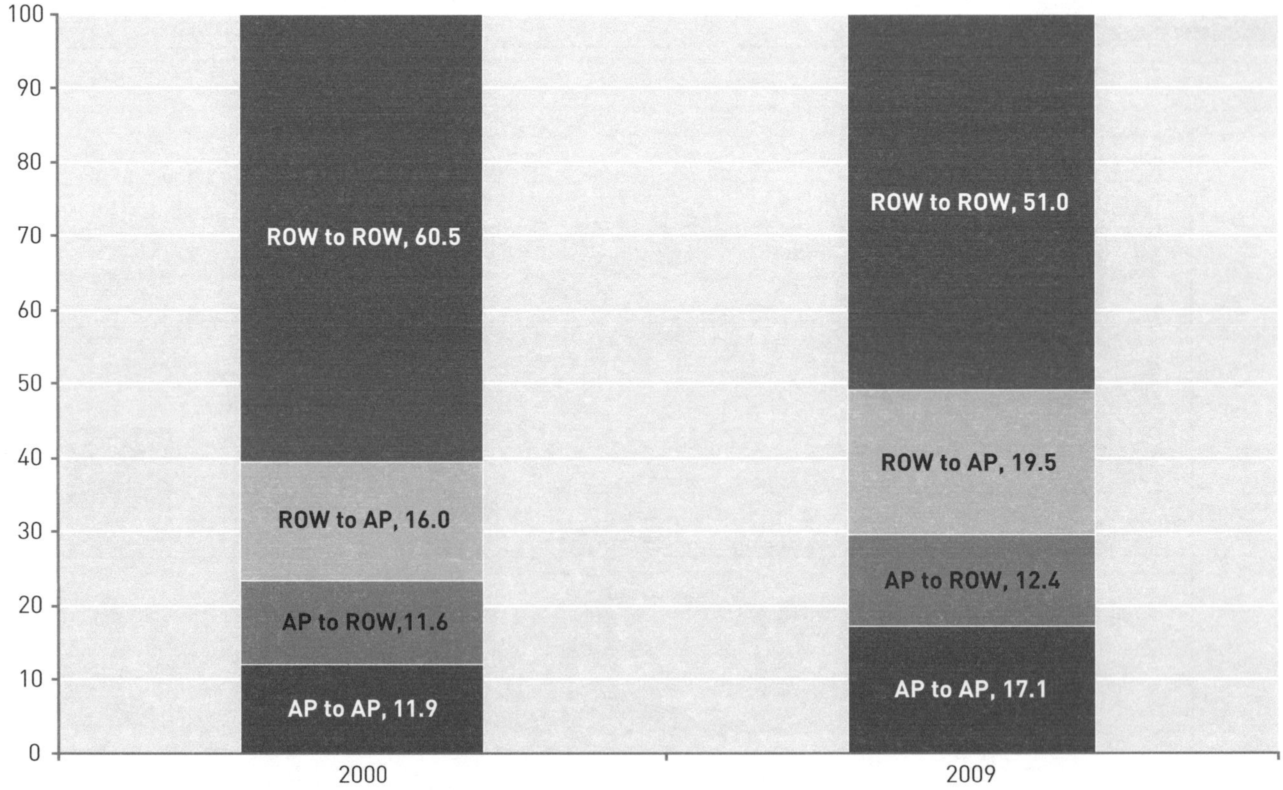

Source: ESCAP calculation, based on OECD-WTO TiVA database (2013).

Note: AP - Asia-Pacific; ROW - rest of the world.

FIGURE 2.11 Flows of traded services inputs contained in global value chain and non-global value chain industrial exports, 2000 and 2009

(Percentage of traded services inputs of industrial exports)

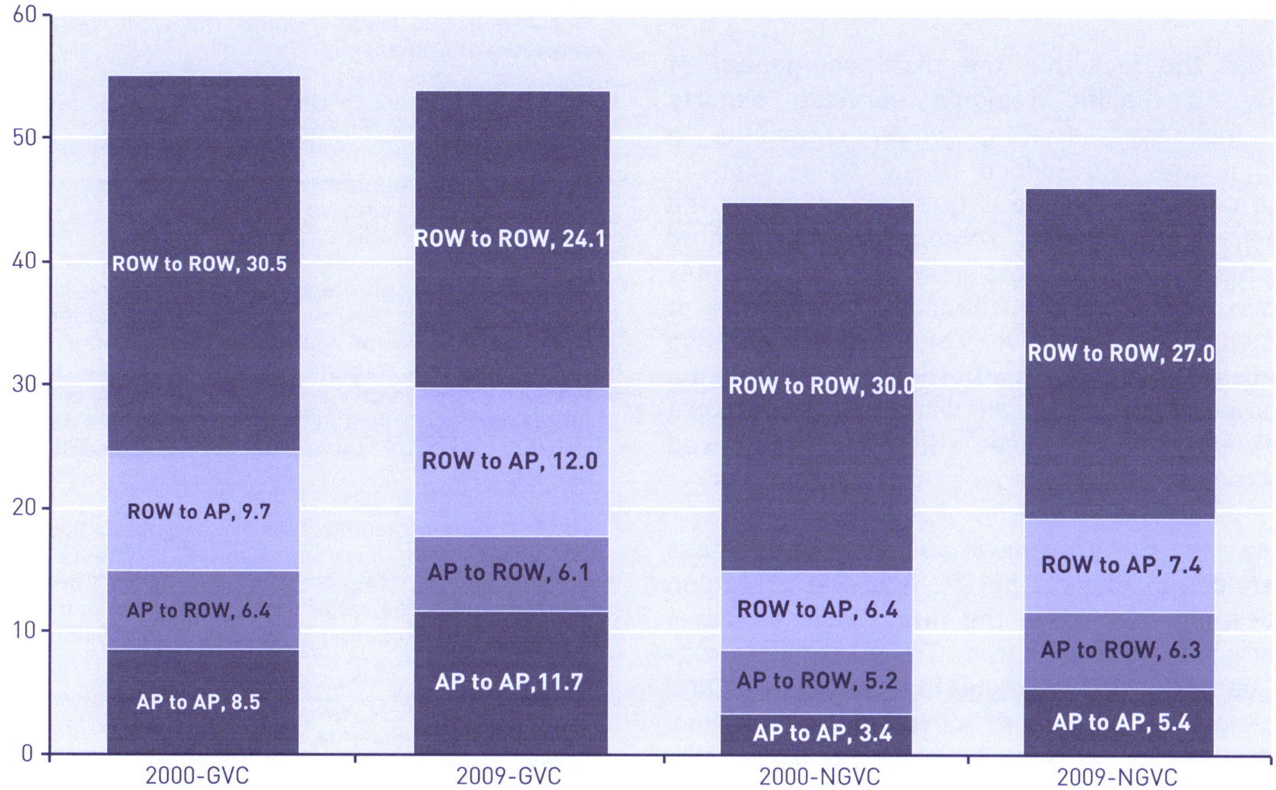

Source: ESCAP calculation based on OECD-WTO TiVA database (2013).

Notes: - GVC exports are the exports of electrical equipment, transport equipment, textiles and textile products, leather products and footwear. Non-GVC exports are industrial exports of the remainder.
- AP - Asia-Pacific; ROW - rest of the world.

the year 2000. A major portion (80%) of this increase came from the expansion of offshoring services inputs demanded by exports of GVC-prominent industries. These activities included: electrical and optical equipment; machinery and equipment; transport and equipment; textiles and textile products; and leather and footwear.

In addition, the region's intraregional trade contributed the most to this rise of intermediate services exports by Asia and the Pacific. The share of intraregional trade increased its share by 6 percentage points, from 11.9% to 17.1%, in overall imported intermediate services embedded in global manufacturing exports during those years (figure 2.11).

CONCLUSION

The Asian and Pacific region's growth of commercial services exports lagged behind the world average in 2013. The slowing of export growth was driven by the diverse performance of leading exporting economies in the region. While export growth of China and India remained strong other exporters, especially the relatively advanced ones, were unable to maintain their export growth momentum.

Although the fluctuation in export growth is discouraging, a pressing concern about Asia-Pacific trade is the uneven use of trade opportunities in the region. The concentration of exports and imports is extremely high, with 65% of exports attributed to just six economies in the region, i.e. China, India, Japan, the Republic of Korea, Singapore and Hong Kong, China. This implies that a large gap exists in trade competitiveness between the leading actors and the rest of the region.

Given the fact that the main component of the Asia-Pacific region's services exports is business services, which contribute a significant value-added to industrial exports, the performance gap is quite alarming for the rest of Asia-Pacific region. Lagging behind in the area of business services does not only have a negative implication for the balance of payments of respective economies; it could also indicate that there is a bottleneck in improving competitiveness of an economy's industrial exports unless services efficiency is enhanced by the removal of services trade restrictions.

However, the growing importance of business services in exports by the Asia-Pacific region does not mean that the importance of travel services can be ignored. Travel services play a particularly vital role in the small island economies and least developing countries. Through its strong backward and forward linkages with domestic activities, the sector has strong implications for improved employment and environment. It is encouraging that, in contrast to services trade in general, Asia-Pacific trade in travel services has continued its strong growth trend during recent years. There is also a great detail of room for improving tourist arrivals in emerging economies including the Pacific island countries through the improvement of tourism infrastructure.

ENDNOTES

1 In order to deal with the lack of data on trade in commercial services by many economies in Asia and the Pacific, the analysis in this chapter uses data compiled from different sources, including mirror data. However, even with this approach, it is not possible to provide an up-to-date and detailed account of intraregional services trade flows. Because of data limitation, this report cannot provide the forecasts for trends of trade in commercial services in 2014 and 2015.

2 Commercial services are total services excluding government services.

3 These numbers are estimates by ESCAP, based on WTO data at the time of preparing this report. More recent revisions of trade data by WTO may result in different values. In addition, using trade data of other sources may also produce different amounts. The total value for Asia-Pacific trade includes the trade of Taiwan Province of China.

4 When intra-European Union export is excluded, this share comes to slightly more than 36% (WTO, 2014).

5 When the intra-European Union imports are excluded, this share comes close to 40% (WTO, 2014).

6 The other commercial services category, in turn, contains eight subcategories, but the data are not readily available for all countries. In addition, the number of years for which data are available is very different across countries, and in most cases limited to just a few years. See box 2.3 of the Asia-Pacific Trade and Investment Report 2012 for a more detailed explanation of this service category (ESCAP, 2012, pp. 38-39).

7 Other commercial services comprise eight subcategories including communication services, computer and information services, construction, financial services, insurance services, other business services, personnel, cultural and recreational services, and royalties and license fees.

8 Database is available from http://stats.oecd.org/Index.aspx?DataSetCode=TIVA_OECD_WTO .

9 The OECD-WTO TiVA database (released May 2013) cover data on trade in value added of 57 economies (including all OECD countries and key trading partners of OECD countries including Argentina, Brazil, Brunei Darussalam, Bulgaria, Cambodia, China, India, Indonesia, Latvia, Lithuania, Malaysia, Malta, the Philippines, Romania, Russian Federation, Saudi Arabia, Singapore, South Africa, Thailand, Viet Nam, Hong Kong, China, and Taiwan Province of China). The dataset covers the years 1995, 2000, 2005, 2008 and 2009 and includes 18 sectors based on 2-digit ISIC revision 3.

REFERENCES

Chen H., and others (2014). Pacific island countries: in search of a trade strategy. IMF Working Paper No. 14/158. Washington, D.C.: International Monetary Fund. Available from www.imf.org/external/pubs/ft/wp/2014/wp14158.pdf .

Economic and Social Commission for Asia and the Pacific (2012). *Asia-Pacific Trade and Investment Report 2012: Recent Trends and Developments*. Bangkok. Available from www.unescap.org/resources/asia-pacific-trade-and-investment-report-2012-recent-trends-and-developments .

_____ (2013). *Asia-Pacific Trade and Investment Report 2013 – Turning the Tide: Towards Inclusive Trade and Investment*. Sales No. E.14.II.F.2. Available from www.unescap.org/resources/asia-pacific-trade-and-investment-report-2013-turning-tide-towards-inclusive-trade-and .

United Nations Conference on Trade and Development (2013). Sustainable tourism: contribution to economic growth and sustainable development. 28 January. TD/B/C.1/EM.5/2. Geneva. Available from http://unctad.org/meetings/en/SessionalDocuments/ciem5d2_en.pdf .

United Nations World Tourism Organization (2014a). *World Tourism Barometer*, vol. 12, January. Madrid. Available from www.wtoelibrary.org/home/main.mpx .

_____ (2014b). *World Tourism Barometer*, vol. 12, April. Madrid. Available from www.wtoelibrary.org/home/main.mpx .

_____ (2014c). *World Tourism Barometer*, vol. 12, June. Madrid. Available from www.wtoelibrary.org/home/main.mpx .

World Trade Organization (2014). Modest trade growth anticipated for 2014 and 2015 following two year slump. WTO 2014 Press Releases, No. 721, 14 April. Available from www.wto.org/english/news_e/pres14_e/pr721_e.htm .

Online databases

Economic and Social Commission for Asia and the Pacific. ESCAP Online Statistical Database. Available from www.unescap.org/stat/data/ .

OECD-WTO Trade in Value Added Database. Available from http://stats.oecd.org/Index.aspx?DataSetCode=TIVA_OECD_WTO .

World Trade Organization. International Trade Statistics Database. Available from http://stat.wto.org/Home/WSDBHome.aspx?Language=E .

_____ Short-term trade in commercial services. Available from www.wto.org/english/res_e/statis_e/short_term_stats_e.htm .

3 FOREIGN DIRECT INVESTMENT SHOWS SIGNS OF RECOVERY FOR ASIA AND THE PACIFIC[1]

A. GLOBAL AND REGIONAL TRENDS

Global foreign direct investment (FDI) showed signs of recovery in 2013 increasing by 9.1% to $1.46 trillion. This followed a weak global economic performance in 2012.

Developing and developed economies experienced similar increases in FDI inflows at 9.5% and 8.9%, respectively. In 2013, for the second year in a row, more than a half of global FDI inflows went to developing economies, amounting to an estimated $886 billion (figure 3.1) which was 61% of the global total. In comparison with the 41.3% fall in FDI inflows to developed economies in 2012, the performance of developed economies was significantly improved, driven by increased intra-company loans and reinvested earnings in addition to an improvement in the tax environment for investment in some European countries.[2] As developed economies are projected to strengthen further but with uneven recovery within the Euro area, the distribution of future FDI flows are expected to revert to a more "traditional" situation in which the majority of flows are to developed economies. Macroeconomic fragility and structural impediments in some emerging markets may also dampen future investment prospects. Nevertheless, FDI inflows to developing economies are projected to remain at a high level.

FIGURE 3.1 Foreign direct investment inflows to developed and developing economies, 2004-2013

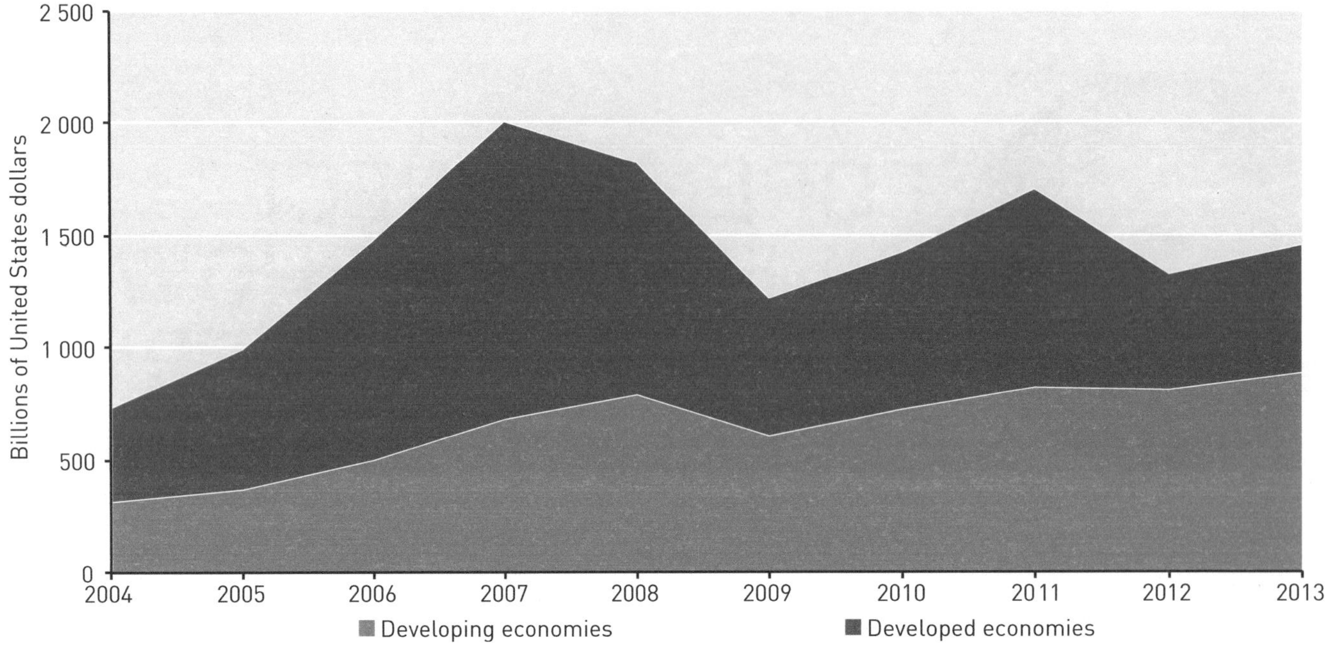

Source: ESCAP calculation based on UNCTADStat and UNCTAD (2014).

Developing countries also continued to represent an increasing share of global FDI outflows, reaching a new record of 39.2% of global FDI outflows in 2013 (figure 3.2). This represents a yearly growth of 12%; the increase was mostly led by transnational corporations (TNCs) in the developing Asia-Pacific region.

FIGURE 3.2 Foreign direct investment outflows from developed and developing economies, 2004-2013

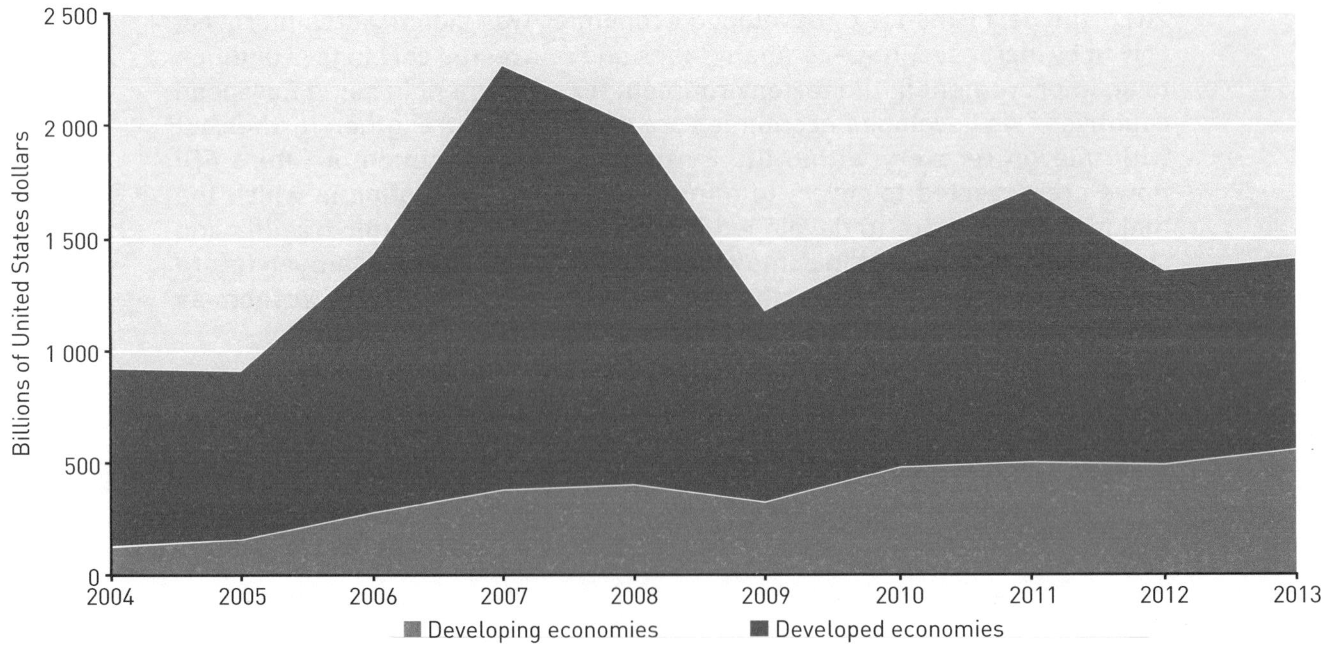

Source: ESCAP calculation based on UNCTADStat and UNCTAD (2014).

The Asia-Pacific region continued receiving significant FDI inflows; however, FDI inflows growth rate of 6.6% was lower than the global average in 2013.

The Asia-Pacific region demonstrated its resilience in the challenging economic climate; however, whether it will continue its strong performance in attracting FDI inflows is not certain. The Asia-Pacific region remains a favourable investment destination for FDI, attracting $549 billion of FDI inflows in 2013 (figure 3.3) and accounting for more than one third of global inflows (37.8%) in 2013. FDI inflows to the Asia-Pacific region rose by 6.6% in 2013, following a fall of 4.9% in 2012. This growth rate, however, was lower than the global average, and much lower than that of Latin America, where a 14.2% increase of FDI inflows was recorded, marking four consecutive years of rising FDI inflows.

FDI outflows from countries in the Asia-Pacific region have significantly increased in 2013, proving that the region is an important source of FDI.

FDI outflows from countries in the Asia-Pacific region were more noticeable in 2013, recording an increase of 15.1% increase. Collectively these economies accounted for a 38.3% share of global FDI outflows. Despite a small dip in 2012, FDI outflows from the Asia-Pacific region have been increasing continuously since 2009.

FIGURE 3.3

Foreign direct investment inflows, 2011-2013

(Total inflow and net flow values in millions of United States dollars)

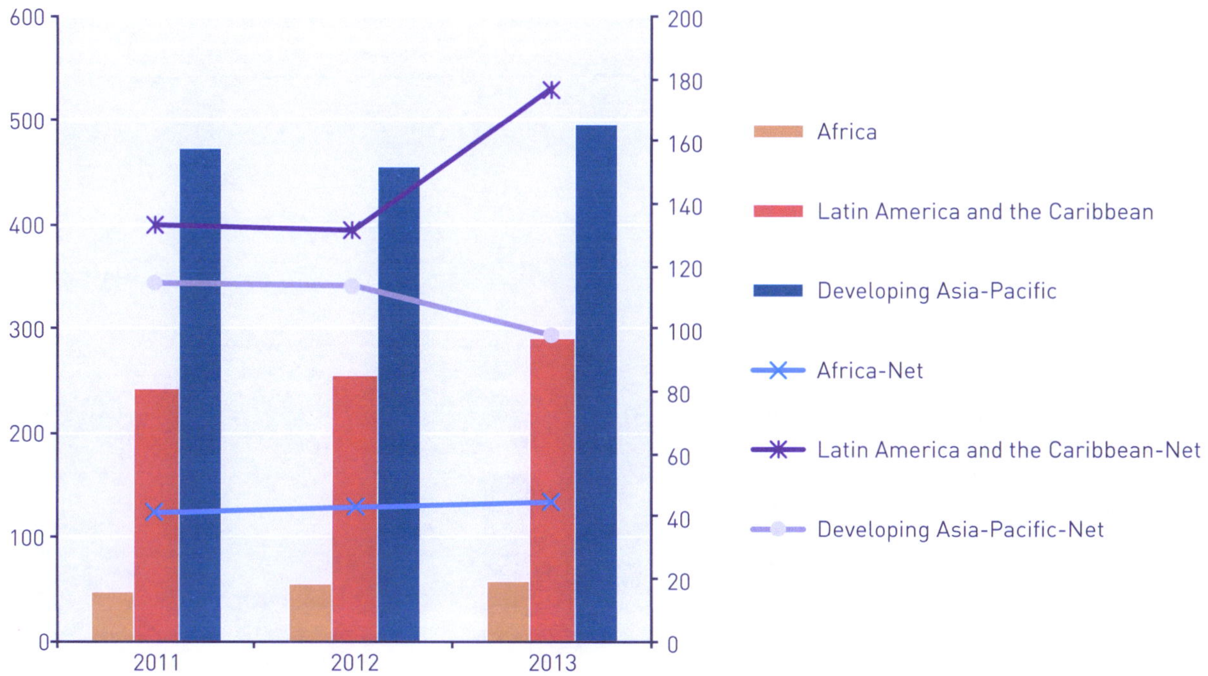

Source: ESCAP calculation based UNCTAD (2014).

CHAPTER 3

B. SUBREGIONAL PERFORMANCE

In 2013, the East and North-East Asia experienced the biggest growth of FDI inflows with 36% increase. However, it was the South-East Asia which proved to be the most resilient, with undisrupted growth in FDI inflows since 2009.

FDI inflows to Asia-Pacific developing subregions picked up in 2013 with North and Central Asia experiencing the largest increase (figure 3.4). Inflows to North and Central Asia grew by 36% whereas those to East and North-East Asia, South-East Asia, and South and South-West Asia experienced much smaller increases of 2.3%, 6.7% and 6%, respectively.

East and North-East Asia continued to attract the largest FDI inflows, reaching $221 billion in 2013 and accounting for 44.6% of all inflows to the developing Asia-Pacific subregions. That success can be attributed to China, which accounted for more than half of the East and North-East Asia subregion's FDI inflows in 2013.

South-East Asia comprising all ASEAN members and Timor-Leste has experienced undisrupted growth in FDI inflows since 2009. Inflows to the subregion amounted to $125 billion in 2013, accounting for a quarter of the inflows to developing Asia-Pacific economies. Although Singapore dominates inflows to the subregion, attracting over half of total investment, other countries in the subregion exhibited higher growth rates in FDI inflows in 2013. FDI inflows into Malaysia, the Philippines and Thailand all grew at more than 20% compared with Singapore's 4.3% increase. The resilience of this subregion in terms of attracting steady FDI inflows is linked to the role ASEAN plays as a hub for many preferential trade agreements (PTAs) (ASEAN has a number of "ASEAN+1" agreements with regional economies as well

FIGURE 3.4 Foreign direct investment inflows to Asia-Pacific developing subregions and developed economies, 2011-2013

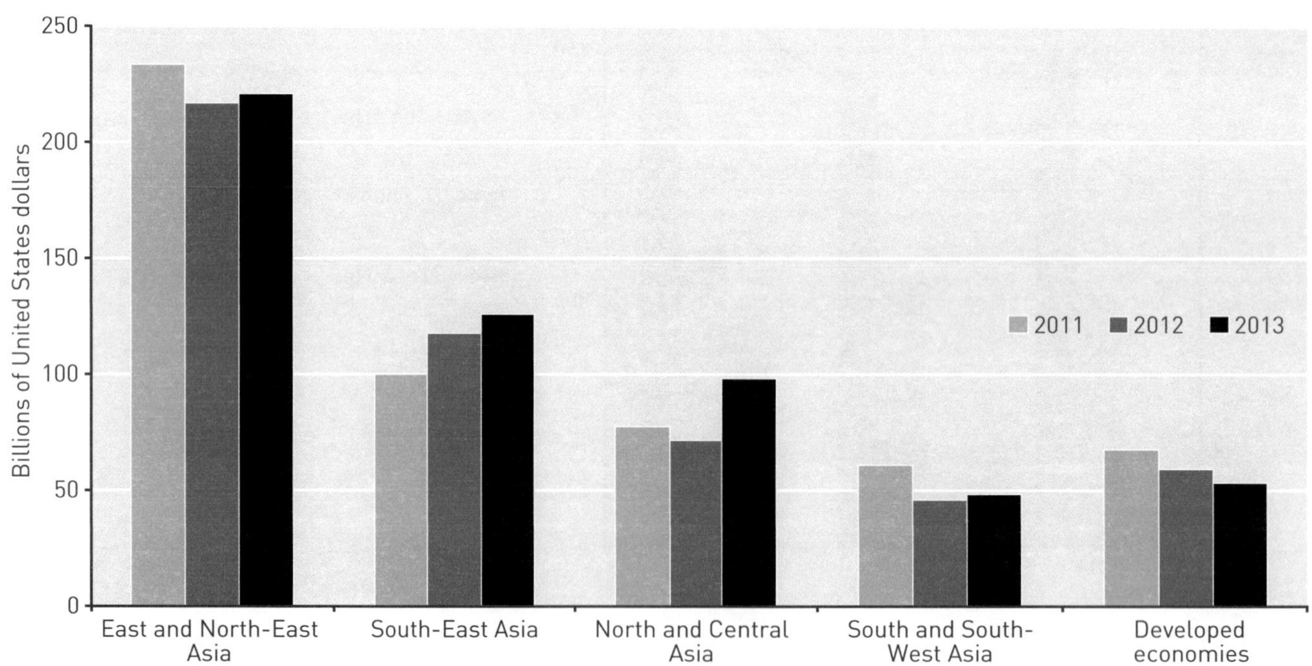

Source: UNCTAD (2014).

Note: Due to the small share of inflows to the Pacific subregion, it is not represented in this figure.

as other PTAs between ASEAN members and countries outside the region). Looking ahead, the completion of the two large "mega-regional" PTAs involving some, or all, ASEAN countries, could give further impetus to regional inward investment.[3]

In North and Central Asia, a 56.7% increase in FDI inflows to the Russian Federation was behind the large growth in inflows experienced by that subregion in 2013. In 2013, inflows to the subregion reached $98 billion, finally surpassing the peak of $94 billion reached prior to the global financial crisis in 2008. Other countries enjoying the positive trend in 2013 included Uzbekistan, Azerbaijan, Georgia and most notably Kyrgyzstan where FDI inflows more than doubled in 2013 to reach $1.9 billion.

FDI inflows to South and South-West Asia amounted to $48 billion in 2013, rising by 6% from the preceding year. Although FDI inflows to Pakistan, Bangladesh and India rose by 52.2%, 23.7% and 16.5%, respectively, lower FDI inflows recorded in Afghanistan (26.6%), the Islamic Republic of Iran (34.6%) and Nepal (19.6%) had a moderating effect on the total inflows to the subregion.

For developed countries in the Asia-Pacific region, the past few years have been challenging. FDI inflows had, by 2011, recovered quite well from the global financial crisis of 2008-2009 reaching $68 billion. However, since then, inflows have been declining, and amounted to only $53 billion in 2013. Australia, accounting for large share of inflows to the Asia-Pacific developed countries, was the main reason for the downturn. During 2011-2013, FDI inflows to Australia dropped by 23.6% from $65 billion to $50 billion, mainly because of the slowing of investment in the natural resources sector.

FDI outflows from the Asia-Pacific region grew by 15.1% in 2013. In East and North-East Asia and South-East Asia the rise was quite moderate; outflows from those two subregions grew by 8.5% and 4.7%, respectively. Outflows from North and Central Asia, on the other hand, nearly doubled due to the large increase in FDI outflows from the Russian Federation. FDI outflows rose to $95 billion partially driven by the acquisition of TNK-BP by the Russian oil company Rosneft (Neate, 2013). Contrary to this, Indian companies scaled back their investments, which led to FDI outflows from the South and South-West Asian subregion declining by 58.2%. Outflows from the Asia-Pacific region's developed countries continue to be dominated by Japan, which accounted for 95.1% of outflows.

FDI outflows from ASEAN are relatively low compared with the Asia-Pacific average. Rising by only 4.7% in 2013, they reached $56 billion. Indonesia, Malaysia, the Philippines and Thailand all experienced a decrease in outflows, but Singapore stood out as its FDI outflows doubled to $27 billion.

C. COUNTRY HIGHLIGHTS

1. China

> *China, an important investment destination and also a source of investment, recorded 15% increase in FDI outflows in 2013, with the support of the Government's "going global" strategy.*

China remained the second-largest recipient of FDI in the world in 2013, following the United States, having $124 billion – 2.3% more than in the previous year (figure 3.5). Although economic growth in China has shown signs of moderation, and despite rising wages making labour-costs more expensive, investor confidence in that country's economy remains strong. The Ministry of Commerce of China (China, 2014) estimated that, in 2013, a total of 22,773 new enterprises invested in China, mostly from Hong Kong, China as well as Singapore and Japan.

With growth of 15%, Chinese outward FDI proved much more dynamic than inflows in 2013. Outflows have increased significantly since 2005, when Chinese investments amounted to $12 billion. In 2013, the value of investments rose to more than $100 billion. Outward FDI

FIGURE 3.5 Foreign direct investment inflows and outflows in China, 2004-2013

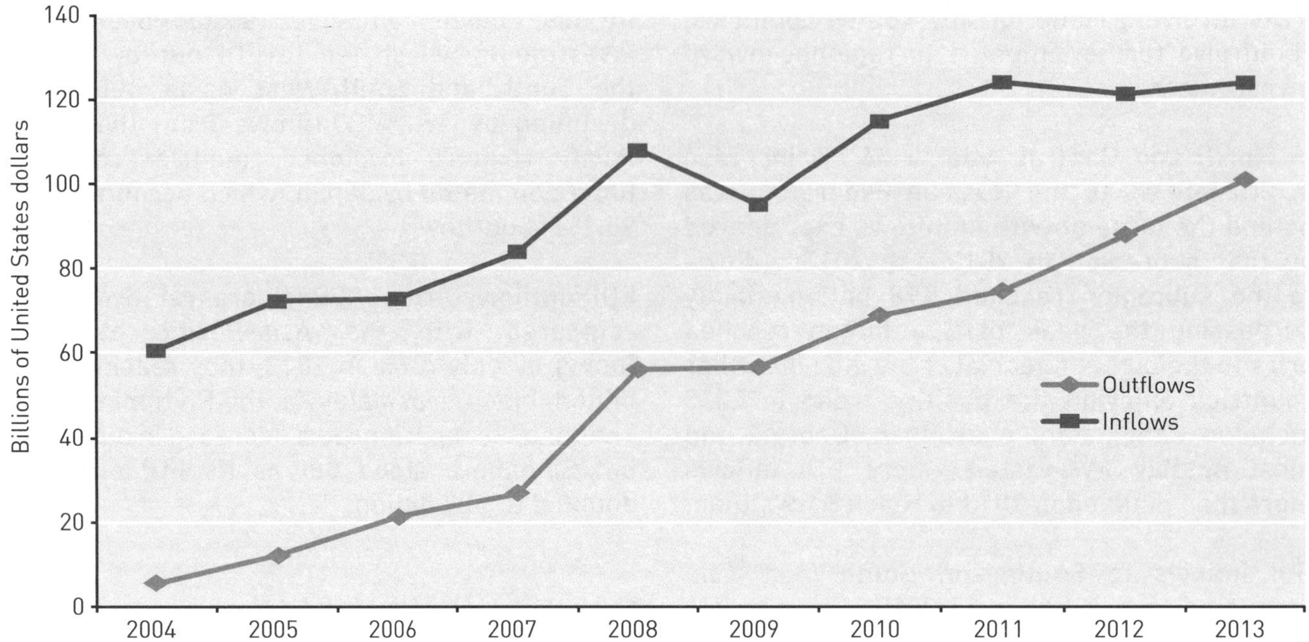

Source: ESCAP calculation based on UNCTADStat and UNCTAD (2014).

predominantly takes the form of mergers and acquisitions (M&A), and is increasingly targeting Europe and the United States (China, 2014). In 2013, China was the third-largest source of outbound FDI in the world after the United States and Japan.

This increasing trend in outward FDI is the result of the "going global" strategy adopted by the Government of China in 2001, under which Chinese firms are encouraged to look for opportunities overseas. This strategy took a further step forward in 2013 with adjustments in the regulatory framework for outward FDI to help Chinese firms be competitive abroad (Sauvant and Chen, 2013). In terms of investment liberalization agreements, China has agreed, as part of the United States-China Strategic Economic Dialogue, to continue negotiations on an investment treaty (United States, 2014).

2. India

Macroeconomic uncertainties and structural constraints in India continue to concern foreign investors. India is experiencing slower economic growth, running a high current account deficit, and enduring high inflation (UNCTAD, 2014). In spite of these worries, FDI inflows grew by 16.5% to $28 billion in 2013 (figure 3.6). However, with reforms there is potential for attracting higher rates of investments (India, 2014a). FDI could help strengthen the economy, provide more decent and productive employment and encourage technological upgrading (ESCAP, 2013).

Elements of the Indian business environment continue to deter foreign investors. For example, India levies a 34% corporate tax rate, substantially higher than in several of its Asian neighbours (Balakrishnan, 2014). Although restrictions on foreign investment in several sectors have been lifted in recent years, many sectors retain equity limits on foreign ownership. For example, FDI in the insurance sector is capped at 26%, while a 49% ceiling is imposed on FDI in the power sector (India, 2014b). While limits on foreign ownership are not unusual in the region, the requirement to find suitable joint venture partners risks hampering FDI inflows.

The retail sector, in particular, has been in the spotlight as a test case for reforms aimed at encouraging foreign investment (ESCAP, 2013). The FDI cap imposed by the Government of India in multi-brand retailing – currently set at 51% – is a major obstacle to the FDI inflows to the sector. In addressing that issue, in 2013 the Government relaxed FDI rules applicable to the sector, reducing the pre-conditions that foreign retailers were required to fulfil. Foreign investors are now waiting for positive signals from the new Government elected in early 2014.[4]

Indian FDI outflows plummeted by 80.2% in 2013, a decline that had continued since the start of the global financial crisis in 2008 (figure 3.6). Indian TNCs invested $1.7 billion overseas in 2013, which is the country's weakest performance since the start of the current millennium.

3. Japan and the Republic of Korea

Although FDI inflows to Japan experienced a sharp rise of 33%, reaching $2.3 billion in 2013, they remained sluggish; the 2013 figure is less than one tenth of 2008 volumes (Japan Times, 2014). The Government of Japan has strived to stimulate economic growth by fiscal and monetary stimulus and "national strategic economic zones" with loosened regulations in particular industries have been developed to further encourage foreign investments (Soble, 2014, and ESCAP, 2014). In addition, new incentives will be implemented, such as corporate tax breaks, simplified investment procedures and improved assistance to foreign investors. (The Economist, 2014a).

As for FDI outflows, Japan remains the second-largest investor behind the United States, increasing its outward FDI by 10.8% in 2013 to $136 billion. The rise could indicate that Japanese firms are seeking to avoid volatility in the domestic economy by investing overseas.

FDI inflows to the Republic of Korea continued their upward trend. Inflows rose by 28.7% to $12 billion in 2013 (Korea Eximbank, 2014). The United States and China are the largest sources of FDI inflow to the Republic of Korea. Several policies that have recently been put in place may have played a role in boosting inflows (Republic of Korea, 2014): the Telecommunication Business Act and the Investment Promotion Act have

FIGURE 3.6 Foreign direct investment inflows and outflows in India, 2004-2013

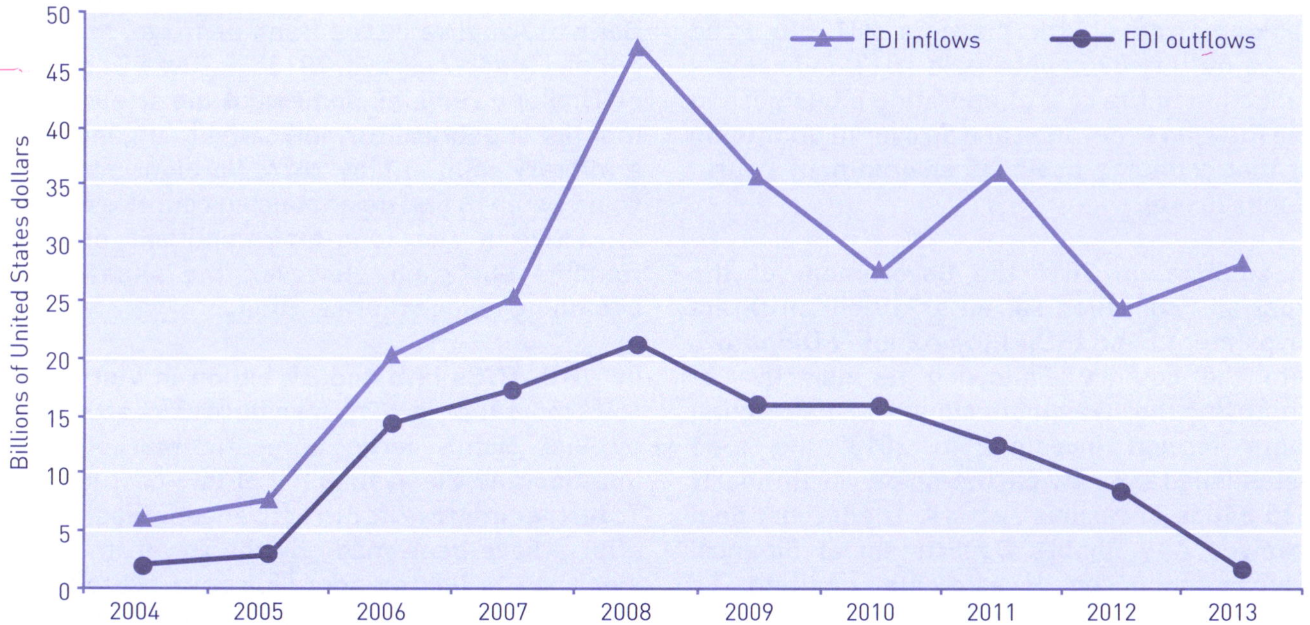

Source: ESCAP calculation based on UNCTADStat and UNCTAD (2014).

been amended, eliminating several constraints concerning the telecommunications sector and joint investments between subsidiaries of holding companies and foreign investors. In addition, the United States-Republic of Korea free trade agreement that entered into force in 2012 has likely further supported FDI inflows from the United States (Manyin and others, 2013).

4. Russian Federation

While the Russian Federation saw its economic growth dip from 3.4% in 2012 to 1.3% in 2013, in the latter year 2013 foreign investors continued to find the economy an attractive destination (World Bank, 2014a). In 2013, the Russian Federation was the third-most attractive location for foreign investors, behind the United States and China. FDI inflows to the Russian Federation increased by 56.7% in 2013, reaching $79 billion. Although the United States and China are ranked as the top investors, 80% of FDI in the Russian Federation originates from Europe. Accession to WTO in 2012 has likely contributed to the upturn.

The liberalization of the service sector has additionally sent a positive signal to foreign investors (Evseev and Wilson, 2012). The country's advancement in the "Doing Business" ranking, from 111th place in 2012 to 92nd place out of 189 countries in 2013, indicates a reduction in the cost of operating a business in the Russian Federation and an overall upgrading of that country's business environment (World Bank, 2014b).

In addition, in 2011 the Government of the Russian Federation set up a $10 billion Direct Investment Fund (RDIF) to promote FDI inflows into the country. Following its objective of improving the investment climate and attracting more foreign investors in 2013, the fund established six new partnerships worth nearly $10 billion in various sectors. The largest deal involved Abu Dhabi's Department of Finance, which announced investments totalling $5 billion in Russian infrastructure projects (Russian Direct Investment Fund, 2014).

However, in 2014, geopolitical tensions and foreign sanctions against the Russian Federation had an impact on the prospects for growth and have seriously dimmed the attractiveness of the country as an investment destination. It is likely that FDI in the Russian Federation from European countries and the United States will be significantly reduced in 2014 (The Economist, 2014b).

5. Selected economies in the Association of Southeast Asian Nations

In the Philippines, inward FDI increased by 20.1% in 2013, reaching almost $4 billion, thus revealing increased confidence in the economic prospects of the country, thanks to a sound economic performance (Bangko Sentral ng Pilipinas, 2014). The manufacturing sector, boosted by the Philippines Development Plan implemented in 2011, accounted for 40% of FDI inflows to the country (National Economic and Development Authority, 2014).

In Thailand, FDI inflows surged in 2013, growing by 20.9% to reach $13 billion. FDI in Thailand has been mainly driven by a rise in M&A activities. In 2013, Thailand was the second-largest target of M&A purchases in South-East Asia, behind Singapore, with concluded sales worth $6 billion. A major deal was the acquisition of the Bank of Ayudhya by the Bank of Tokyo, for $5.3 billion (Tudor-Ackroyd, 2013). Future FDI trends of Thailand remains somewhat uncertain after months of political turmoil came to an end with a military coup in May 2014. Foreign investors could begin to find neighbouring countries more attractive if the long-term political outlook remains uncertain. However, the situation is beginning to look more settled.

In 2013, TNCs invested $9 billion in Viet Nam, 6.4% more than in 2012. Investors were attracted by Viet Nam's large domestic market, low inflation and the availability of low-cost labour. To further improve its attractiveness, substantial efforts have been made by the Government of Viet Nam to lighten administrative procedures and promote a sound business environment.

FDI inflows into Indonesia decreased slightly, from $19 billion in 2012 to $18 billion in 2013. The major sources of investment were Japan and Singapore (Indonesia Investment Coordinating Board, 2014). Most inflows were directed to the automotive manufacturing, mining, oil and gas sectors. The Government of Indonesia also took steps to increase the appeal of the country to foreign investors. For example, a fiscal package dedicated to the promotion of FDI was implemented in 2013, while several regulations were relaxed, such as FDI caps in the pharmaceutical industry (VN, 2013). Whether Indonesia can sustain FDI inflows depends on how successful the new Government will be in addressing outstanding problems, particularly infrastructural constraints.

D. TRENDS IN GREENFIELD FOREIGN DIRECT INVESTMENT AND MERGERS AND ACQUISITIONS[5]

Greenfield FDI, of crucial importance for economic development, is a significant mode of entry for investors in the Asia-Pacific region. Since 2004, the region has attracted more than $3 trillion in greenfield FDI compared with $1.4 trillion through M&A (figure 3.7).

During the past decade, greenfield FDI peaked in 2008 at $518 billion. However, the growth of greenfield FDI declined notably since then, reaching a low of $222 billion in 2013, as a result of the persistent economic slowdown in developed countries. Comparing 2013 with the peak year in 2008, outflows from the United States and the United Kingdom of Great Britain and Northern Ireland to the Asia-Pacific region declined by more than 50% while outflows from Germany and Japan fell by more than 30%. These countries were the top four greenfield investors during 2004-2013.

> *M&A is gaining higher importance as a mode of entry for investors in the Asia-Pacific region. On the other hand, greenfield FDI has decreased by 43% between 2011 and 2013.*

FIGURE 3.7 Greenfield foreign direct investment and merger and acquisition inflows to the Asia-Pacific region, 2004-2013

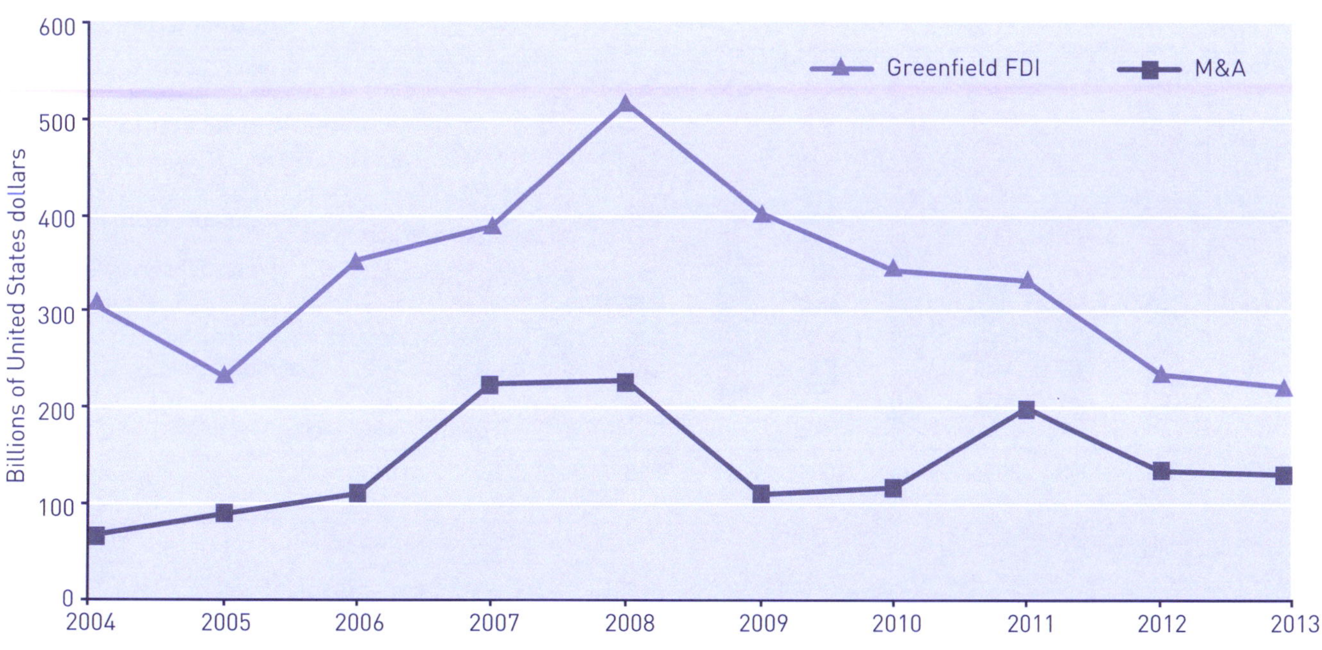

Source: ESCAP calculation based on fDi Intelligence and Thomson Reuters.

At the same time, M&A is gaining in importance as a mode of entry for investors in the Asia-Pacific region, although historically it has not been as significant as greenfield FDI. During the last decade, FDI inflows to the Asia-Pacific region through M&A doubled from $66 billion in 2004 to $130 billion in 2013.

However, FDI inflows to the Asia-Pacific region through M&A stagnated in 2013, when they registered a slight decline of 3.6%. However, going against the overall trend, China and Thailand both attracted a record value of deals in 2013, when China reached a total of $25 billion while Thailand recorded slightly more than $6 billion. In the same year, Myanmar recorded its three first M&A deals ever. A breakdown of the Asia-Pacific region into developing and developed countries reveals that developing economies are following a different trajectory to that of developed economies. Whereas FDI inflows through M&A to developed economies in the Asia-Pacific region declined by 38.6% in 2013, inflows to the developing Asia-Pacific economies increased by 18.4%.

There are significant differences in the industries targeted by greenfield and M&A FDI. Greenfield FDI tends to be spread over multiple industries, each accounting for a small share of the total (figure 3.8). From 2004 to 2013, the top industry of coal, oil and natural gas accounted for a 16.3% share of total greenfield FDI in the Asia-Pacific region, while the second-largest industry, real estate, only accounted for a 8.7% share (figure 3.8). On the other hand, M&A activity was more clearly focused on a few key sectors. Most M&A activity from 2004 to 2013 took place in the financial industry, followed by consumer products and energy and power (figure 3.9). The top seven industries accounted for 82% of total M&A.

FIGURE 3.8 Greenfield foreign direct investment inflows in the Asia-Pacific region, by industry, 2004-2013

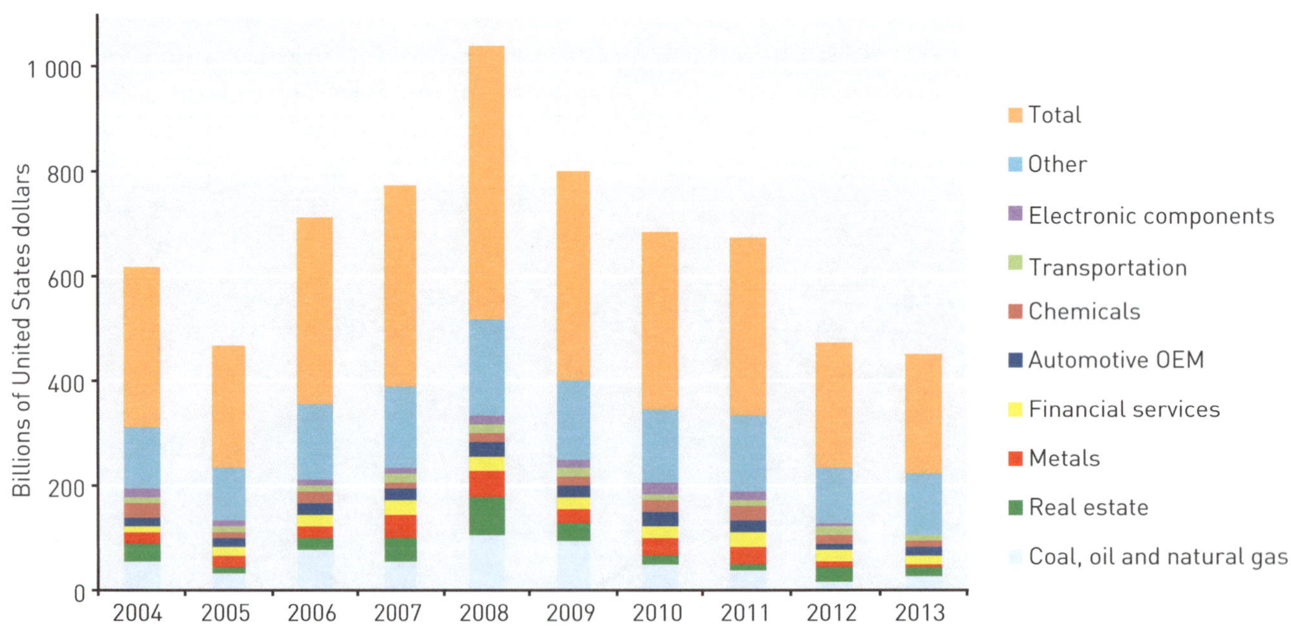

Source: fDi Intelligence.

FIGURE 3.9

Foreign direct investment inflows to the Asia-Pacific region through mergers and acquisitions, by industry, 2004-2013

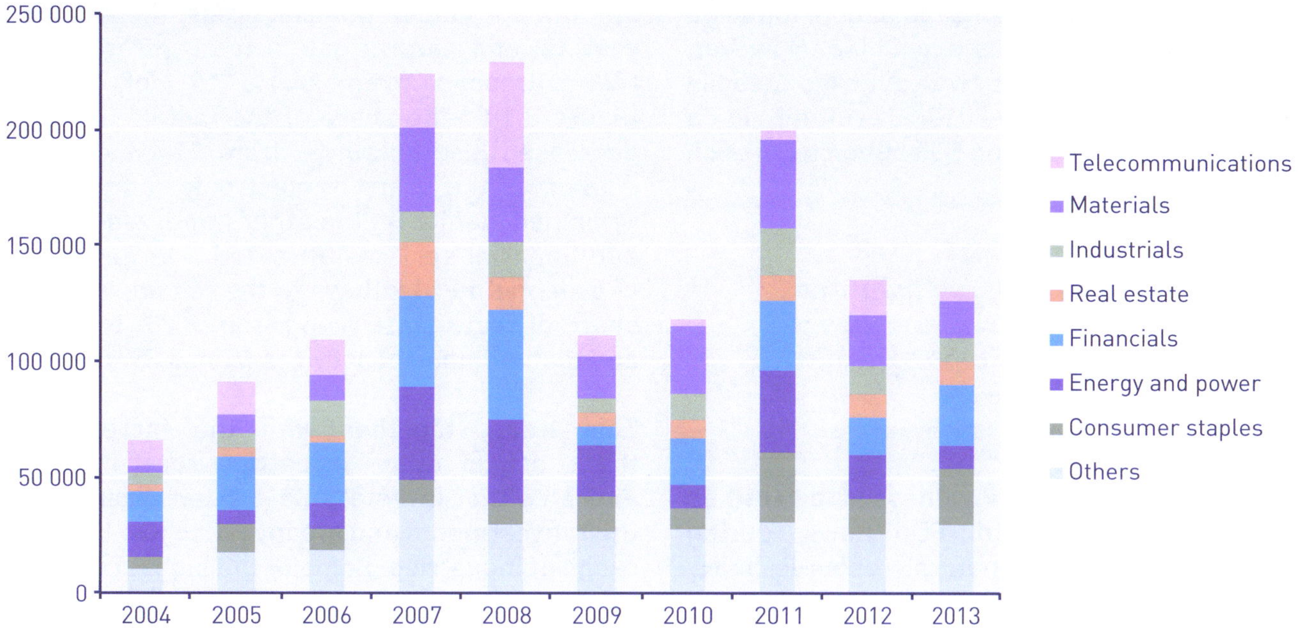

Source: Thomson Reuters.

E. INTRAREGIONAL FOREIGN DIRECT INVESTMENT TRENDS IN THE ASIA-PACIFIC REGION

1. Intraregional greenfield foreign direct investment

(a) Inflows

> *Intraregional investors are increasingly replacing traditional big investors from European countries and the United States.*

Intraregional greenfield FDI in the Asia-Pacific region continues to be significant, totalling $336 billion during 2011-2013. However, between 2011 and 2013, intraregional greenfield FDI inflows to the region dropped by 43%. This downward trend was visible in all major destination economies. China remained the largest destination for intraregional greenfield FDI with a total of $100 billion in FDI inflows during 2011-2013. ASEAN as a group, however, was not far behind having $99 billion in greenfield FDI from Asia-Pacific sources outside ASEAN during the same period.

The only economies showing a substantial increase in intraregional greenfield FDI inflows during 2011-2013 were Japan and Myanmar. Greenfield FDI inflows to Japan more than tripled during this period, reaching more than $3.3 billion. FDI in Japan mainly originated from the Republic of Korea and Singapore. Japan's interest in alternative and renewable energy was sparked by the Fukushima Daiichi nuclear accident, after the 2011 Tohoku earthquake and tsunami. As a likely result, during 2011-2013, greenfield FDI in alternative and renewable energy was quite high, totalling $820 million, second only to greenfield FDI in real estate at $840 million. Greenfield FDI inflows to Myanmar rose from a meagre $500 million to slightly more than $12 billion, but this was due mainly to a single $9.9 billion project by Mitsubishi Corporation from Japan for building a fossil fuel power station in the Dawei special economic zone.

(b) Outflows

Japan remained the top source of intraregional greenfield FDI with a share of 30% of total intraregional greenfield outflows. During 2011-2013, outflows from Japan to the Asia-Pacific region reached more than $100 billion, followed by the Republic of Korea and China. However, outflows from the latter two countries steadily declined during 2011-2013, resulting in a cumulative total of around $35 billion from each country.

Intraregional greenfield FDI go to a broader range of industries, away from natural resource-heavy industries to more knowledge-based industries and services.

The Asia-Pacific region witnessed diversified intraregional greenfield FDI flows during 2011-2013, away from natural resource-heavy industries to more knowledge-based industries and services. During that period, intraregional greenfield FDI inflows to most of the top industries declined, including the top industry of coal, oil and natural gas. Compared with the three-year period from 2005 to 2007 running up until the global financial crisis, the share of coal, oil and natural gas in total intraregional FDI dropped from 24.1% to only 13.7% (figure 3.10). The share of the metals industry decreased less notably – from 11.4% to 8.7% – whereas the share of electronic components remained stable. On the other hand, real estate and financial services attracted a larger share of greenfield FDI inflows to the region, with the share of real estate rising from 8.7% to 10.6% and that of financial services from 5.3% to 6.9%.

This trend, together with the increase in the share of other industries receiving FDI, indicates that investors have been diversifying their investments and are investing in a broader range of industries. Some of the biggest gainers have been health care, pharmaceuticals and biotechnology, reflecting the increase in the ageing population and higher demand for health-care products. Building and construction,

FIGURE 3.10 Intraregional greenfield foreign direct investment, by industry share, 2005-2013

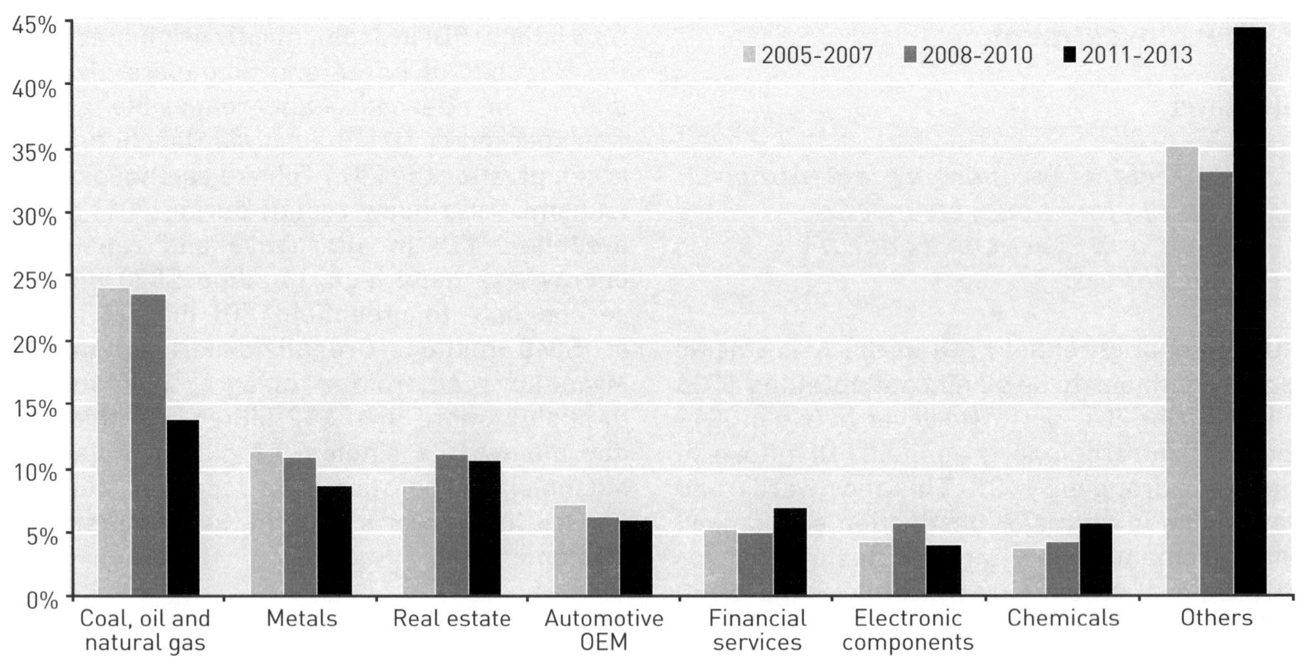

Source: fDi Intelligence.

consumer products and business services have also largely benefitted. Despite these increases, however, the amounts invested in these industries still remained small compared with the top industries.

2. Intraregional mergers and acquisitions

(a) Inflows

M&A activity among the Asian economies remained quite intensive during 2011-2013 (table 3.1). During that period, intraregional FDI inflows through M&A accounted for 40% of total FDI inflows through M&A in the Asia-Pacific region. Companies in the East and North-East Asian and South-East Asian subregions were the main sources of intraregional FDI flows. Twenty-three per cent of intraregional FDI inflows through M&A during 2011-2013 targeted the financial sector ($28.3 billion), followed by materials and real estate, accounting for 18% and 13%, respectively, of intraregional inward FDI through M&A.

In China, companies from Hong Kong, China, and ASEAN are replacing acquiring companies from Europe and the United States. During 2011-2013, 71.5% of M&A deals in China were concluded with investors from the Asia-Pacific region, with the total deal value reaching $41 billion. In terms of the number of deals, close to half were concluded with Asian investors. This indicates that the deals concluded in China by companies from other parts of the Asia-Pacific region tend to be of higher value than those concluded by companies from outside the region. Intraregional M&A investments in China were mostly in the financial sector, with more than $4.7 billion invested. In addition, companies in the real estate and consumer goods sectors were popular M&A targets, accounting for 21.6% and 12% of intraregional inflows, respectively.

Trends in Hong Kong, China have been quite similar, with the territory receiving 66% of its FDI inflows through M&A from the Asia-Pacific region. China accounted for a half of these intraregional inflows and Singapore for one fifth. During 2011-2013, of the total $19 billion intraregional FDI inflows through M&A to Hong Kong, China almost one third was into the financial sector, followed by the real estate sector (20.7%), and consumer goods and services (16.2%).

In the Republic of Korea, intraregional FDI inflows through M&A also played a significant role. During 2011-2013, intraregional FDI inflows through M&A totalled $4 billion, which amounted to 45.1% of total FDI inflows through M&A to the country, and targeted the financial sector, real estate and materials.

In the case of Japan, one fifth of total FDI inflows through M&A came from the Asia-Pacific region, driven mainly by China and the Republic of Korea, amounting to $7.6 billion during 2011-2013. The most attractive sectors in Japan were the real estate, industry and high technology, which together accounting for almost three quarters of the intraregional inflows.

From 2011 to 2013, ASEAN members attracted $22.5 billion of FDI in the form of M&A from other Asian countries outside ASEAN, representing close to one third of all FDI inflows through M&A to ASEAN. Japanese companies were involved in 51.6% of intraregional FDI inflows through M&A to ASEAN, while enterprises from Hong Kong, China accounted for 21.6%. The most attractive economies in ASEAN for FDI through M&A were Singapore and Thailand, both of which attracted $6.7 billion from Asia-Pacific firms outside ASEAN. Even low-income economies took part in the intraregional dynamic; all M&A in Cambodia, the Lao Peoples' Democratic Republic and Myanmar involved companies from the Asia-Pacific region. Popular industries among investors in ASEAN were the financial, materials, and energy and power. The telecommunications sector attracted the most investments in low-income economies. For higher-income economies, the financial sector was the main driver for intraregional flows.

By far the largest destination for intraregional FDI through M&A from the region during 2011-2013 was Australia, with intraregional M&A deals totalling more than $45 billion, representing 39.1% of total inward M&A activities in the Asia-

TABLE 3.1 Top five destinations and sources of intraregional mergers and acquisitions, 2011-2013

(Billions of United States dollars)

Top destinations	Total deal value	Top sources	Total deal value
Australia	45 783	China	34 992
China	40 941	Hong Kong, China	34 980
ASEAN	22 544	Japan	33 532
Hong Kong, China	19 155	ASEAN	31 269
Japan	7 628	Republic of Korea	8 670

Source: Thomson Reuters.

Pacific region. The main sources of M&A in Australia were China (almost $15 billion), Japan ($9 billion) and Hong Kong, China (almost $7 billion). Investors mainly focused on materials, and energy and power.

The Russian Federation and India, the two "giants" of the North and Central Asian and South and South-West Asian subregions, attracted fewer intraregional investors. During 2011-2013, Russian intraregional FDI inflows through M&A reached $4.2 billion, accounted for only 8.2% of total FDI inflows through M&A. Similarly, in India, intraregional FDI through M&A accounted for only 11.3% of total FDI inflows through M&A in the Asia-Pacific region, just short of $5 billion.

(b) Outflows

With regard to FDI outflows through M&A, China was the biggest contributor to intraregional M&A activities in the Asia-Pacific region during 2011-2013. With the conclusion of deals valued at close to $35 billion, China accounted for one fifth of intraregional FDI outflows through M&A within the Asia-Pacific region. During 2011-2013, one half of Chinese outward FDI through M&A comprised purchases of Australian firms. The main industries targeted by Chinese TNCs were the materials, energy and power, and financial sectors.

Hong Kong, China as well as Japan and ASEAN were substantial sources of investment through M&A, with each investing more than $30 billion in other Asia-Pacific economies. Intraregional purchases by companies in Hong Kong, China represented 26.1% of total FDI outflows from Hong Kong, China through M&A. During that period, ASEAN countries took an increasing part in M&A activity in the region with 36.7% of outward FDI through M&A from ASEAN targeting companies in the Asia-Pacific region. China was the top destination for FDI outflows through M&A from ASEAN. Of the ASEAN members, Singapore and Thailand were the most active intraregional investors, accounting for 80% of ASEAN M&A purchases in Asia and the Pacific.

Companies in the Russian Federation and India were also active in investing in their Asia-Pacific neighbours, although the total value of their intraregional M&A deals was far behind that of the top countries. Intraregional FDI outflows through M&A from both countries reached close to $6 billion each during 2011-2013. Of the total M&A outward activity of the Russian Federation, 23.8% concerned other countries in the Asia-Pacific region, mainly Turkey and China. During 2011-2013, Indian companies mainly targeted investment in Australia, which accounted for 73% of intraregional M&A outflows from India.

CONCLUSION

In 2013, global FDI showed signs of recovery, recording $1.46 trillion, following a weak year in 2012. Developing economies, in particular, continued to share an increased portion of global FDI as well as attract more than a half of global FDI inflows.

The Asia-Pacific region experienced a 6.6% increase in FDI inflows, which was lower than the 9.1% increase in global FDI. Although the Asia-Pacific region remained attractive to investors, who accounted for 37.8% of total global FDI, it did not reach the level of high growth seen in the past or compared with other fast-growing regions such as Latin America.

Whether the number and the size of investments to the Asia-Pacific region are reaching their saturation point, or only forming a temporary trend, is not certain. In any case, some changes are being noticed, including (a) the trend of traditional big players either showing stagnated or slow levels of expansion, and (b) more foreign investors being attracted by small players resulting in diversified investments.

FDI inflows varied greatly among different subregions and economies. Among the subregions, East and North-East Asia experienced the biggest growth of FDI inflows, attracting 36% more inflows compared with 2012. However, South-East Asia proved to be the most resilient, having experiencing undisrupted growth in FDI inflows since 2009.

In terms of FDI outflows, the Asia-Pacific region experienced a significant increase of 15.1% in 2013. The subregion accounted for 38.3% of share of the global FDI outflows, thus gaining greater importance as investors. There were some key players, such as China and the Russian Federation, which contributed to the stiff increase.

In Asia and the Pacific, China is undoubtedly one of the most important players in the region, not only as an investment destination but also as a source of investment. China continuously increased its FDI outflows during the past decade and shows no sign of stopping, with the government strategy of "going global" encouraging the trend ever further. Japan also played a major role recording a 33% increase in 2013. However, not all economies experienced positive trends. India, for example, is still suffering from macroeconomic uncertainties and an unfavourable business environments that are discouraging investors. Its FDI plummeted in 2013, following a continuous decline since 2008.

Varied performances in FDI in different subregions and economies are the result of a combination of several factors. One is government policies that encourage or hinder foreign investments. As seen from the examples of several economies, government policies played an important role.

Another trend identified is that while the traditional big players in the Asia-Pacific region still continue to lead the way, small players are increasing their importance as FDI destinations. This is leading to more diverse Asia-Pacific FDI inflows and outflows.

The significance of the roles played by greenfield FDI and M&A is also changing. Traditionally, for the Asia-Pacific region, the greenfield FDI was a significant mode of entry for investors. However, since 2008 a decline has been noticed; on the other hand, M&A is gaining in importance.

Between 2011 and 2013, intraregional greenfield FDI inflows in the region dropped by 43% with the downward trend visible in major destination countries, due to the effect of the economic crisis in 2012.

Intraregional FDI will not be immune to global macroeconomic factors such as global economic slowdown, political tensions and a global credit crunch. However, there are indications that the role of intraregional FDI activities remains significant.

First, intraregional FDI investors are increasingly replacing investors from European countries and the United States – which were traditionally the top investors in the Asia-Pacific region. As stated above, popular investment destinations that recorded significant amounts of M&A deals with investors from the Asia-Pacific region included, for example, China (71.5%), Hong Kong, China (66%), and the Republic of Korea, (45.1%).

Second, intraregional FDI investors are investing in a broader range of industries, away from natural resource heavy industries to more knowledge-based industries and services. Investments increased in industries such as health care, pharmaceuticals and biotechnology, construction, consumer products and business services.

Third, the share of FDI inflows through M&A to the Asia-Pacific in overall intraregional FDI inflows has increased. Although global FDI inflows through M&A to the Asia-Pacific region decreased in 2012 and 2013, intraregional FDI inflows through M&A have remained substantial at a total of $153.8 billion, accounting for almost one third of total FDI inflows through M&A to the Asia-Pacific region.

Fourth, a number of mega-treaties involving FDI are currently under negotiation in the region; these treaties will provide a solid basis for more open trade and investment, thus improving future economic prospects in the region. These factors are expected to contribute to increased levels of intraregional FDI activities in the foreseeable future.

ENDNOTES

1 All FDI data are from UNCTADStat, except for greenfield FDI data which are from fDi Intelligence, and data on mergers and acquisitions which are from Thomson Reuters.

2 Belgium, Luxemburg, Ireland and the Netherlands. See UNCTAD (2014).

3 These are the Trans-Pacific Partnership Agreement (TPPA) and Regional Economic Comprehensive Partnership (RCEP) which are discussed in chapter 6 of this Report.

4 The concerns remain, especially from local small-scale producers, with ensuring equal opportunities to be a part of production value chain effectively to increase their share of profit.

5 The data on greenfield FDI are provided by fDi Intelligence, which track greenfield FDI project announcements on a global basis. The data are based on information available at the time of the project announcement and, therefore, differ from official FDI flows that are often based on balance of payments statistics. Discrepancies may arise from the timing of the investment as the database does not take any phasing of the investment into account. In addition, fDi Intelligence uses its own estimates of capital investment if those data have not been given in the announcement. Additionally, some of the announced investment capital may be raised locally, meaning that only a part of the capital invested may manifest itself as actual FDI flows.

REFERENCES

Balakrishnan, Bhaskar (2014). India's next Government can boost the economy - OPED. 19 May. Available from www.eurasiareview.com/19052014-indias-next-government-can-boost-economy-oped/ .

Bangko Sentral ng Pilipinas (Central Bank of the Philippines) (2014). Selected economic indicators – Asian countries, 2010-2014. Available from www.bsp.gov.ph/statistics/spei_pub/Table%2060.pdf .

China, Ministry of Commerce (2014). Statistics of FDI in China in January-December 2013. Available from http://english.mofcom.gov.cn/article/statistic/foreigninvestment/201402/20140200498911.shtml .

Economic and Social Commission for Asia and the Pacific (2013). *Asia-Pacific Trade and Investment Report 2013 – Turning the Tide: Towards Inclusive Trade and Investment*. Sales No. E.14.II.F.2. Available from www.unescap.org/resources/asia-pacific-trade-and-investment-report-2013-turning-tide-towards-inclusive-trade-and .

_____ (2014). *Economic and Social Survey of Asia and the Pacific 2014: Regional Connectivity for Shared Prosperity*. Sales No. E.14.II.F.4. Available from unescap.org/resources/economic-and-social-survey-asia-and-pacific-2014 .

Evseev, Viacheslav, and Ross Wilson (2012). WTO accession: implications for Russia. Russian Analytical Digest, No. 119, 21 October. Available from www.css.ethz.ch/publications/pdfs/Russian_Analytical_Digest_119-2.pdf .

India, Ministry of Commerce, Department of Industrial Policy and Promotion (2014a). Fact sheet on foreign direct investment (FDI) from April 2000 to December 2013. Available from http://dipp.nic.in/English/Publications/FDI_Statistics/2013/india_FDI_December2013.pdf .

_____ (2014b). Consolidated FDI policy (effective from 17 April 2014). Available from http://dipp.nic.in/English/Policies/FDI_Circular_2014.pdf .

Indonesia Investment Coordinating Board (2014). Domestic and foreign direct investment realization in quarter IV and January-December 2013. 21 June. Available from http://www2.bkpm.go.id/file_uploaded/public/Press%20Release%20TW%20IV%202013%20-%20eng%20wartawan_01.pdf .

Japan Times (2014). Increasing FDI in Japan. 28 July. Availablefromwww.japantimes.co.jp/opinion/2014/07/23/editorials/increasing-fdi-japan/#.U_Vgt_mSwaA .

Korea Eximbank (2014). Foreign investment statistics. Available from www.koreaexim.go.kr/en/fdi/invest_02.jsp .

Manyin, Mark E., Remy Jurenas, and Michaela D. Platzer (2013). The U.S.-South Korea Free Trade Agreement (KORUS FTA): provisions and implications. CRS Report for Congress. Washington, D.C.: Congressional Research Services. Available from http://fas.org/sgp/crs/row/RL34330.pdf .

Neate, Rupert (2014). Rosneft takes over TNK-BP in $55bn deal. Guardian. 21 March. Available from www.theguardian.com/business/2013/mar/21/rosneft-takes-over-tnk-bp .

National Economic and Development Authority (2014). Philippine Development Plan 2011-2016. Available from www.neda.gov.ph/?p=1128 .

Republic of Korea, Ministry of Trade, Industry and Energy (2014). Trade policies. Available from www.motie.go.kr/language/eng/policy/Tpolicies_02.jsp .

Russian Direct Investment Fund (2014). Partnerships. Available from http://rdif.ru/Eng_Partnership/ .

Sauvant, Karl P., and Victor Zitian Chen (2014). China's regulatory framework for outward foreign direct investment. *China Economic Journal*, vol. 7, Issue 1, pp. 141-163.

Soble, Jonathan (2014). Japan to pursue reforms in six economic zones. *Financial Times*. Available from www.ft.com/cms/s/0/f902773a-b6a2-11e3-8695-00144feabdc0.html#axzz3BjsdLTIF .

The Economist (2014a). Have the three arrows of Abenomics hit their targets? 25 April. Available from http://country.eiu.com/article.aspx?articleid=81760792&Country=Japan&topic=Economy .

_____ (2014b). Tipping the scales. 3 May. Available from www.economist.com/news/finance-and-economics/21601536-crisis-ukraine-hurting-already-weakening-economy-tipping-scales .

Tudor-Ackroyd, Alison (2013). Japan's MUFG to Buy Bank of Ayudha Stake for $5.6 billion. *Finance Asia*. 3 July.

United Nations Conference on Trade and Development (2014). *World Investment Report 2014*. Sales No. E.14.II.D.1. Available from http://unctad.org/en/pages/PublicationWebflyer.aspx?publicationid=937 .

United States, Department of the Treasury (2014). U.S. - China Strategic and Economic Dialogue. Available from www.treasury.gov/initiatives/Pages/china.aspx .

VN, Sreeja (2013). Indonesia's Government to relax foreign direct investment norms to boost economy as growth sputters. *International Business Times*. 24 December. Available from www.ibtimes.com/indonesias-government-relax-foreign-direct-investment-norms-boost-economy-growth-sputters-1519258 .

World Bank (2014a). Data – GDP growth. Available from http://data.worldbank.org/indicator/NY.GDP.MKTP.KD.ZG .

_____ (2014b). Economy rankings. Available from www.doingbusiness.org/rankings .

Online databases

Financial Times Ltd. fDi Intelligence. fDi Markets – Crossborder investment monitor. Available from www.fdimarkets.com. Accessed May and June 2014.

Thomson Reuters Datastream Professional database. Available from www.datastream.com/. Accessed April 2014.

United Nations Conference on Trade and Development, UNCTADStat. Available from http://unctadstat.unctad.org/ReportFolders/reportFolders.aspx?sCS_referer=&sCS_ChosenLang=en. Accessed May and June 2014.

4 TRADE FACILITATION IN THE ASIA-PACIFIC REGION: A BRIGHT OUTLOOK

The Trade Facilitation Agreement (TFA), accomplished at the ninth WTO Ministerial Conference in December 2013, is the first major global trade agreement to have been concluded since the establishment of WTO in 1995. Although implementation of the TFA remains uncertain, the agreement provides evidence of a global consensus on the importance of trade facilitation for sustainable economic development as well as a narrow but concrete framework through which countries may simplify and enhance the transparency of their trade procedures.

At the regional level, progress made towards a regional arrangement on the facilitation of cross-border paperless trade (since the adoption by ESCAP member States in May 2012 of a resolution on enabling the cross-border recognition of electronic data and documents for inclusive and sustainable intraregional trade facilitation) also suggests that the region is committed to making significant progress in this area in the future.

This chapter provides a preliminary regional assessment of the implementation of trade facilitation measures included in the TFA as well as the development of trade services and systems for paperless trade facilitation based on surveys carried out by the ESCAP secretariat since 2012.[1] Taking into account the particular importance of the agricultural sector to inclusive trade and development and the earlier finding that agricultural trade costs were typically twice as high as those for manufacturing goods (ESCAP, 2013), this chapter also presents recent findings from country- and product-specific agricultural trade process analyses. The chapter concludes with a way forward for countries of the region to make further progress in trade facilitation.

A. TRADE FACILITATION MEASURES IN THE WTO TRADE FACILITATION AGREEMENT: IMPLEMENTATION STATUS

The TFA is regarded as "one of the biggest reforms of WTO since its establishment in 1995" (WTO, 2014a, p.10) although its implementation still remains uncertain.[2] The key components of the WTO TFA are summarized in box 4.1.

In an effort to provide a basis for countries to design and prioritize their own trade facilitation implementation plans and strategies, the

Box 4.1 Introduction to the WTO Trade Facilitation Agreement

Negotiations on a new TFA were launched in July 2004 as an addition to the Doha Development Agenda formulated in 2001. The aim of the agreement is to expedite the movement, release and clearance of goods (including goods in transit) as well as to ensure effective cooperation between customs and other appropriate authorities. Particular attention was paid to developing and least developed countries, which stand to benefit from far-reaching flexibilities and considerable technical assistance and capacity-building support. After nearly 10 years, the negotiations were successfully concluded in December 2013 at WTO's ninth Ministerial Conference in Bali, Indonesia.

While discussions are still ongoing when the TFA will be implemented, the text of the TFA has been finalized. The TFA has two sections. Section I contains provisions for expediting the movement, release and clearance of goods. It clarifies and improves the relevant Articles (V, VIII and X) of the General Agreement on Tariffs and Trade (GATT) 1994. Section II contains special and differential treatment provisions for developing and least developed countries, which are aimed at helping them to implement the provisions of the Agreement. More specifically, the TFA includes the following Articles:

Section I

Article I: Publication and availability of information.
Article II: Opportunity to comment, information before entry into force and consultation.
Article III: Advance rulings.
Article IV: Appeal or review procedures.
Article V: Other measures to enhance impartiality, non-discrimination and transparency.
Article VI: Disciplines on fees and charges imposed on or in connection with importation and exportation.
Article VII: Release and clearance of goods.
Article VIII: Border agency cooperation.
Article IX: Movement of goods under customs control intended for import.
Article X: Formalities connected with importation and exportation and transit.
Article XI: Freedom of transit.
Article XII: Customs cooperation.
Article XIII: Institutional arrangements.

Section II

- Special and differential treatment provisions for developing country members and least developed country members.
- Final provisions.

Source: WTO, 2014b.

ESCAP secretariat has set out to systematically collect and analyse information on the actual implementation of trade facilitation measures in the region since 2012.

While the scope of ESCAP data collection work on trade facilitation implementation goes beyond that of the provisions listed in the TFA, the results from the 2013-2014 ESCAP survey on trade facilitation and paperless trade implementation that pertain to the 13 articles included in the TFA are presented below.

1. Implementation of general trade facilitation measures

> *A key concern is whether there is a mechanism in place to ensure information is published and updated on a regular basis and in a coordinated manner.*

General trade facilitation measures included in the ESCAP survey, most of which relate to Articles I through X of the TFA, are being at least partially implemented by more than half of the 29 countries surveyed (figure 4.1). The measure referring to publication of existing import and export regulations on the Internet has been fully or partially implemented by all countries surveyed. A key concern, however, is whether there is a mechanism in place to ensure information is published and updated on a regular basis and in a coordinated manner.[3] Another concern is the level of difficulty in finding the required information. Although information on existing import and export regulations may be available, it is often scattered, which makes it complicated or impossible for traders to easily access and utilize it.

Implementation of single window[4] is arguably one of the most far-reaching, but also most

FIGURE 4.1 General trade facilitation measures implemented by Asia-Pacific countries

(Percentage)

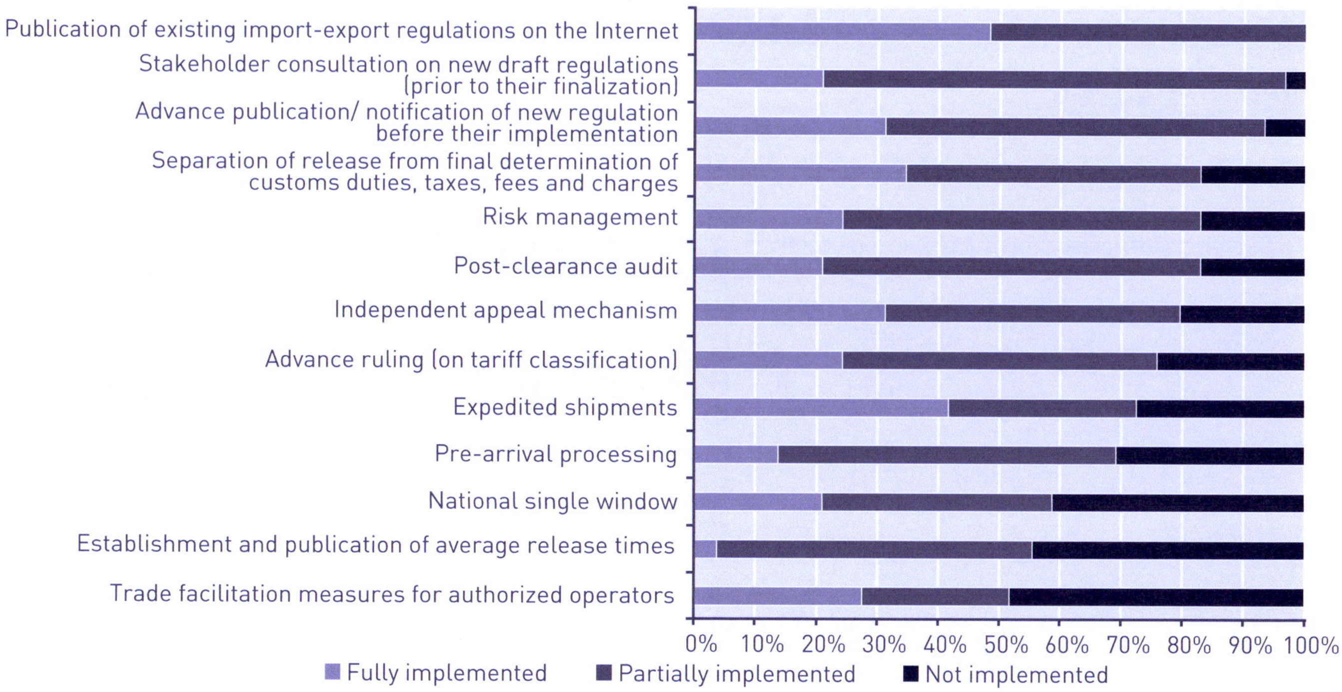

Source: Wang and Duval (2014).

complex, measures included in the TFA. The fact that (a) partial implementation of national single windows is ongoing in more than half of the countries surveyed, and (b) trade facilitation measures related to automation and paperless trade procedures (including development of national single windows) were identified by the respondents of the survey as an area where the most progress had been made over the past 12 months,[5] is promising. The leadership of the region in implementing single window facilities can be explained in part by the ASEAN members' commitment made in 2005 to implement a regional ASEAN Single Window by 2012.[6]

Measures found to be the least implemented include authorized economic operators (AEO), followed by measures to establish and publish average release times. Only Japan has conducted and published results on a regular basis of studies on release times whereas most other countries conduct these studies on an ad hoc basis (if at all), and/or often do not publish the results.

2. Implementation of transit facilitation measures

Despite the utmost importance of transit facilitation for many landlocked developing economies of the region, some international and regional agreements dealing with transit have not been effectively implemented.

Article XI of the TFA is related to transit facilitation. The survey results reveal that the relevant information on transit fees and charges has seldom been published on the Internet. Such information in most cases is available at the concerned offices and bureaux. Shippers, freight forwarders and transport operators who were surveyed indicated that such information was either rarely available in the public domain or transparent to them.

In terms of transit operation (figure 4.2), in 23 countries (almost 80% of those surveyed),

FIGURE 4.2 Measures for facilitating transit (Percentage)

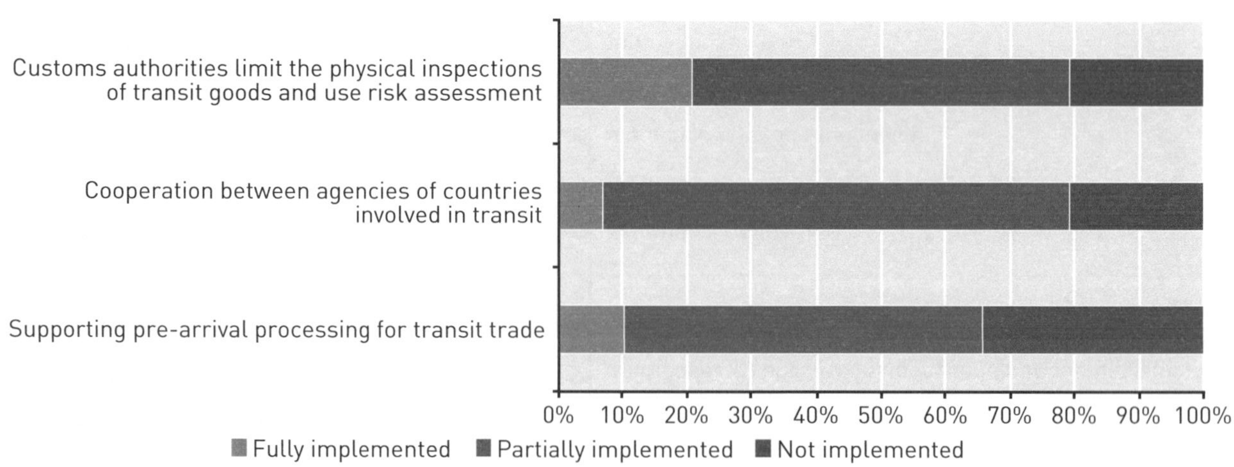

Source: Wang and Duval (2014).

customs authorities limit the physical inspections of transit goods to some extent. Similarly, in 23 countries, various border agencies cooperate on transit to some extent. Pre-arrival processing for transit trade is also partially or fully supported in 19 countries (66% of those surveyed).

3. Implementation of measures on cooperation at the borders

> *Cooperation within a country on trade facilitation is more widely spread than cooperation with neighbouring countries.*

Article XII of the TFA addresses issues on cooperation at the borders. Figure 4.3, not surprisingly, shows that cooperation within a country is more widely spread than cooperation with neighbouring countries. It indicates that in 12 countries (more than 40% of those surveyed), different border agencies fully cooperate with each other, while in another 17 countries the border agencies cooperate with each other to some extent. In 24 countries (82% of those surveyed), controls are either fully or partially delegated to customs authorities.

The measure referring to alignment with neighbouring countries of working days and hours at border crossings has been fully implemented in only 12 countries (41% of those surveyed). Alignment of formalities and procedures with neighbouring countries at border crossings has also been fully implemented in just four countries (13% of those surveyed), although 17 countries (59%) are reportedly working on this issue.

4. Establishment of a national trade facilitation body

Article XIII of the TFA states that: "Each Member shall establish and/or maintain a national committee on trade facilitation or designate an existing mechanism to facilitate both domestic coordination and implementation of provisions of this Agreement." Establishment of a national trade facilitation body (NTFB) is crucial to the involvement of all relevant stakeholders in trade facilitation, and is often regarded by international organizations[7] as one of the most important factors for sustaining progress in trade facilitation.

FIGURE 4.3

Cooperation at the borders

(Percentage)

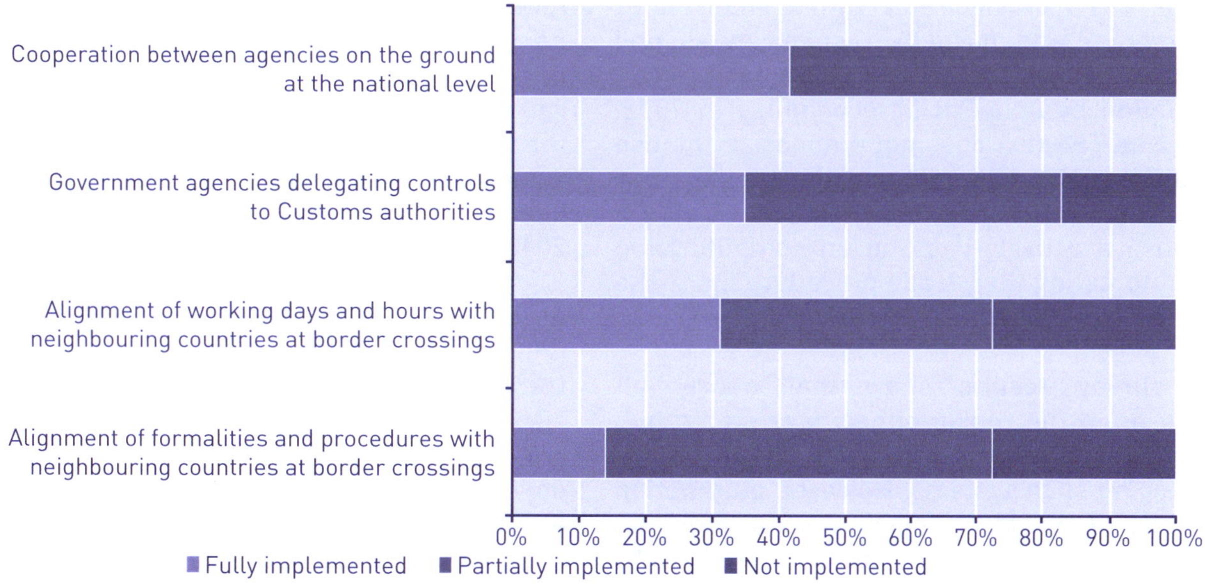

Source: Wang and Duval (2014).

CHAPTER 4

The results of the survey reveal that, as of 2014, at least 10 countries[8] have an NTFB. In seven countries, either NTFBs have been partially established or a mechanism for coordination of trade facilitation has been put in place.[9] Among those countries, China, Indonesia and Malaysia have cross-sectoral coordination mechanisms in place in order to facilitate trade and logistics, although there is no official trade facilitation body. In India, Japan, the Republic of Korea and Viet Nam the committees for paperless trade facilitation (including a single window) partially fulfill the functions of trade facilitation bodies but comprise fewer representatives from either the Government or the private sector, rather than a fully-fledged trade facilitation committee.

In the remaining 11 countries surveyed, a trade facilitation body has not yet been established, suggesting that coordination of trade facilitation may have taken place on an ad hoc basis.

B. IMPLEMENTATION OF PAPERLESS TRADE

Good progress appears to have been made in establishment of a supportive legal framework for the development and use of paperless trade services.

Enabling paperless trade, or conducting trade on the basis of electronic rather than paper documents, was formally recognized as one of the keys to inclusive and sustainable trade facilitation by Asia-Pacific economies in 2012. While the TFA text does not emphasize the use of information and communications technology for trade facilitation, many countries of the region are actively working on computerizing and automating their trade procedures to make them more efficient.

The survey results show that nearly all countries in the region either have electronic/automated customs systems in place or are developing such systems. However, automation and use of electronic documents beyond the customs declaration is more limited, with only 17 countries either already have or are actively engaged in the development of electronic "single-window systems" for one-time submission of information to all trade regulatory agencies.

The establishment of a supportive legal framework is essential to the development and use of paperless trade services, and good progress appears to have been made in this area. The survey results show that 22 countries (76% of those surveyed) have fully or partially promulgated laws and regulations for electronic transactions. At the same time, only 6 countries (21%) have recognized certification authorities that can issue digital certificates to traders for conducting electronic transactions while another 10 countries are developing such certification authorities. Almost half of the countries surveyed (13) do not have such certification authorities.

Most of the paperless trade systems in the region have also been focused on facilitating information exchange between stakeholders domestically, while facilitating international trade inherently requires trade information to flow across borders along international supply chains. As a result, the flow of electronic trade information generated domestically encounters both technical and legal barriers beyond the border, requiring traders to maintain conventional paper-based trade practices and reducing the overall benefits and return on investment from paperless trade systems. The need to find effective ways to address these barriers has been regularly and increasingly raised by public and private stakeholders in the region and region-wide export gains from achieving cross-border paperless trade have been estimated at $257 billion annually (ESCAP, 2014).

As figure 4.4 shows, no country reported "full implementation" of cross-border paperless trade measures. More than half of the countries surveyed (15) have engaged in some form of cross-border exchange of electronic trade documents, essentially on a pilot basis or with a very limited number of partner countries. Specifically, 12 countries (about 40% of those surveyed), have engaged in some electronic exchange of Certificates of Origin with other countries. Similarly, in 12 of the countries

FIGURE 4.4

Cross-border paperless trade practice

(Percentage)

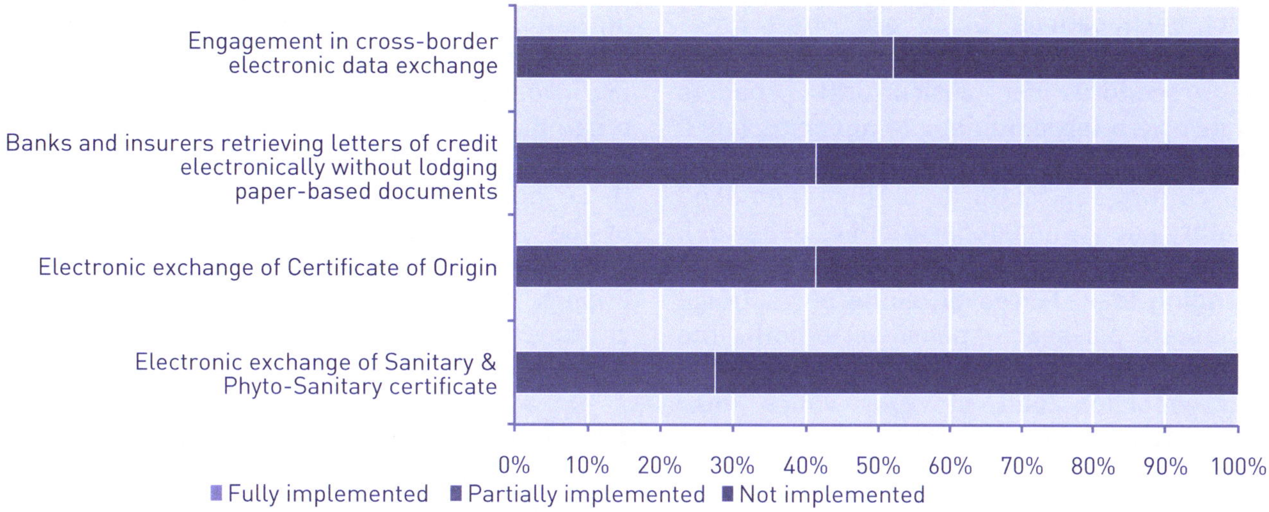

Source: Wang and Duval (2014).

surveyed, measures are being taken to allow banks and insurers to retrieve letters of credit electronically without lodging paper-based documents. Only 8 countries (28% of those surveyed) have been engaged in the electronic exchange of Sanitary and Phytosanitary (SPS) Certificates with other countries.

C. COSTS AND PROCEDURES OF AGRICULTURAL PRODUCTS TRADING

The trade costs of agricultural products are often higher than those of other products such as in manufacturing (figure 4.5). This can largely be explained by the characteristics

FIGURE 4.5

Average trade costs (excluding tariffs) for agricultural and manufacturing products between China and selected countries in Asia, 2000-2011

(Percentage)

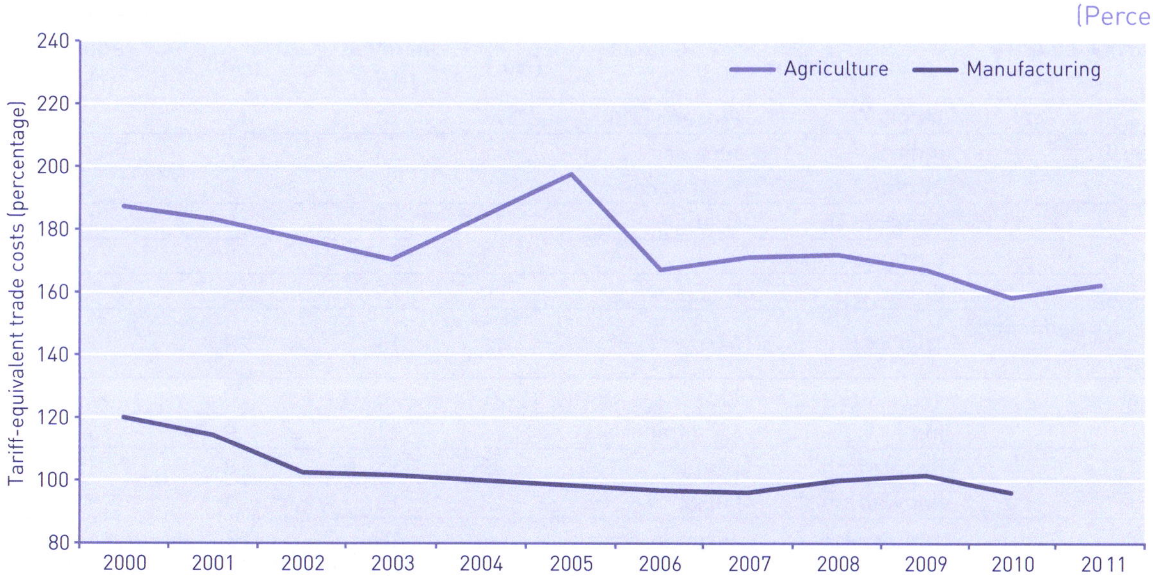

Source: ESCAP-World Bank Trade Cost Database, updated August 2013.

Note: Average costs in this figure refer to average costs between China and selected countries in the region (Georgia, India, Indonesia, Japan, Kazakhstan, Kyrgyzstan, Lao People's Democratic Republic, Malaysia, Nepal, Philippines, Republic of Korea, Russian Federation, Sri Lanka, Thailand, Turkey and Viet Nam).

of the industry. Exporting and importing agricultural products involves regulatory trade procedures such as laboratory tests and product certifications which are often time-consuming. From an institutional perspective, trade procedures for agricultural products often involve a large number of agencies (such as customs, ministry of commerce, ministry of agriculture, agricultural product and food regulatory agency and department of fisheries). Coordination of multiple agencies can be a challenging task. Moreover, some agricultural products are perishable, sensitive to both time and temperature, and require special handling for transportion and storage, which may increase trade costs.

A whole-supply-chain approach is essential to making significant progress in reducing trade transaction costs and improving competitiveness of agricultural products.

Recent studies of import and export procedures for agricultural products using the business process analysis approach (UNNExT, 2012) facilitated by ESCAP - especially under the SATNET,[10] and SASEC[11] programmes - show that the severity and type of procedural barriers to agricultural trade vary from country to country. For example, in Myanmar, no less than 20 actors are involved in the export of rice (compared with a sample average of 13, as illustrated in table 4.1). In the Lao People's Democratic Republic, three agencies require visiting the premises of the animal feed importer to provide three separate reports for verifying the request for import.[12] In Nepal, local administration still charges an export fee even though there is a national policy for no export fees.

Analysis of trade procedures can shed more light on time and costs required to complete each procedure as well as pinpoint potential areas for improvement. For example, for exporting shrimp from Bangladesh and Thailand, it can take up to 17.5 days and 14 days, respectively to obtain the SPS certificate, including laboratory tests (figure 4.6). This accounts for more than half of the total time required to complete export procedures within those two countries. In Cambodia, it takes between five to seven

TABLE 4.1 Actors, time, costs and documents involved in exporting agricultural products in South and South-East Asia

Exporting country	Importing country/region	Product	Days (No.)	Actors involved (No.)	Procedures (No.)	Documents required (No.)	Cost ($)
Bangladesh	Japan	Frozen shrimp	36.75	14	12	24	500
Bangladesh	India	Jute bag	10	15	12	24	236
Bangladesh	Bhutan	Fruit juice	18	7	9	9	225
Bhutan	Bangladesh	Oranges	12	14	18	14	444
Cambodia	European Union	Rice	32	14	12	24	1 029
Cambodia	China	Maize	20	15	13	22	1 250
Lao People's Democratic Republic	Thailand	Maize	16	11	8	21	735
Myanmar	West Africa	Rice	19-23	20	10	>25	425
Nepal	India	Cardamom	13	11	9	14	1 213
Nepal	Bangladesh	Lentils	13	14	18	18	613
Thailand	Bangladesh	Sugar	13	13	13	31	1 128
Thailand	United States	Jasmine rice	16	16	15	n.a.	n.a.

Source: Derived from SATNET BPA Studies (www.satnetasia.org/theme2.html), SASEC Phase I BPA Study (forthcoming), and other BPA studies available from http://unnext.unescap.org/pub/tipub2615.pdf.

Note: While the studies were conducted on the basis of the UNNExT BPA Guide, the scope and context of each study differs. Accordingly, results may not be used for cross-country benchmarking purposes.

FIGURE 4.6 Days required for export of agricultural products

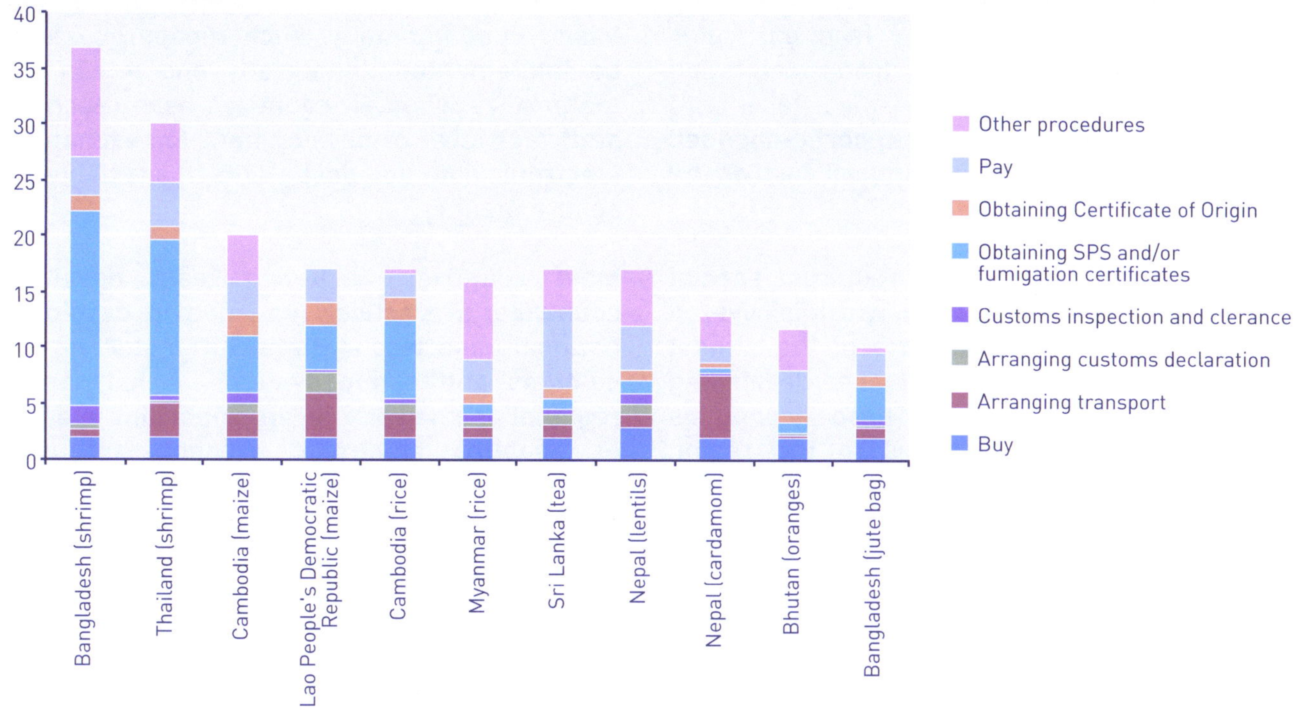

Source: Derived from SATNET studies (www.satnetasia.org/theme2.html), SASEC Phase I BPA Study (forthcoming), and other studies available from unnext.unescap.org/tools/business_process.asp.

Note: While the studies were conducted on the basis of the UNNExT BPA Guide, the scope and context of each study differ. Accordingly, results may not be used for cross-country benchmarking purposes.

days to complete the same procedure. In Nepal, Cambodia, Myanmar and Sri Lanka, only one day is required to obtain the SPS certificate.

The findings from the studies have important implications for policymakers and other stakeholders involved in trade facilitation. First, they confirm that many agricultural trade procedures are not only complex but also specific to the sector or product, suggesting the need for trade facilitation support programmes dedicated to agriculture and food products.[13] Second and more generally, the trade process analysis studies suggest that a whole-supply-chain approach is essential to making significant progress in reducing trade transactions cost and improving competitiveness, as the most important bottlenecks may not be at the border and may also relate to inefficient services by the private sector more than by government agencies. Accordingly, this requires policymakers to monitor the performance along the entire supply chain and identify solutions for streamlining trade process continuously, as proposed by ESCAP and ADB (Duval, Wang and Nguyen, 2014).

CONCLUSION AND THE WAY FORWARD

Given the latest developments in trade facilitation, this chapter highlights the following areas to which the countries need to pay attention in order to further advance trade facilitation in the region.

1. Implementation of the Trade Facilitation Agreement

The TFA provides a unique global framework for trade facilitation. By nature, it only needs to be implemented by the WTO member States. However, as the WTO member States also trade with non-WTO member, all countries need to strive to implement all the trade facilitation measures included in the WTO agreement. The least developed and land-locked developing countries in the region may face particular challenges for implementing trade facilitation measures; however, they may take full advantage of assistance and support embedded in the TFA[14] as well as other support such as the Aid for Trade initiative.

One particular area that requires special attention is transit facilitation, which is covered by the TFA. Transit issues are of the utmost importance to the many landlocked developing economies of the region. These economies as well as transit countries in the region need to continue to facilitate transit as part of trade facilitation plans and to strengthen collaboration with neighbouring countries. The current international and regional agreements dealing with transit have not been effectively implemented. For example, although the TIR Convention provides a useful framework for implementing transit operations, it has not been widely implemented in the region except in a few cases such as the Islamic Republic of Iran, the Russian Federation and Turkey.[15] Other examples are the ASEAN Framework Agreement on the Facilitation of Goods in Transit (1998) and the Greater Mekong Subregion Cross-Border Transport Facilitation Agreement (CBTA), which have not yet been implemented.

It is noteworthy that, while the TFA does include negotiations on freedom of transit and related issues, bilateral and regional trade and/or economic partnership agreements typically do not contain transit facilitation provisions. Transit is often still treated as a fully separate and distinct issue. However, integrating or clarifying the linkages between bilateral/regional trade and transit agreements, when both exist, would certainly contribute to making international trade procedures more transparent (Cousin and Duval, 2014).

2. Development of cross-border paperless trade

Cross-border paperless trade is still at a nascent stage of implementation. Even in the most advanced countries, cross-border paperless trade has been limited to exchanging selected electronic documents on a pilot basis. Fundamentally, such measures cannot be implemented unilaterally and it can only materialize when all countries have reached a sufficient level of development for exchanging electronic data and documents in a reliable and secure manner.

Most countries, including least developed countries, are actively engaged in developing national paperless systems, often starting with customs automation systems. A harmonized regional framework is an important element of enabling electronic exchange of trade data and documents, as recognized in ESCAP Resolution 68/3.[16] A regional arrangement on the facilitation of cross-border paperless trade, as envisaged in ESCAP Resolution 70/6, would provide the framework needed for developing practical solutions to existing technical and legal barriers through the adoption of common principles and structured knowledge sharing as well as capacity-building mechanisms.[17]

In this context, all countries in the region should be actively involved in the Intergovernmental Steering Group on Cross-Border Paperless Trade established by ESCAP . It should be noted, in particular, that participation at an early stage of adoption of paperless trade would ensure that they could learn from the lessons of more advanced countries and develop systems that would be more readily interoperable.

3. Establishment of a sustainable Trade Facilitation Monitoring Mechanism

Every country needs to establish a continuous, affordable and sustainable monitoring mechanism to regularly monitor the progress in trade facilitation and prioritize measures to advance trade facilitation.

Few countries in the region have put an effective mechanism in place to (a) monitor the actual effectiveness of their trade facilitation reforms, and (b) identify the trade and transport process and procedures that should be prioritized for simplification or streamlining. The global trade facilitation performance surveys and databases now available are useful benchmarking and awareness-raising tools, but they do not provide sufficient detailed information to enable the development or updating of national trade facilitation action plans. In addition, while trade and transport facilitation assessments ranging in scope are often conducted in least developed or landlocked developing countries, these assessments are typically ad hoc in nature, with little coordination among development partners and limited buy-in by the governmental agencies concerned.

In order to regularly monitor progress in trade facilitation and prioritize measures to advance trade facilitation, every country needs to establish a continuous, affordable and sustainable monitoring mechanism. It is recommended that the national trade facilitation body should be the executive body of such a monitoring mechanism, and that monitoring trade facilitation should be regarded as one of its functions. It is also recommended that national human resources should be used to conduct assessment studies and exercises in order to reduce the costs and maintain the sustainability of such mechanism.

In this regard, countries in the region may take advantage of the existing work carried out by ESCAP and ADB on a sustainable and integrated approach to monitor trade facilitation (box 4.2).

Box 4.2

Towards a national integrated and sustainable Trade and Transport Facilitation Monitoring Mechanism

Despite the efforts made by many developing countries to facilitate trade and transport, few have effective mechanisms in place to (a) monitor the actual effectiveness of their trade and transport facilitation reforms, and (b) identify the trade and transport process and procedures that should be prioritized for simplification or streamlining. To bridge this gap, ESCAP and ADB have jointly developed a guide on establishing a national integrated and sustainable Trade and Transport Facilitation Monitoring Mechanism (TTFMM) to enable the countries to monitor progress in trade facilitation and adapt their strategies to the changing national, regional and global environments.

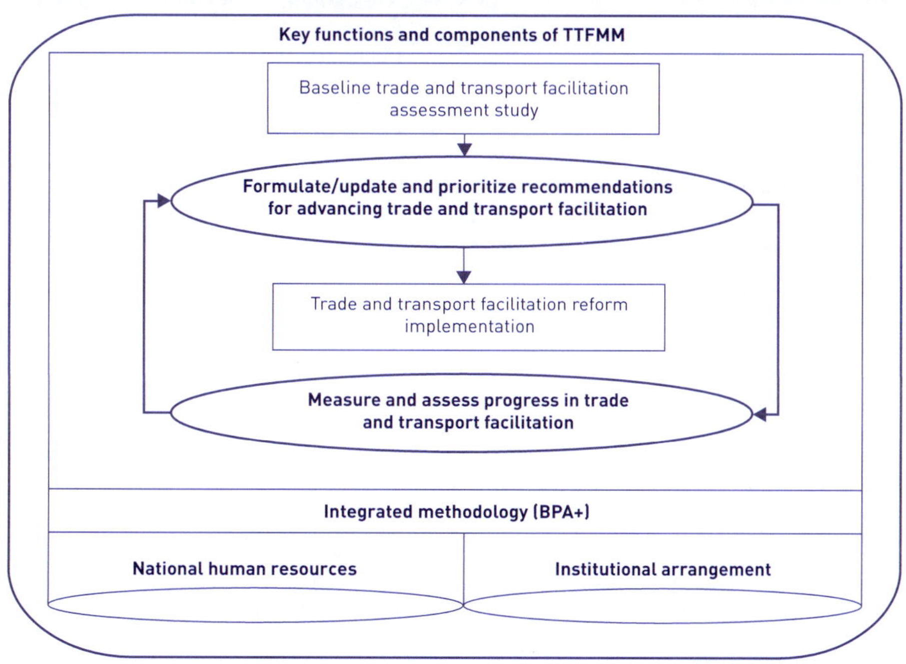

CHAPTER 4

Box 4.2 (continued)

The key functions of the TTFMM are two-fold: (a) to formulate/update and prioritize recommendations for advancing trade facilitation; and (b) to measure and assess progress in trade facilitation. It is emphasized that TTFMM should be anchored within a national trade and transport facilitation committee (or an equivalent institution) and rely upon national resources to make it sustainable and affordable. Underpinning TTFMM is the methodology called Business Process Analysis Plus (BPA+) which is built on the Business Process Analysis methodology, supplemented by Time Release Studies (TRS) and Time-Cost-Distance (TCD) methodologies.

TTFMM is being implemented in Bangladesh, Bhutan and Nepal. In these three countries, national trade (and transport) facilitation committees take the lead in implementation, with support from ESCAP and ADB. National training workshops on the implementation of TTFMM in these countries were held in March-April 2014. The TTFMM baseline studies will be carried out during 2014-2015.

Source: Duval, Wang and Nguyen (2014).

ENDNOTES

1 More information on the survey is available from Wang and Duval (2014).

2 The adoption of the protocol on the Trade Facilitation Agreement, scheduled to be done by the end of 31 July 2014, did not take place. See details at www.wto.org/english/news_e/news14_e/tnc_infstat_31jul14_e.htm .

3 For example, Lao People's Democratic Republic has established a trade portal that is aimed at providing a one-stop-point for all information on trade-related procedures and enquiry points and has set up a mechanism to ensure relevant data and information are collected and uploaded to the portal.

4 Article X of the TFA states that "Members shall endeavor to establish or maintain a single window, enabling traders to submit documentation and/or data requirements for importation, exportation or transit of goods through a single entry point to the participating authorities or agencies."

5 Of the respondents from 19 countries who provided information on progress and challenges, respondents from 16 countries stated that the greatest progress had been made in trade facilitation measures related to automation and paperless trade (including development of a national single window). Progress was also identified in the areas of risk management, legislation and regulations on trade facilitation, publication of trade-related information and post-clearance audit, as identified by the respondents.

6 Agreement to Establish and Implement an ASEAN Single Window. Available from http://asw.asean.org/archives/agreements/item/agreement-to-establish-and-implement-the-asean-single-window .

7 For example, for details of the work of UNCTAD on establishment of trade facilitation bodies see unctad.org/en/DTL/TLB/Pages/TF/Committees/default.aspx .

8 Azerbaijan, Bangladesh, Bhutan, Cambodia, Lao People's Democratic Republic, Mongolia, Nepal, Pakistan, Singapore and Thailand.

9 China, India, Indonesia, Japan, Malaysia, Republic of Korea and Viet Nam.

10 SATNET refers to the Network for Knowledge Transfer on Sustainable Agricultural Technologies and Improved Market Linkages in South and Southeast Asia (SATNET). Studies are available from www.satnetasia.org/theme2.html as well as unnext.unescap.org/tools/business_process.asp .

11 SASEC refers to the South Asia Subregional Economic Cooperation (SASEC) Program under the auspices of the Asian Development Bank. BPA studies were jointly conducted by ESCAP and ADB under that programme in 2012-2013.

12 More detailed information is provided in SATNET Business Process Analysis Studies (Bangladesh, Nepal, Cambodia, Myanmar, Nepal, Lao People's Democratic Republic) (various dates), ESCAP, Bangkok. Available from unnext.unescap.org/tools/business_process.asp.

[13] This is consistent with the conclusions reached in the macro-level analysis of trade costs in developing countries conducted by Arvis and others (2013).

[14] A new initiative, entitled the WTO Trade Facilitation Agreement Facility (TFAF), was launched on 22 July 2014 to provide developing countries and least developed countries with trade facilitation-related technical assistance and capacity-building support. TFAF will complement existing efforts by regional and multilateral agencies, bilateral donors, and other stakeholders. It will become operational when the protocol to insert the TFA into the existing regulatory framework is adopted by WTO member States (www.wto.org/english/news_e/news14_e/fac_22jul14_e.htm .

[15] Fifteen ESCAP member States are contracting parties of TIR. In 2013, among 1.26 million TIR Carnets issued to ESCAP member states, 1.18 million TIR Carnets (93% of the total) were used in the Islamic Republic of Iran, the Russian Federation and Turkey. Data are derived from the Economic Commission for Europe (2014).

[16] ESCAP Resolution 68/3: Enabling paperless trade and the cross-border recognition of electronic data and documents for inclusive and sustainable intraregional trade facilitation, available from www.unescap.org/commission/68/documents.html .

[17] ESCAP Resolution 70/6: Implementation of the Decision of the Ad Hoc Intergovernmental Meeting on a Regional Arrangement for the Facilitation of Cross-border Paperless Trade, available from www.unescap.org/commission/documents .

REFERENCES

Arvis, Jean-François, Yann Duval, Ben Shepherd, and Chorthip Utoktham (2013). Trade costs in the developing world: 1995-2010. World Bank Working Paper Series, No. 6309, January. Available from http://elibrary.worldbank.org/doi/book/10.1596/1813-9450-6309 .

Cousin, Louis, and Yann Duval (2014). Trade facilitation potential of Asian transit agreements in the context of the WTO negotiations. TID Working Paper No. 01/14, 27 January 2014. Bangkok: ESCAP Trade and Investment Division. Available from www.unescap.org/resources/trade-facilitation-potential-asian-transit-agreements-context-wto .

Duval, Yann, Tengfei Wang, and Cuong Minh Nguyen (2014). *Towards a National Integrated and Sustainable Trade and Transport Facilitation Monitoring Mechanism: BPA+*. ST/ESCAP/2683. Bangkok: ESCAP. Available from www.unescap.org/resources/towards-national-integrated-and-sustainable-trade-and-transport-facilitation-monitoring .

Economic and Social Commission for Asia and the Pacific (2013). *Asia-Pacific Trade and Investment Report 2013 – Turning the Tide: Towards Inclusive Trade and Investment.* Sales No. E.14.II.F.2. Available from www.unescap.org/resources/asia-pacific-trade-and-investment-report-2013-turning-tide-towards-inclusive-trade-and .

______ (2014). *Estimating the Benefits of Cross-Border Paperless Trade*. Bangkok: ESCAP. Available from www.unescap.org/resources/estimating-benefits-cross-border-paperless-trade .

Economic Commission for Europe (2014). TIR Carnets. Geneva. Available from www.unece.org/tir/tircarnets.html .

SASEC Business Process Analysis Studies (Bangladesh, Nepal, Bhutan) (forthcoming). Manila: ADB and Bangkok: ESCAP.

SATNET Business Process Analysis Studies (Bangladesh, Nepal, Cambodia, Myanmar, Nepal, Lao People's Democratic Republic). (various dates). Bangkok: ESCAP. Available from http://unnext.unescap.org/tools/business_process.asp .

UNNExT (2012). *Business Process Analysis Guide to Simplify Trade Procedures – updated September 2012*. Bangkok: ESCAP. Available from http://unnext.unescap.org/pub/tipub2558new.asp .

Wang, Tengfei, and Yann Duval (2014). Trade facilitation and paperless trade implementation: 2013/14 Asia-Pacific Update. TID Working Paper No. 02/14, 27 June. Bangkok: ESCAP Trade and Investment Division. Available from www.unescap.org/resources/trade-facilitation-and-paperless-trade-implementation-201314-asia-pacific-update .

World Trade Organization (2014a). *Annual Report 2014*. Geneva. Available from www.wto.org/english/res_e/booksp_e/anrep_e/anrep14_e.pdf .

______ (2014b). Trade Facilitation Agreement. Geneva. Available from www.wto.org/english/tratop_e/tradfa_e/tradfa_e.htm (accessed 8 August 2014) .

5

LIBERALIZATION OR PROTECTION: TRADE POLICY AT A CROSSROADS

A. RECENT TRADE POLICY DEVELOPMENTS

Trade policies in the Asian and Pacific economies show signs of both protectionist and liberalizing tendencies with the overall outlook uncertain. The latter half of 2013 and the first half of 2014 have seen some positive signs of renewed interest in liberalization suggesting that post-2008 crisis pressures for the protection of domestic producers may be weakening. In the major G20 economies, the pace of introducing new trade-restrictive measures recorded by WTO had at least plateaued in the six months up to May 2014 (WTO, 2014a). At the same time, more liberalizing efforts were also recorded. Separately, the regional trade policy environment continues to be shaped by the negotiation of large preferential trade agreements such as the Trans-Pacific Partnership (TPP) and Regional Comprehensive Economic Partnership (RCEP) (see chapter 6 for more details).

On the other hand, the failure to move forward with the Trade Facilitation Agreement means that potential reductions in trade costs will, for now, go unrealized. Similarly, it has reduced hopes that the Doha Development Round of multilateral negotiations might be concluded in the near-term. Furthermore, investigation of developments globally and in the Asia-Pacific region suggests that the autonomous introduction of new liberalizing measures is occurring infrequently. While Asia-Pacific countries adopted both liberalizing and trade-restrictive measures, from October 2012 to November 2013 (henceforth, the reporting period) the balance tipped further towards trade-restrictive measures (WTO, 2014b).

> *Arresting and reversing the trend towards greater barriers to trade should be a priority for large and small economies in the Asia-Pacific region alike.*

As the impact of trade-restrictive policy changes is cumulative, the imposition of new measures without rolling back previously instituted measures makes the overall trade environment increasingly protectionist and difficult. Among trade-restrictive measures, the continued use of less-transparent measures (often not notified to WTO) is of continuing concern. Many of these changes, not least the usage of less-transparent measures (also known as "murky" protectionism), have an impact on the region's least developed countries as they are especially vulnerable to trade restrictions, given the limited diversification of their export baskets and their difficulties in meeting export requirements, for example, product standards (see more details below). Arresting and reversing these trends towards greater barriers to trade through actions at the national, regional, and global levels should be a priority for large and small economies in the Asia-Pacific region alike.

Assessing the overall landscape of trade policy on the basis of recent policy changes requires the assembly of data from several sources. While WTO is a principal source of information on trade policy changes, not all measures are reported to WTO. Further, WTO does not report on all categories of measures that could be called trade restrictive – notably those measures for which there is no WTO agreement. This chapter, therefore, builds on WTO data together with information from various other sources. Trade policy changes that, since 2009, are monitored by WTO include: trade-restrictive measures, such as tariff increases and export restrictions; the initiation of trade remedies, for example anti-dumping investigations; and trade liberalizing measures such as tariff reductions or the removal of import quotas.

According to WTO, at the global level, during the last reporting period 407 new trade restrictions or initiations of trade remedies were introduced compared with 308 in the equivalent period a year earlier (WTO, 2014b). These new measures cover an estimated 1.3% of world merchandise imports, valued at $240 billion, although their precise impact on trade flows is difficult to estimate (ESCAP, 2014). In the Asia-Pacific region 72 new trade-restrictive measures were recorded compared with 37 liberalizing measures. A simple counting of trade-restrictive and liberalizing measures alone does not, however, provide a sufficient indicator of the direction and impacts of trade policy as the effect of individual policies can vary widely.

In terms of trade-restrictive measures, globally, for every five import restrictive measures there was one export restrictive measure; however, in the Asia-Pacific region this ratio was only 3:1. The greater relative use of export restrictions by Asia-Pacific economies is accounted for by the usage of export restrictions on food and other agricultural products as well as other commodities such as tin and rare earth metals. Overall, tariff increases were the most common trade-restrictive measure (table 5.1); the reporting period saw 106 tariff increases globally, 28 of which were in the Asia-Pacific region (25 in the region's developing countries).

TABLE 5.1 New trade and trade-related restrictive measures, mid-October 2012 - mid-November 2013

Type of measure	World	Asia-Pacific
Import	153	55
of which, tariffs	*106*	*28*
Export	27	17
Other	10	0
Total	190	72

Source: ESCAP calculation, based on data from WTO, (2014b).

Fewer trade-liberalizing than trade-restrictive measures were introduced, both globally and in the Asia-Pacific region.

Trade liberalizing measures were fewer in number than trade-restrictive measures both globally and in the Asia-Pacific region. Tariff reductions (mainly unilateral) were the most common form of liberalizing measures accounting for around two thirds of liberalizing measures in the Asia-Pacific region (table 5.2). Compared with the areas where restrictive measures were introduced, countries liberalized most in the machinery and equipment sectors. This may reflect policies designed to facilitate imports in order to assist manufacturers integrate into global supply chains (WTO, 2014b).

During the reporting period, 217 new trade remedies were initiated, with 70 in the Asia-Pacific region. This was greater than the number of terminations meaning that the overall number of barriers to trade increased, although this trend may be turning (box 5.1). Anti-dumping initiations were by far the most common form of action. This continues the rising trend of anti-dumping investigation initiations since 2011, although the total number is still below the peak of 2001.

Asia-Pacific countries were active players in initiating anti-dumping investigations: India (35) was the single biggest initiator, while other significant regional initiators were Australia (20), China (12) and Turkey (10). China was the country most targeted by anti-dumping investigations (28% of all investigations). The Republic of Korea was the next most targeted at 8%. Likewise, China was also the subject of the most initiations of countervailing duty investigations, accounting for 43% of the total new investigations during the reporting period.

In addition to measures reported by WTO, other measures can also distort trade and give domestic producers an advantage at the expense of foreign rivals. For example, state financial support for particular industries ("bail-outs") can disadvantage foreign competitors. Monitoring by Global Trade Alert (GTA) suggests that the use of trade-restrictive measures

TABLE 5.2 New trade liberalizing measures, mid-October 2012 - mid-November 2013

Type of measure	World	Asia-Pacific
Import	101	35
of which, tariffs	*82*	*21*
Export	6	2
Total	107	37

Source: ESCAP calculation, based on data from WTO (2014b).

TABLE 5.3 Trade remedy measures, mid-October 2012 - mid-November 2013

Trade remedies		World	Asia-Pacific
Initiation		217	70
	Anti-dumping		51
	Safeguarding		14
	Countervailing		5
Termination		138	30
	Anti-dumping		25
	Safeguarding		5
	Countervailing		0

Source: ESCAP calculation, based on data from WTO (2014b).

Box 5.1

Has the crisis-driven use of trade remedies by major economies peaked?

Temporary trade barriers (TTBs), also known as trade remedies, include anti-dumping, safeguards and countervailing duties. These tools allow Governments some policy flexibility (also known as policy space) in responding to harm to domestic industries caused by imports; however, they can also be exploited as a tool for protectionism. While differing in their application, these three remedies allow the temporary imposition of tariffs on specific products where criteria for damage to domestic industries have been met. As many economies apply import tariffs that are now relatively low and cannot be substantially raised without violation of multilateral or preferential trade disciplines, temporary trade remedies are an increasingly deployed tool of trade policy.

As expected, the reduction in growth rates and rise in unemployment during the recent global financial crisis triggered an upsurge in pressure for protection of domestic industries. Given the restrictions on the use of conventional tariff policies, many Governments initiated investigations leading to the introduction of TTBs – particularly in emerging economies (Bown, 2011).

In the Asia-Pacific region there was a substantial increase in the number of new investigations by Governments of emerging economies in 2008 and 2009, leading to a cumulative increase to more than 1.8% in the "stock" of import products covered by TTBs from below 1% in the years prior to the crisis (see figure below). Among major Asia-Pacific economies, in 2013 India had the highest share of imports covered by TTBs (5.3%), followed by Indonesia (2.4%) and China (1.9%) (table A).

FIGURE

Use of temporary trade barriers: selected Asia-Pacific high-income and emerging economies

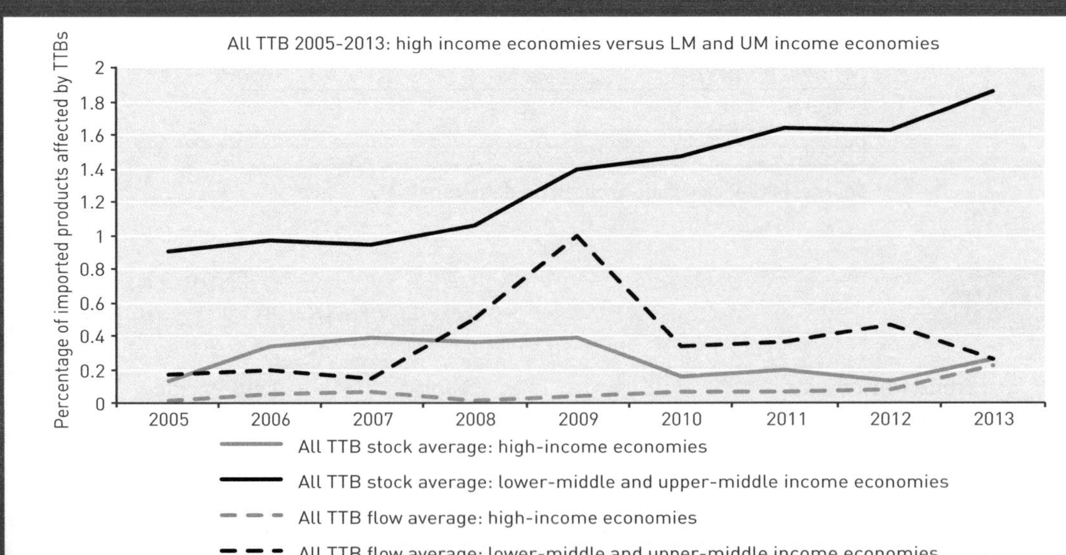

Source: ESCAP calculation based on World Bank Temporary Trade Barriers Database (accessed July 2014).

Note: Share of non-oil imports on a trade-weighted basis. High income economies: Australia, Japan, New Zealand, Republic of Korea and Taiwan Province of China. Emerging economies: China, India, Indonesia, Malaysia, Pakistan, Philippines and Thailand.

Box 5.1 (continued)

TABLE A Share of import products by value subject to temporary trade barriers, by selected Asia-Pacific economy

(Percentage)

Policy-imposing economy	Share of imports subject to TTBs in effect	Share of import products subject to new TTB investigations	Average annual share of import products subject to new TTB investigations
	2013		2005-2012
India	5.3	0.9	1.4
Indonesia	2.4	0.1	0.5
China	1.9	0.2	0.2
Thailand	1.7	0.0	0.1
Pakistan	1.3	0.1	0.4
Australia	0.9	0.5	0.1
Republic of Korea	0.4	0.1	0.1
Malaysia	0.4	0.1	0.1
Taiwan Province of China	0.3	0.4	0.0
New Zealand	0.1	0.0	0.0
Philippines	0.1	0.5	0.0
Japan	0.0	0.0	0.0

Source: ESCAP calculation based on World Bank Temporary Trade Barriers Database (accessed July 2014).

Note: Share of non-oil imports on a trade-weighted basis.

Unlike other trade barriers, anti-dumping and countervailing duties can be imposed on the exports of particular countries rather than being made applicable to all WTO members. Looking at exports to all G20 economies from the Asia-Pacific region, China is the most affected by the use of TTBs in other G20 economies; 6.4% of exports in 2013 were covered by TTBs. The Republic of Korea and the Russian Federation also face a significant impact, with each having 3.5% of exports covered (table B).

TABLE B Asia-Pacific countries with the largest share of exports subject to G20-imposed temporary trade barriers, 2013

(Percentage)

Exporting country	TTB-affected share of exports to G20 countries
China	6.4
Republic of Korea	3.5
Russian Federation	3.5
India	2.7
Indonesia	1.6
Thailand	1.5
Pakistan	1.2
Iran (Islamic Republic of)	1.2

Source: World Bank Temporary Trade Barriers Database (accessed July 2014).

Note: Trade-weighted share of non-oil exports to the G20, excluding exports to and TTBs imposed by the Russian Federation or Saudi Arabia.

Box 5.1 (continued)

However, the tide of TTB usage may be turning. A recent review of the global use of TTBs found that 2013 was marked by a relatively low share of imports being subject to newly initiated TTB investigations by major economies compared with the years since the global financial crisis (Bown, 2014). This suggests that some of the pressure for new protectionism may be diminishing. In the Asia-Pacific region the share of import products subject to new TTB investigations was also below the average annual level between 2005 and 2012 in all the top five users of TTBs (table A).

The next several years will also be a particularly important market-opening opportunity for trade policymakers; many of the TTBs currently in effect are anti-dumping policies and, as such, are subject to a five-year "sunset" review to determine whether to extend or eliminate the policy. The next few years could thus be used to dismantle many of the barriers put in place during the global financial crisis.

increased after the global financial crisis as countries found themselves under pressure to support domestic firms affected by the slump in global demand. In general, increases in restrictions bound by multilateral rules were more modest than more "murky" measures that were not subject to binding disciplines. Overall, since 2008, globally the ratio of new restrictive measures to liberalizing ones has been around 3:1. GTA estimates are that 45% of all protectionist measures implemented worldwide since November 2008 were aimed at China (Evenett, 2013). Examining the usage of less-transparent measures shows that during the same reporting period, the Asia-Pacific region saw the introduction of 236 trade-restrictive measures. After manufacturing, the agricultural sector was the most commonly affected (figure 5.1).

FIGURE 5.1 Sectoral composition of less-transparent measures, mid-October 2012 - mid-November 2013

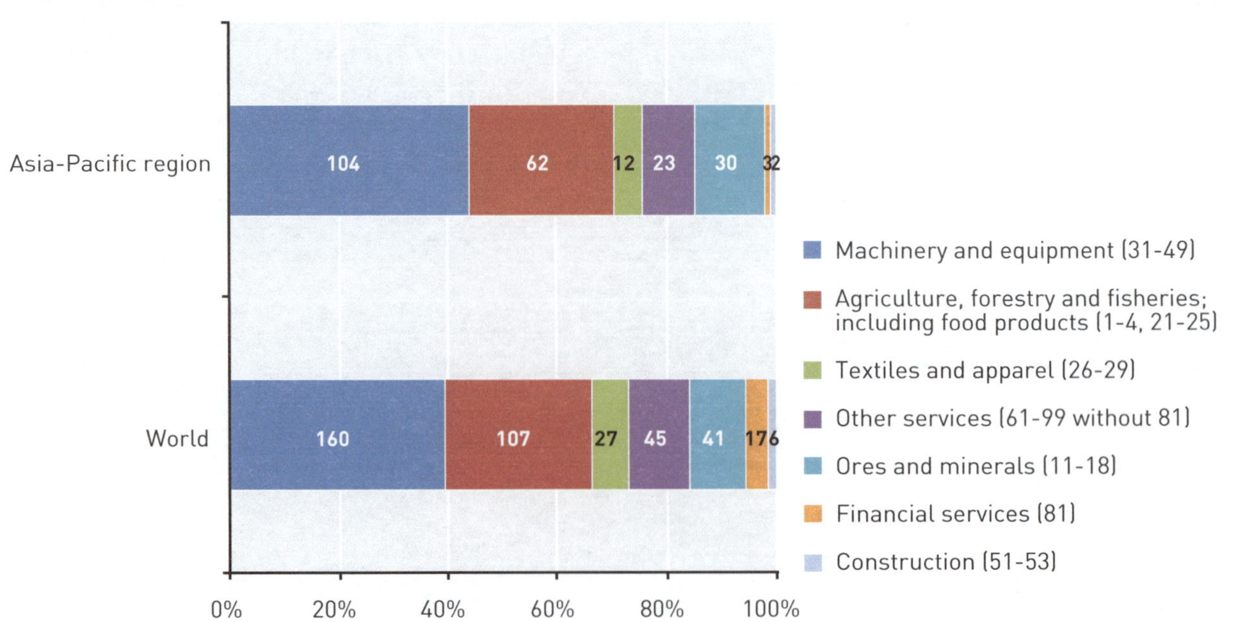

Source: Global Trade Alert database (accessed June 2014).

B. TARIFF AND NON-TARIFF MEASURES

Changes to trade policy shape the environment in which businesses attempt to export and import. While monitoring trends in recent changes gives an important indicator of the direction in which the trade environment is moving, it is important to remember that trade policy changes are cumulative. While the section above reviews the most recent changes, in this section these changes are put in a broader context and the amount of policy flexibility still available to regional economies is considered.

In most regional economies the tariff rates have, on average, fallen significantly in recent decades as a result of: (a) successive rounds of multilateral liberalization; (b) the spread of preferential trade agreements; and (c) unilateral market opening. Trends since the turn of the century (figure 5.2) indicate both that average applied tariffs have fallen since 2000, and that there was no widespread resorting to higher tariffs in response to increased pressures for protectionism following the global financial crisis. Average figures, however, conceal large disparities in tariff protection across sectors – some, such as agriculture, are still frequently subject to high tariff rates.

As applied tariff rates have generally fallen, the gaps between applied rates and bound rates, which are committed to under WTO agreements, has also widened. These gaps, sometimes referred to as "water" in tariff rates means that countries retain significant policy flexibility (or "policy space"); if necessary they can raise rates on particular products to protect domestic industries without violating multilateral agreements.

In general, developing countries have more policy space than developed countries as the bound rates they have committed to are higher (figures 5.3 and 5.4). Degrees of policy space in Asia-Pacific economies range from close to zero in some economies (such as Hong Kong, China and Macao, China) to more than 100% in the case of agriculture in Bangladesh. Agricultural products generally retain higher degrees of policy space than non-agricultural products.

FIGURE 5.2 Trends in applied tariff rates in selected Asia-Pacific economies, 2000-2012

(Percentage)

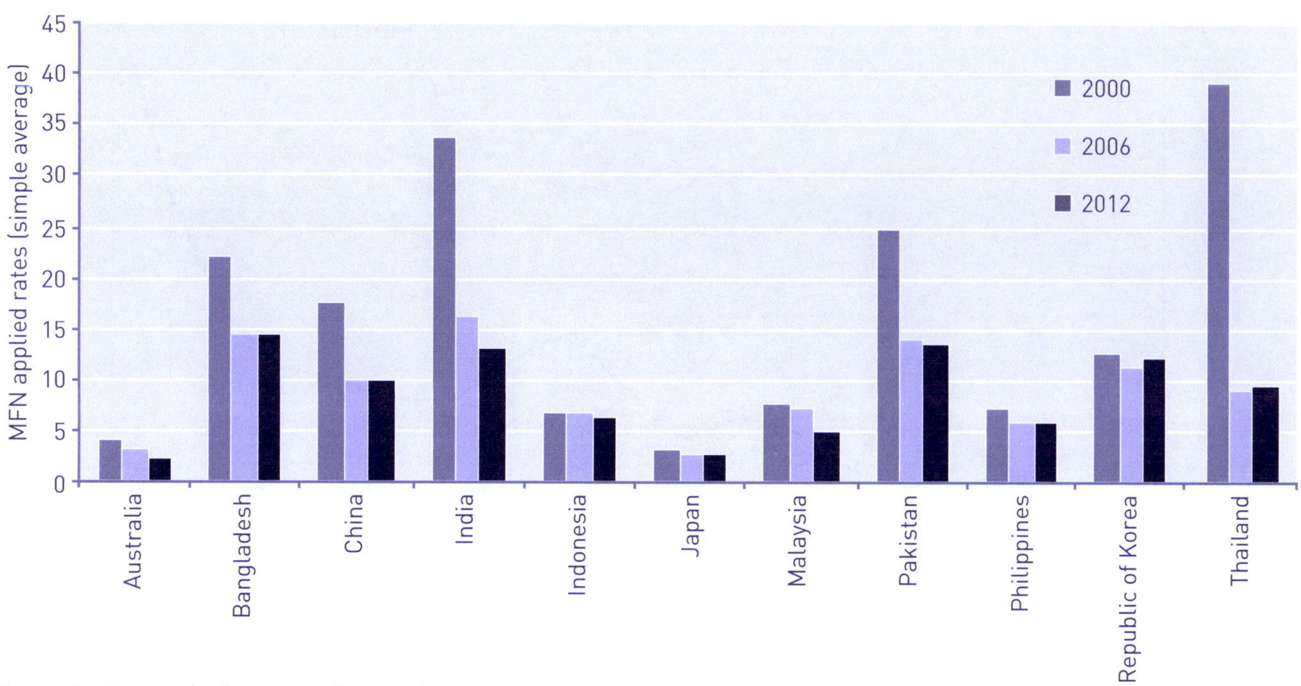

Source: WTO Integrated Data Base (accessed via WITS July 2014).

FIGURE 5.3 Policy flexibility in selected Asia-Pacific economies: non-agriculture

(Percentage)

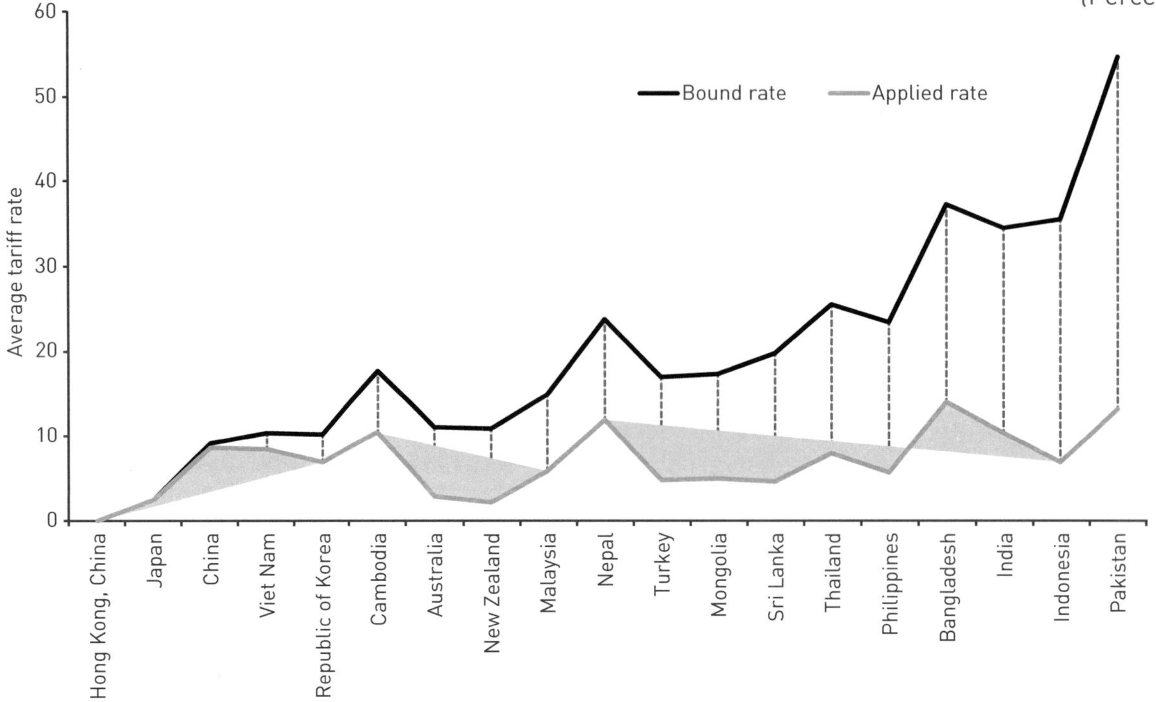

Source: WTO World Tariff Profiles, 2013.

FIGURE 5.4 Policy flexibility in selected Asia-Pacific economies: agriculture

(Percentage)

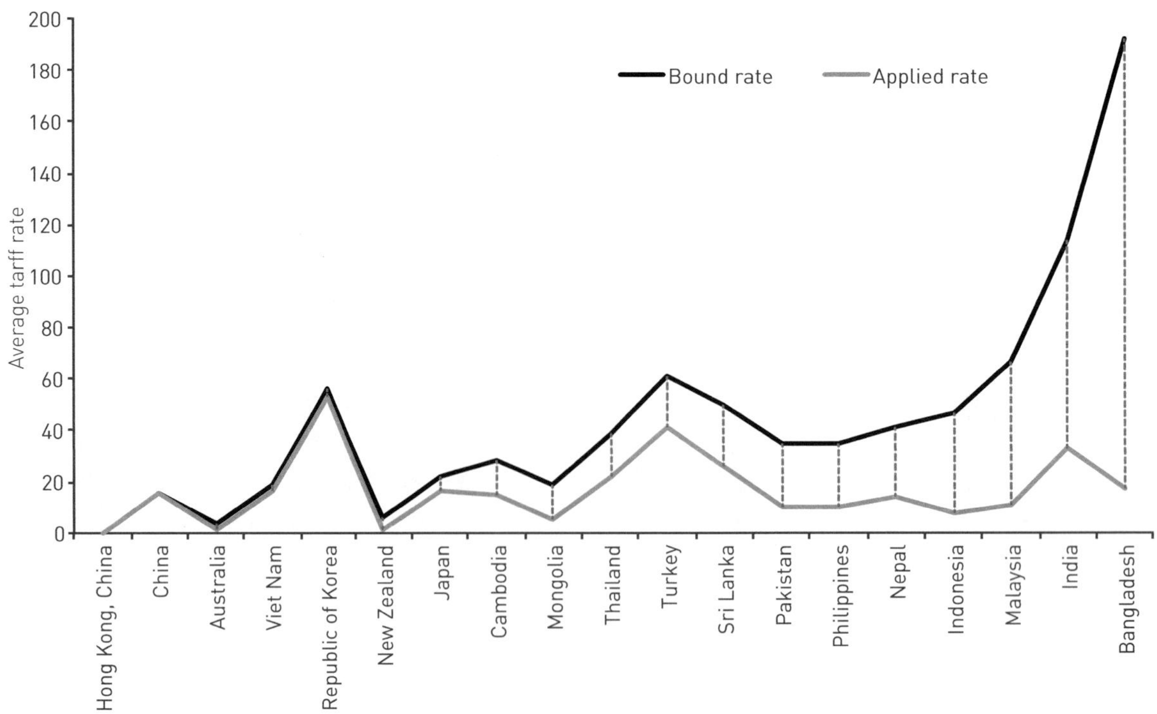

Source: WTO World Tariff Profiles, 2013.

Box 5.2 Measuring "water" in services commitments

Recent research has revealed that services play a more important role in trade than had previously been appreciated. In addition to direct cross-border trade in services, much of the value of the goods traded across borders also embodies the value of services inputs. For example, in the case of countries wishing to integrate into international production networks, increased attention to the availability of efficient and competitive services that support value chain activities is important (OECD, 2013). However, compared to merchandise trade, the data available to measure and analyse trade in services are patchy (see chapter 2).

In addition to measuring trade in services itself, it is also difficult to measure the scale of barriers to services trade; comparing alternative regulations in two different countries is much harder than simply comparing tariff levels. This makes comparisons across countries as to their level of restrictiveness difficult, although some comparative studies have been undertaken and comparative measures are available from the World Bank and OECD.

Similarly, in services trade, it is more difficult to measure the extent to which countries have policy space or "water" in between their commitments to WTO members through the General Agreement on Trade in Services (GATS) and their "applied" levels of restrictiveness - that is, the extent to which the regulations that govern services trade in practice are liberalized. While countries may be reluctant to make commitments to liberalize services trade in GATS, many Governments maintain levels of openness that go beyond these commitments.

Using approximations of the level of "water" based on a comparison of the World Bank's Services Trade Restrictiveness Index and the GATS commitments in the World Trade Indicators, it is clear that as with tariffs on goods, significant policy flexibility remains in services trade, particularly for developing countries (figure below).

Box 5.2 (continued)

FIGURE "Water" in services commitments

(Percentage)

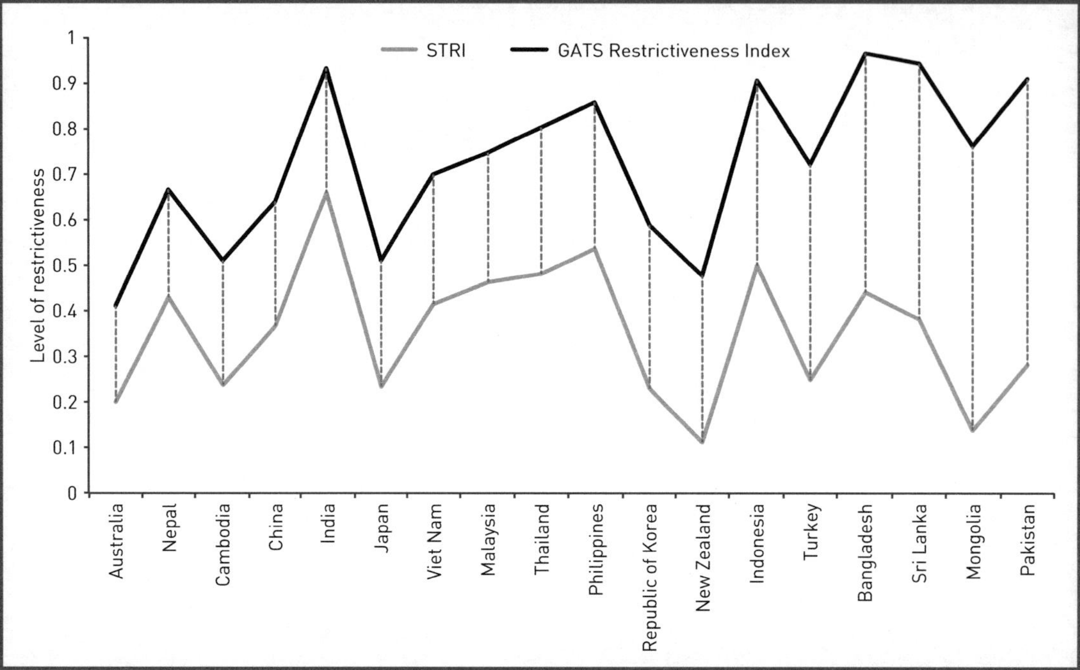

Source: ESCAP calculation based on the World Bank Services Trade Restrictions Database and World Bank World Trade Indicators.

Note: Services Trade Restrictiveness Index (STRI) scores are based on the World Bank assessment of openness across five sectors: finance, transport, telecoms, professional services and retailing. The degree of restrictiveness of GATS commitments is based on World Bank Trade Indicators indices that cross the 12 standard service sectors in GATS. Scores have been adjusted to put them in the same range (0-1) as STRI scores.

Non-tariff barriers to trade are now more important for many products than remaining tariff barriers.

Nonetheless, as tariff rates have generally fallen, non-tariff measures (NTMs) to trade have become relatively more important. NTMs cover a large number of diverse policies, regulations and practices that vary for each product, thereby creating difficulties in assessing their restrictive impact and making comparisons across countries. Some efforts to calculate the tariff equivalent costs of NTMs have been made and found that they are significant (figure 5.5). In many cases, the tariff-equivalent of non-tariff measures can exceed the tariff rate.

Sanitary and phytosanitary (SPS) measures are among the most common NTMs. These are often deployed by Governments to protect human or animal health from diseases or pests that might arrive via traded goods. As such they are usually applied to agricultural and food products. While often motivated by legitimate public interest concerns SPS measures can degenerate into a barrier to trade. Additionally, meeting SPS requirements can be a particular burden for developing or least developing countries which often lack the laboratory facilitates or certification processes to ensure compliance.

From October 2012 to September 2013, a total of 1,260 new SPS notifications were submitted

FIGURE 5.5 Estimates of the tariff equivalents (ad-valorem equivalent) of non-tariff measures in selected economies, 2009

(Percentage)

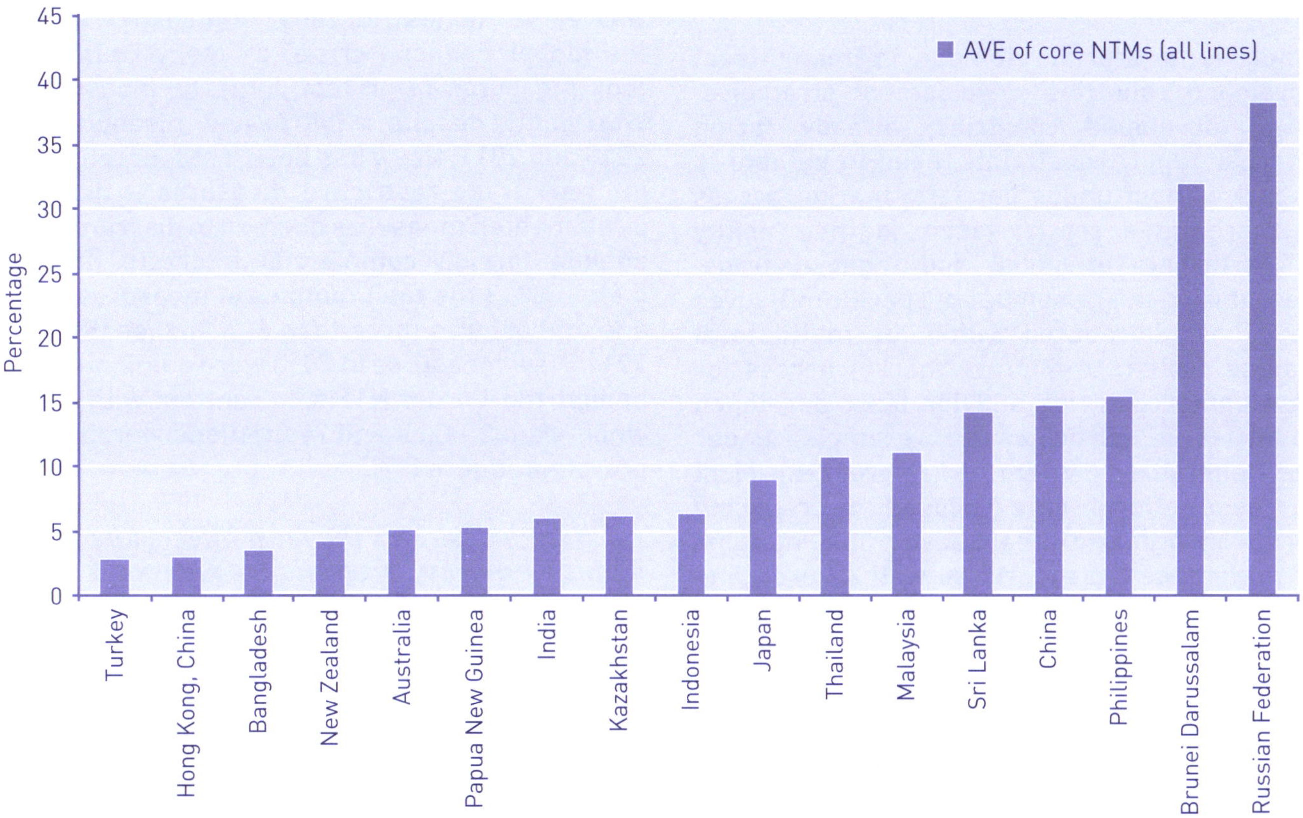

Source: World Bank, Trade Restrictiveness Index.

Note: AVE – ad valorem equivalent.

to WTO (which is probably an underestimation of the total introduced during the reporting period). Of these, the proportion submitted by developing country members rose to 63%. Developing country members accounted for 90% of all emergency SPS measures. The frequent usage of emergency SPS measures by developing countries reflects the underdeveloped nature of their regular monitoring and regulatory systems with regard to adequate management of SPS-related risks. As a result, urgent challenges must often be met with new regulations since existing practices are insufficient.

Technical barriers to trade (TBT) are generally regulations and standards governing the sale of products that have as their prima facie the objective of dealing with market inefficiencies resulting from externalities linked with the production, distribution, and consumption of these products. They can include, for example, labelling standards for foods or automobile exhaust emissions standards. During the reporting period, WTO members submitted 1,704 regular TBT notifications (again probably an underestimation of the total number). The majority of these measures had as their stated objective the "protection of human health and safety" with "protection of the environment" as the second most common objective.

WTO members can raise concerns over TBT that they believe go beyond what is reasonable and act as an unnecessary barrier to trade. In the recent reporting period, among the Asia-Pacific countries Indonesia was the most frequently challenged at WTO with five concerns raised, followed by China (3) and the Russian Federation (3). The challenged TBT of Indonesia mainly targeted food products while China's TBT that were under challenge were imposed mainly on medical instruments and medical devices.

C. LEAST DEVELOPED COUNTRIES: ACCIDENTAL VICTIMS OF MURKY PROTECTIONISM

Trade is a crucial element in many least developed countries' development strategies. Least developed countries, already facing internal supply constraints, need to be able to export without undue barriers; market access is therefore a crucial factor in their ability to participate in global and regional trade. Recognizing this, a number of specific initiatives have been introduced within the multilateral trading system to improve market access for developing countries and for least developed countries in particular (for example, under the Generalized System of Preferences). Most of these efforts have focused on reducing tariffs in order to create favourable margins of preference for exports as well as providing "Special and Differential Treatment" in relation to other commitments. The "Least developed countries' package" agreed at the ninth WTO Ministerial Conference in 2013 in Bali, Indonesia also agreed on measures of importance for this group of countries which should improve duty-free quota-free access for their export products as well as contribute to the simplification of rules of origin.

Tariffs, including those faced by the Asia-Pacific region's least developed countries, have declined during recent years (WTO, 2013). While this is to be broadly welcomed, it should be recognized that preferential market access alone is not sufficient. Even where tariff preferences are available, other non-tariff barriers may be substantial deterrents to the participation of least developed countries in global trade. Complex rules of origin are one of the major obstacles faced by least developed countries attempting to utilize existing preferences and in this context the recent decision at the ninth WTO Ministerial Conference will be helpful. However, other forms of "murky" or "less transparent" measures can worsen market access for exporters, including least developed countries, thereby reversing or lessening the positive impacts of tariff preferences.

The total number of new less-transparent measures having an impact on at least one of the Asia-Pacific least developed countries was at its highest in 2009, immediately after the global financial crisis, as many countries took measures to protect domestic industries. Worryingly, despite a fall in new measures in 2010 and 2011, there has been a recent rebound in "red" trade-restrictive measures – that is, implemented measures deemed to discriminate against foreign commercial interests (figure 5.6). In 2013 the total number of measures (red and amber) was more than 60% higher than in 2011. New measures in 2013 were dominated by behind-the-border NTMs, in contrast with 2011 when export taxes and restrictions were more prevalent (figure 5.7).

> *Bangladesh was the most affected by new "murky" protectionist measures among the Asia-Pacific least developed countries.*

Among the Asia-Pacific least developed countries, Bangladesh remains the most affected by new "murky" protectionist measures followed by Afghanistan and Cambodia. Bangladesh's exports were potentially affected by 24 new "murky" measures in 2013, bringing the total number of measures introduced since 2009 to 134 (table 5.4). Of the countries implementing measures that have an impact on Asia-Pacific least developed countries, India introduced the most measures (26) in 2013, followed by Indonesia (11) and Argentina (11).

The sectoral distribution of measures that have an impact on Asia-Pacific least developed countries has remained broadly constant for every year since 2009. In general, agriculture, forestry and fishery products, food products, beverages and tobacco, textiles, apparel and leather products are the sectors most frequently targeted sectors for less-transparent protectionist measures.

FIGURE 5.6

New "murky" measures affecting at least one Asia-Pacific least developed country, by year, 2009-2013

(Percentage)

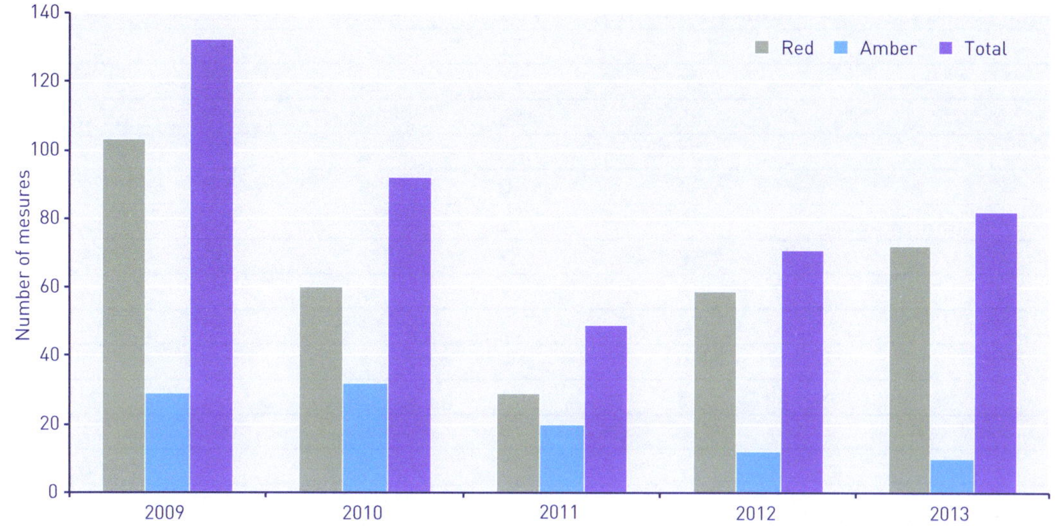

Source: ESCAP calculation based on the Global Trade Alert Database (accessed June 2014).

Note: A measure is classified as "red" when it has been implemented and almost certainly discriminates against foreign commercial interests. It is classified as "amber" when it has been: (a) implemented and may involve discrimination against foreign commercial interests, (b) announced, or (c)is under consideration and would (if implemented) almost certainly involve discrimination against foreign commercial interests.

FIGURE 5.7

Types of measures affecting Asia-Pacific least developed countries

(Percentage as shares in total number)

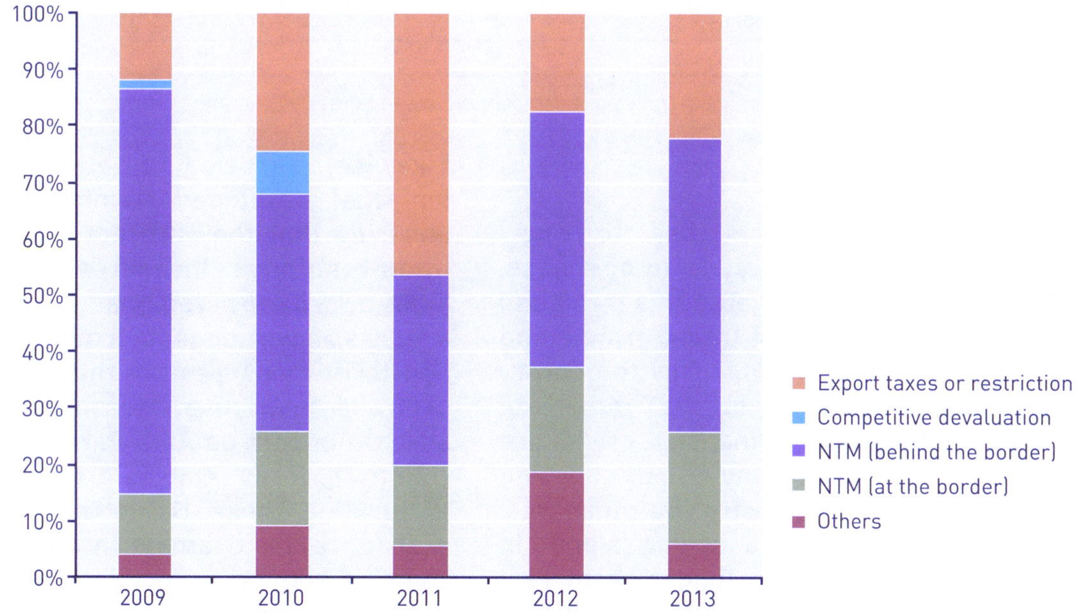

Source: ESCAP calculation based on the Global Trade Alert Database (accessed June 2014).

Notes: NTM (at the border) includes quotas, import ban, TBT, non-tariff barriers. NTM (behind the border) includes consumption subsidies, local content requirements, public procurement, bailout/state aid measures, export subsidies, trade finance support, SPS measures, and support to state-owned trading enterprises and state-controlled companies. Others include investment, migration, intellectual property protection and other service sector measures.

CHAPTER 5

TABLE 5.4 Number of red and amber "murky" measures affecting Asia-Pacific least developed countries, 2009-2013

Least developed country	Total (2009-2013)	2009	2010	2011	2012	2013
Bangladesh	134	31	33	21	25	24
Afghanistan	60	21	13	2	9	15
Myanmar	53	16	13	7	6	11
Cambodia	51	21	11	3	7	9
Nepal	34	10	5	6	7	6
Lao People's Democratic Republic	29	12	7	2	2	6
Samoa	16	7	3	0	3	3
Bhutan	14	4	2	2	3	3
Solomon Islands	9	3	1	0	4	1
Vanuatu	9	3	3	1	1	1
Timor-Leste	8	1	1	0	3	3
Tuvalu	4	2	0	1	1	0
Kiribati	2	1	0	1	0	0

Source: Global Trade Alert database (accessed June 2014).

TABLE 5.5 Less transparent measures targeting Asia-Pacific least developed countries, by country of introduction

Name of country	Number of less transparent measures		
	Red	Amber	Total
India	22	4	26
Indonesia	11	0	11
Argentina	11	0	11
Pakistan	4	1	5
Viet Nam	4	1	5
Japan	5	0	5

Source: Global Trade Alert database (accessed June 2014).

CONCLUSION

Regional trade policy continues to show worrying signs of a drift away from openness. New energy is needed to reverse this trend and seize opportunities to boost trade, growth and prosperity. In the near-term, many temporary trade barriers introduced in the immediate aftermath of the global financial crisis are approaching their "sunset clauses". By choosing not to renew these trade restrictive measures, Governments could send a strong signal in favour of openness. In the longer term real progress is needed both through the negotiation of effective regional trade agreements as well as a commitment to implementing the WTO "Bali Package" as a first step towards further multilateral liberalization.

Likewise, securing greater market access for least developed countries' products and ensuring that they are not affected unduly by trade-restrictive measures should be given high priority by regional policymakers. The analysis above suggests that behind-the-border non-tariff measures are the principal category of trade-restrictive measures that have an adverse impact on Asia-Pacific least developed countries. In addition to greater commitments to tackling these NTMs, scaled-up technical assistance, for example through Aid for Trade, can also help least developed countries realize their trade and development potential.

REFERENCES

Bown, Chad P., ed. (2011). *The Great Recession and Import Protection: the Role of Temporary Trade Barriers*. Washington, D.C.: World Bank, Centre for Economic Policy Research.

_____ (2014). Temporary trade barriers database: update through 2013. Washington, D.C.: World Bank.

Economic and Social Commission for Asia and the Pacific (2014). *Economic and Social Survey of Asia and the Pacific 2014: Regional Connectivity for Shared Prosperity*. Sales No. E.14.II.F.4. Available from www.unescap.org/resources/economic-and-social-survey-asia-and-pacific-2014 .

Evenett, Simon J. (2013). What restraint? Five years of G20 pledges on trade: the 14th GTA report. London: Centre for Economic Policy Research. Available from www.globaltradealert.org/sites/default/files/GTA14_0.pdf .

Organisation for Economic Co-operation and Development (2013). Implications of global value chains for trade, investment, development and jobs. OECD, WTO and UNCTAD paper prepared for the G-20 Leaders Summit, Saint Petersburg (Russian Federation), September 2013. Available from www.oecd.org/trade/G20-Global-Value-Chains-2013.pdf .

World Trade Organization (2013). *World Trade Report 2013: Factors Shaping the Future of World Trade*. Geneva. Available from www.wto.org/english/res_e/booksp_e/world_trade_report13_e.pdf .

_____ (2014a). Report on G-20 trade measures (mid-November 2013 to mid-May 2014). Available from www.wto.org/english/news_e/news14_e/g20_wto_report_jun14_e.pdf .

_____ (2014b). Overview of developments in the international trading environment: Annual Report by the Director-General. Trade Policy Review Body (WT/TPR/OV/16). Available from www.wto.org/english/news_e/spra_e/spra8_e.htm .

ONLINE DATABASES

Global Trade Alert. Available from www.globaltradealert.org/advanced-search .

World Bank. Temporary Trade Barriers Database. Available from http://go.worldbank.org/J3R2BHEE70 . Accessed July 2014.

_____ Trade Restrictiveness Index. Available from http://go.worldbank.org/FG1KHXSP30 .

_____ World Trade Indicators 2009/10. Available from http://info.worldbank.org/etools/wti/2a1.asp.

_____ Services Trade Restrictions Database. Available from http://iresearch.worldbank.org/ServiceTrade/home.htm .

World Trade Organization. Tariff Profiles Database. Available from http://stat.wto.org/TariffProfile/WSDBTariffPFHome.aspx?Language=E .

_____ Integrated Data Base. Available via WITS from http://wits.worldbank.org/ .

6 PREFERENTIAL TRADE POLICIES AND AGREEMENTS

After a temporary slow-down in 2012, the proliferation of preferential trade agreements (PTAs), which for Asia-Pacific economies began in earnest in the early 1990s, is continuing.[1] There is no single reason for this preoccupation with PTAs; rather, it is a combined role of: (a) lack of progress in securing lower trade barriers and/or opening new areas of liberalization through multilateral trade negotiation;[2] (b) contracting import demand in most of the developed country markets that, on average, have low tariff barriers and need to open new markets that might be more protected; and (c) recognition of the benefits of South-South PTAs.

The content and membership composition of PTAs have also been changing. For example, recent PTAs have increasingly included areas that are outside multilateral obligations, such as competition, government procurement and investment, one explanation for which is that countries have a preference to opening these areas through such agreements. Also, the geographical proximity of PTA members is no longer a factor in seeking membership, as many agreements are interregional or even inter-continental in nature. This is also due to the fact that many countries have already concluded PTAs with many of their neighbours and thus now have to look for partners further afield.

Are Asia-Pacific economies running out of prospective partners for negotiating new PTAs?

Globally, there are 253 "physical" trade agreements in force,[3] of which 150 involve Asia-Pacific economies.[4] During 2013 and the first half of 2014, the Asia-Pacific region almost reached a plateau on PTAs. This was due to the fact that most of the economies have already engaged in PTAs with partner economies in which they have current and potential trade interests.

The ESCAP secretariat has continuously monitored the PTA landscape in Asia and the Pacific. It regularly assesses the trends in the creation of new PTAs as well as changes in the patterns and nature of PTAs involving Asian and Pacific economies. Following previous analyses,[5] this investigation into the features of preferential trade policies and their impacts has been extended to cover the most recent period. This chapter revisits some stylized facts and features of PTAs that are common across the region's economies. Agreements have been classified with regard to the number of partners, the nature of agreements[6] and their status.[7] Other agreement features of interest to analysts and decision-makers are linked to their liberalization content and the range of areas covered, which together define the type of agreement. By looking at all these characteristics, this chapter explores how effective preferential trade policies have been in connecting countries in the region, not only in terms of establishing PTA networks but also in considering the coverage of overall exports and imports with PTA partners. Efforts have been made to establish which subregions are the main drivers of the Asia-Pacific PTAs. In that context, due attention is given to the Asia-Pacific Trade Agreement (APTA), which is at present the only functioning agreement connecting the three subregions of East and North-East, South-East, and South Asia through its seven members; however, it has a potential to become an Asia-Pacific-wide bloc if it is opened to the developed countries of the region as well as converted from the partial coverage to a high standard free trade agreement.[9] In addition, negotiations for establishing two mega-blocs – the Trans-Pacific Partnership Agreement and the Regional Comprehensive Economic Partnership – are already ongoing, so this chapter also provides an update on those processes.

A. TRENDS IN PREFERENTIAL TRADE AGREEMENTS: STYLIZED FACTS

1. Continuing reliance among developing economies on preferential trade policies

As stated above, because of the slow progress of the Doha Round and the search for new trade opportunities (markets and products), many economies have continued to pursue preferential trade policies in the post-2008 crisis years. As of July 2014, there were 227[10] agreements associated with Asian and Pacific economies, of which 150 were in force and the remainder at various stages of negotiation or consideration. Figure 6.1 gives the cumulative number of the PTAs associated with Asian and Pacific economies. It is evident that the drivers of Asia-Pacific PTAs are the developing economies, with more and more agreements being signed with each other, thus establishing a foundation for a stronger bias towards South-South trade. However, it appears that the growth in the number of preferential deals is tapering off and that a plateau is being reached for PTAs in the Asia-Pacific region. This could also be due to the fact that many economies already have agreements with their important trading partners, not only in the region but also outside. Of the 150 PTAs in force, 78 are between the economies in Asia and the Pacific, therefore reflecting a still strong reliance on partners outside the region. Nevertheless, in addition to emphasis that nowadays is placed on mega-bloc negotiations, it appears that finding appropriate bilateral trading partners is becoming more difficult, as during 2009-2013 the regional economies put into force an average of 7.8 trade agreements per year compared with an average of 8.6 during 2004-2008. In the first eight months of 2014 only three agreements came into force and another two signed.

FIGURE 6.1 Cumulative number of preferential trade agreements (notified and non-notified to WTO) enacted by Asia-Pacific economies, 1971-2014 (July)

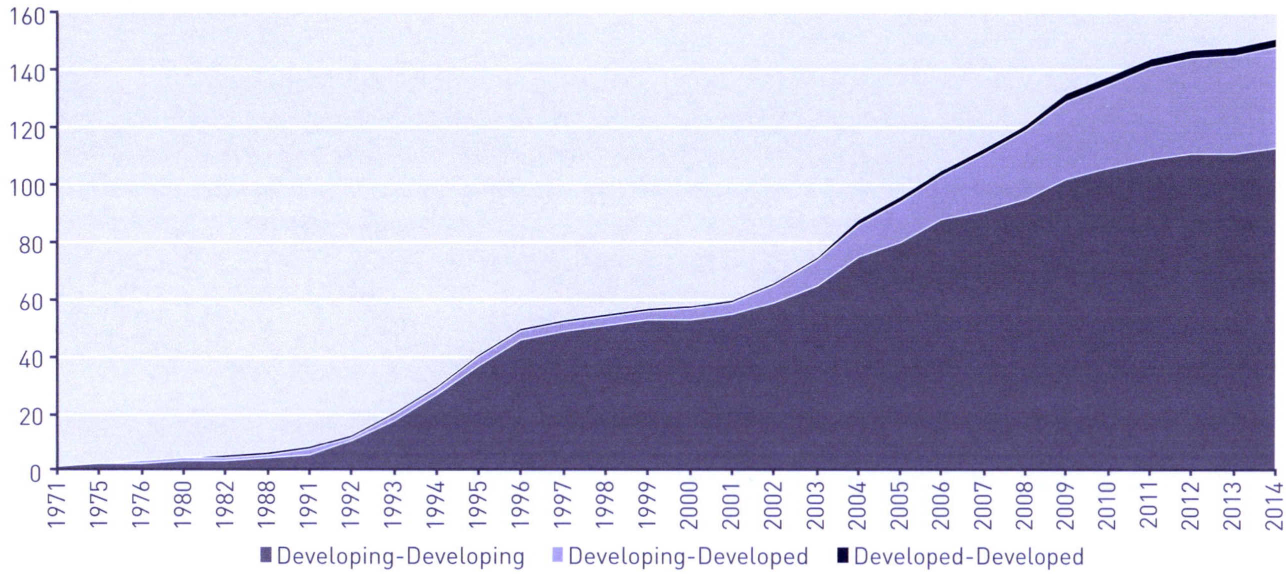

Source: ESCAP calculation, based on data from the Asia-Pacific Trade and Investment Agreements Database (APTIAD).[11]

At present, there are more than 220 agreements associated with Asian and Pacific economies, of which 150 are in force.

The Asia-Pacific economies are divided into subregions, which often serve as target areas for establishing regional blocs. In fact, only the East and North-East Asian subregion does not yet have its "own" regional integration initiative.[12] The three Asian and Pacific developed countries (Australia, Japan and New Zealand) are engaged in both regional and interregional initiatives. Which countries, then, are driving the PTA proliferation? The economies in the North and Central Asian subregion were the major contributors to Asia-Pacific PTAs in the 1990s, when they were trying to replace the single production and trade area under the former Soviet Union with a plethora of bilateral free trade agreements. South-East Asia (minus Timor-Leste), through the Association of Southeast Asian Nations (ASEAN), played a more dynamic role during 2000-2009 (when most of the intiatives were driven by either ASEAN or its individual members and their dialogue partners). The South and South-West Asian subregion also contributed to the rise in PTAs during 2000-2009 (driven mainly by India, Pakistan and Turkey) (figure 6.2).

East and North-East Asia is the only subregion that does not have its "own" single regional integration initiative.

It is also worth mentioning that the surge in PTAs at the global level was initially driven by regions other than Asia-Pacific. This situation existed until 1971, after which the Asia-Pacific economies began engaging in PTAs, thus contributing to an ever larger share of the total number of PTAs in world. The Asia-Pacific share reached more than half of the global PTAs in 1995. The trend more or less continues today.

2. Number of partners, contiguity and regional proximity

Bilateral deals are clearly preferred, often with partners from the same subregion. The four bilateral PTAs involving least developed countries include three between India and Afghanistan, Bhutan and Nepal, and one between Thailand and the Lao People's Democratic Republic. However, other least developed countries are involved in regional blocs.[13] The desire for preferential market access is so strong that even countries that are already members of an established trading bloc still pursue bilateral deals with partners within as well as outside the bloc. This is, perhaps,

FIGURE 6.2 Cumulative number of preferential trade agreements (notified and non-notified to WTO), by Asia-Pacific subregion, 1971-2014 (July)

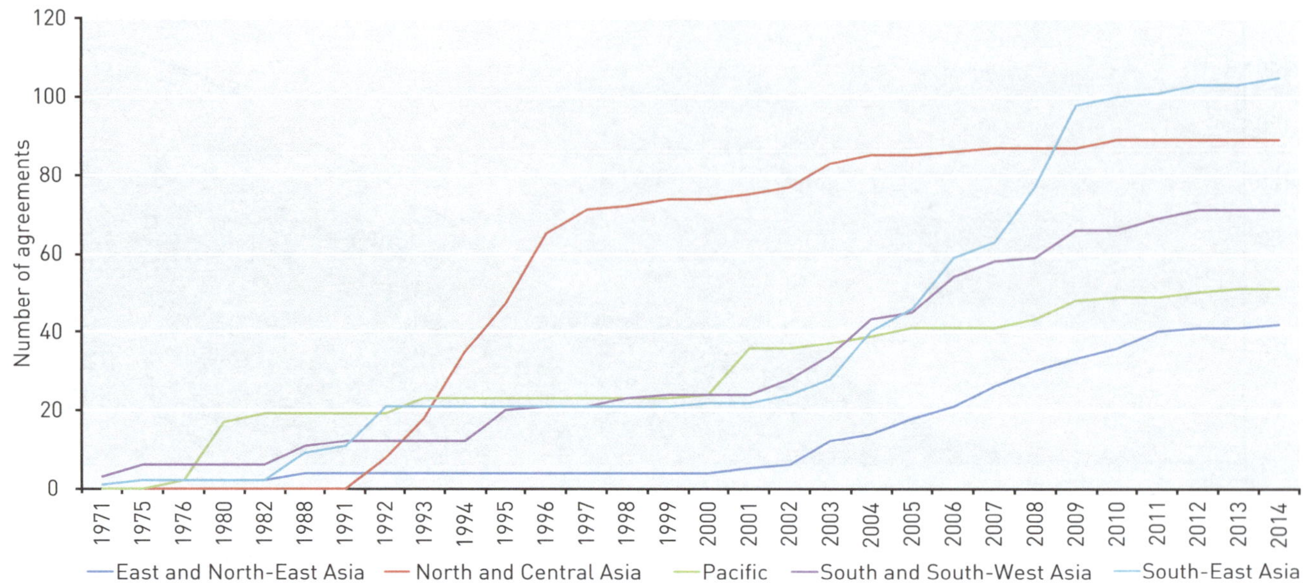

Source: ESCAP calculation, based on data from APTIAD.

most evident for, but not exclusive to, members of ASEAN. While committed to establishing the ASEAN Economic Community (AEC) by December 2015, ASEAN members continue to seek additional bilateral agreements. Another region that demonstrates similar behaviour is the Commonwealth of Independent States (CIS), where bloc agreements are intertwined with numerous bilateral agreements.

The existence of a regional bloc does not prevent its members from searching for further bilateral deals.

This proliferation of bilateral (and other) PTAs contributes to multiple overlapping agreements – the so-called "noodle bowl". This has had an adverse impact on the efficiency of trade among partners in the agreements. In the Asia-Pacific "bowl" there are currently 120 bilateral agreements in force,[14] of which 53 are PTAs signed with partners outside Asia and the Pacific (figure 6.3). More specifically, there are 11 enacted agreements with countries in Africa and the Middle East, and 15 in Latin America. Turkey has the largest number of bilateral trade agreements with "non-regional" partners (although all of them are geographically located relatively close to Turkey); however, it is expected that with the accession of Turkey to the European Union these agreements will be nullified. Central Asian economies are a distant second.

In the Asia-Pacific "noodle-bowl" there are currently 120 bilateral deals, 53 of which are with partners outside the region.

Other Asian countries, when signing agreements with partners outside the region, target mostly: (a) Latin America (Chile and Peru); (b) the United States; (c) Canada and Mexico, the other two North American Free Trade Area (NAFTA) members; and (d) two European blocs – the European Free Trade Association (EFTA) and the European Union. After accounting for all these intercontinental and intraregional bilateral partnerships, the number of bilateral agreements comprising contiguous countries is small – only 21 bilateral PTAs involve countries that share borders, with North and Central Asian countries accounting for the largest number. The small number of deals between contiguous countries is, of course, largely a consequence of the number of Asia-Pacific countries that are islands without land borders. It can also be

FIGURE 6.3 Breakdown of trade agreements, by type and number of partners

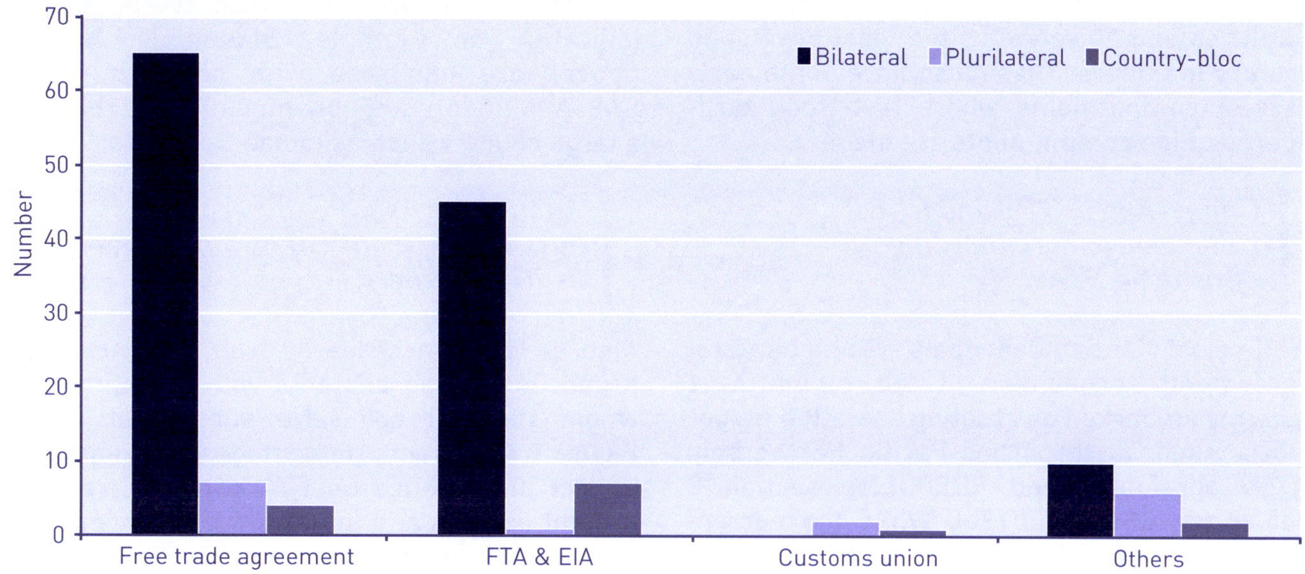

Source: ESCAP calculation, based on data from APTIAD.

Note: FTA – free trade agreement; EIA – economic integration agreement.

attributed to a spirit of "open regionalism" and a willingness to negotiate with partners outside the region.

> *Only 2% of all PTAs are customs unions.*

There are 16 plurilateral trade agreements with an average of 8.1 countries per agreement. As stated above, most plurilateral deals are subregional initiatives that have achieved varying degrees of progress in converting preferential trade into an integrated market. They range from ASEAN – which is preparing to transform itself from a free trade area into the AEC and simultaneously initiated negotiations for the 16-member Regional Comprehensive Economic Partnership (RCEP) – to the Bay of Bengal Initiative for Multi-Sectoral Technical and Economic Cooperation (BIMSTEC), whose members have not been able to finalize negotiations to enable trade under preferential terms to begin.

More than half of all trade agreements put into force by Asia-Pacific economies refer to free trade agreements or areas for trade in (merchandise) goods, while close to a further 35% of agreements allow free trade of both goods and services (figure 6.3). Therefore, more than 86% of PTAs are presented as free trade deals on goods or goods and services. In contrast, only 12% (18 agreements) are declared as having partial scope (i.e. "Others" in figure 6.3), and only 2% of all PTAs are customs unions. Of these three customs unions, two involve North and Central Asian countries. The lack of weight of the "custom unions" category is, on the whole, consistent with the behaviour observed in other parts of the world as well as the acceptance by countries of the obstacles to successfully finishing this type of negotiation.

Countries are becoming increasingly creative in their efforts to label their deals differently, and not as "free trade agreements."[15] As a result, many agreements are identified as economic and/or comprehensive partnership agreements. This is to indicate the intention of engaging in wider integration. Of these, "comprehensive economic partnership" appears to be the most popular designation. The new names signal intent to (a) open markets beyond goods and services trade, and (b) make commitments in other areas of cooperation. However, the actual immediate speed of liberalization remains slow and the coverage is shallow, except trade in goods. The average tariff liberalization timetable is five to seven years among developing countries and 10 years for the least developed country members. These also have some early harvest commitments where fast-track tariff liberalization commitments are made.

> *Completion of TPP and RCEP could lead to the cancelling of up to 54 PTAs.*

While most of the current deals are still bilateral agreements, economies in the region have recently embarked on creating so-called mega-blocs, such as the Trans-Pacific Partnership (TPP) agreement and RCEP (see section C below and ESCAP, 2012b). While the current economic potential of TPP is larger (see table 6.1 in the following section), the members of these prospective mega-blocs currently engage in a similar number of trade agreements among themselves. The 12 negotiating members of TPP share a total of 26 existing (24 bilateral and 2 plurilateral) agreements among themselves, while the 16 RCEP negotiating members are engaged in 28 agreements in total (22 bilateral and 6 plurilateral).[16] Therefore both of these mega-blocs offer a great opportunity for consolidation of existing agreements among the economies that are participating in the negotiations. Of course, it is not a forgone conclusion that if and when these mega-blocs are finalized the other agreements will wither away. However, if this does not happen, the perennial "noodle bowl" problem will continue.

B. INTRA-PREFERENTIAL TRADE AGREEMENT PARTNERS' TRADE

It is difficult to produce exact evaluations of the contributions by PTAs to trade expansion. Often trade between parties to an agreement is simply tracked before and after a deal is done. Using current European Union intra-bloc trade as a benchmark,[17] ASEAN shows very slow growth in intra-PTA trade as a share of total trade, despite its rapid increase in overall trade volume (ESCAP, 2013).

For individual countries, especially small ones, trade with partners could be much more important than aggregate bloc averages may indicate. For example, Bhutan or Nepal's dependence on trade with partners within SAFTA is understandably much higher than for a large country such as India.

> *An average Asia-Pacific economy buys less than 40% of its imports from its PTA partners.*

Also, it is not necessarily true that countries primarily sign agreements with partners with whom they already have substantial trade. Figure 6.4 presents percentages of export and import dependence on PTA partners, relative to total exports and imports. The numbers are average shares from 2010 to 2012 for those Asia-Pacific economies for which trade data are available, including all enacted agreements for those countries. There is great variability in PTAs coverage of exports and imports among the developing economies of the region. On the export side, Brunei Darussalam directs almost 100% of its exports to its PTA partners. On the other hand, some of the Pacific island countries export less than 10% of their total exports to PTA partners (including Australia and New Zealand).[18] While averages can hide important specifics (i.e. the liberalizing quality of the PTAs), it is worth noting that the North and Central Asian countries export only 16% of their total exports to their PTA partners. At the other end of spectrum are some of the South-East Asian countries with much higher dependence on trade with PTA partners.

Developed economies are also dissimilar, with Australia and Japan obviously still relying on much of their trade with non-partners, while New Zealand's PTAs cover half of its trade. Four of the least developed countries in the region (Bhutan, the Lao People's Democratic Republic, Myanmar and Nepal) have very high shares of exports going to PTA partners, which could be mainly due to their dependence on trade with large neighbouring countries.

FIGURE 6.4 Trade share with preferential trade agreement partners, 2010-2012

(Average percentage)

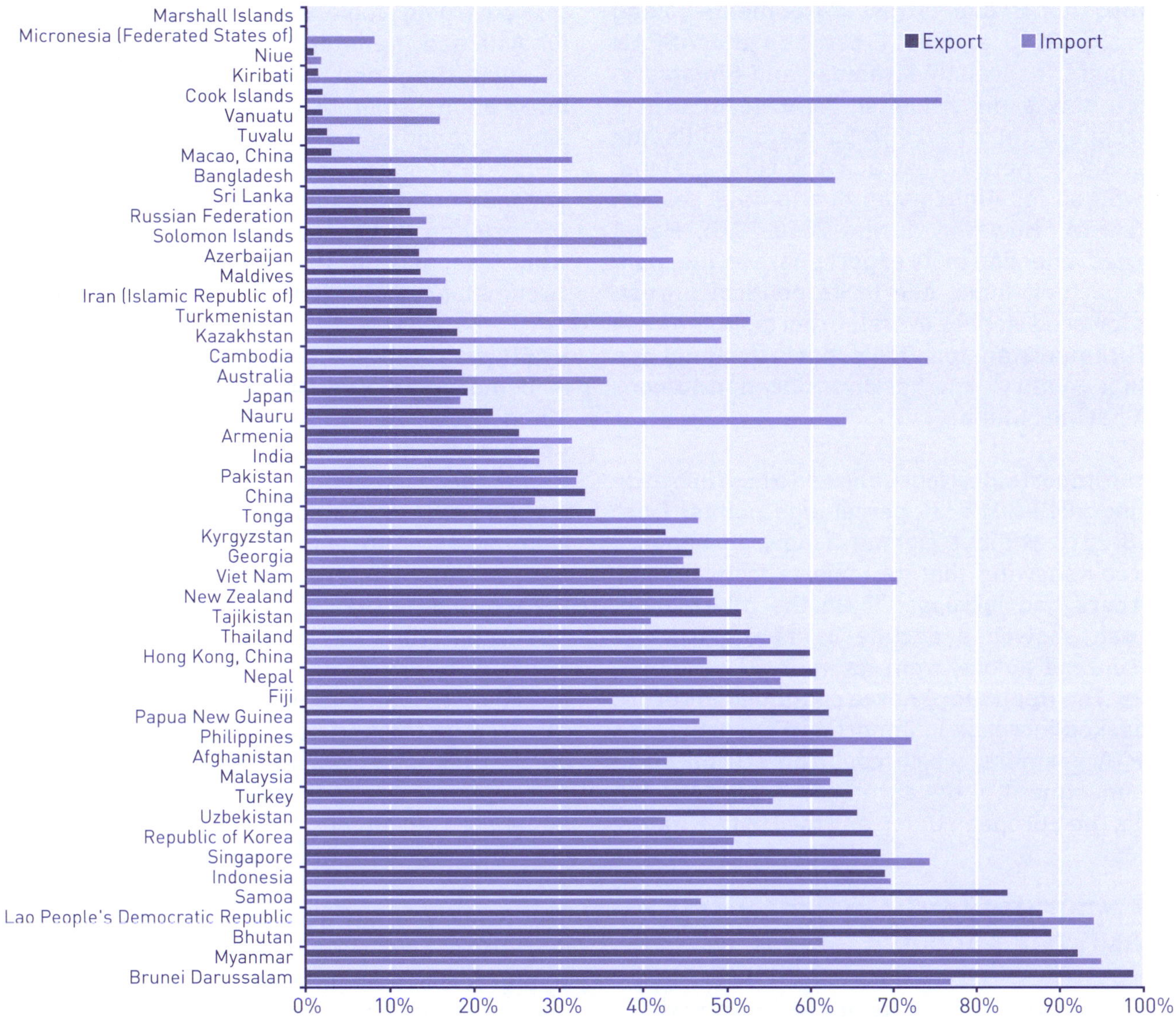

Source: ESCAP calculation, based on United Nations Comtrade data accessed from WITS and APTIAD databases (accessed June 2014).

There is no correlation between the number of PTAs to which a country is a signatory and its share of trade that is attributed to those agreements. For example, the Lao People's Democratic Republic's nine agreements currently in force capture a much larger share of its trade than Singapore's 21 trade agreements. Another example is India, which is a member of the same number of PTAs as Malaysia (14), but which has a significantly lower trade share attributable to its PTA partner countries. Therefore, what is important is identifying how business and economic current and potential linkages are placed, and then trying to deepen those through PTAs. This also explains why many countries continue to depend on trade with non-PTA countries, such as Japan and the United States, Australia and the European Union. It also shows why similar linkages established through global value chains and other business and investment deals will often determine trade flows over and above the directions envisaged under signed PTAs.

Several economies registered much higher shares of trade with PTA partners compared with the previously observed period (ESCAP, 2013). This is due to new agreements taking effect in 2010 and 2011 between the ASEAN members (especially Myanmar and Singapore, which saw a much higher increase in export shares) and their new PTA partners – India, the Republic of Korea, Australia and New Zealand, as well as for Afghanistan due to its accession to SAFTA. However, during 2010-2012, Nepal showed a decline in its export share to the main PTA partner, India, due to its political unrest; this lowered Nepal's overall exports. In the case of Turkmenistan, too, PTA exports declined due to that country's market diversification to non-PTA partner China.

On the import side, Nauru showed a high increase during 2010-2012 (36 percentage points) from 2008-2010 without signing a new agreement, thereby showing that its imports from its PTA partners had increased.[19] On the other hand, Bhutan showed a decline in its imports (15 percentage points) from its main PTA partner, India. The Republic of Korea continued to record a marked increase in import and export values to PTA partners, which could be attributed to the enactment of the agreements with ASEAN, India, the European Union and the United States.

C. EMERGING MEGA-BLOCS IN ASIA AND THE PACIFIC

1. Regional Comprehensive Economic Partnership

> *The RCEP market accounts for around 30% of GDP, 49% of population and 28% of imports globally.*

The Regional Comprehensive Economic Partnership (RCEP) is a logical extension of the East Asia Free Trade Agreement also known as ASEAN+3 and the Comprehensive Economic Partnership in East Asia, known as ASEAN+6 initiatives. The objective of RCEP is to achieve a modern, comprehensive, high-quality and mutually beneficial economic partnership agreement among the ASEAN member States and the main ASEAN's Dialogue Partners. While recognizing the centrality of ASEAN in the emerging regional economic architecture for Asia and the interests of ASEAN's Partners in supporting and contributing to economic integration, equitable economic development and strengthening economic cooperation, RCEP intends to have broader and deeper engagement with significant improvements over the existing ASEAN+1 free trade agreements, while recognizing the individual and diverse circumstances of the participating countries.[20]

RCEP is a comprehensive trade agreement that is being negotiated among 16 countries: the 10 members of ASEAN (Brunei Darussalam, Cambodia, Indonesia, the Lao People's Democratic Republic, Malaysia, Myanmar, the Philippines, Singapore, Thailand and Viet Nam) and the six countries with which ASEAN has existing bilateral free trade agreements (FTAs) under the ASEAN+1 arrangement – Australia, China, India, Japan, the Republic of Korea and New Zealand (figure 6.5). The RCEP negotiations were launched by the leaders of the 16 participating countries on 20 November 2012. Their objective is to achieve a modern, comprehensive, high-quality and mutually-beneficial economic partnership agreement covering a wide range of trade-related issues.

The RCEP market accounts for about 30% of world GDP and 49% of the world's population (table 6.1). If negotiated successfully, RCEP would create the most extensive trading bloc in the world and would have significant implications as an ASEAN-centred regional free trade initiative.

In addition to trade in goods, trade in services and investment comprising its three core areas, the RCEP negotiations encompass other issues including economic and technical cooperation, intellectual property, competition and dispute settlement. Five Rounds of negotiations have been held so far, the latest in Singapore in June 2014.[21] In the Fifth Round, negotiators were able to make progress on the structure and elements, especially with regard to chapter text for the three core areas.

FIGURE 6.5

Current negotiating members in the mega-blocs

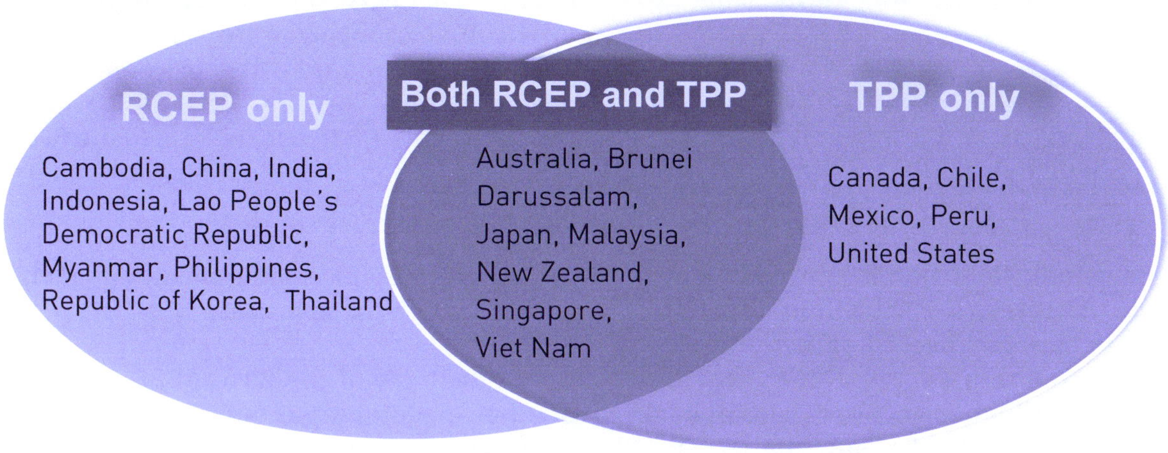

For trade in goods, the key issues that were covered in the negotiations included non-tariff measures, standards, technical regulations and conformity assessment procedures, sanitary and phytosanitary measures, customs procedures and trade facilitation, and rules of origin. For trade in services, negotiators achieved convergence on the main issues, such as the structure and elements of the services chapter and the scheduling of commitments. For investment, progress was made mainly with regard to the approach to scheduling of commitments. The next Round of the RCEP negotiations is to be held in New Delhi, India in December 2014.

As per the information available, India is under heavy pressure to eliminate duties on substantial product coverage. Facing the threat of cheaper goods flooding across its borders, especially from China, India is having to negotiate on lowering its barriers under pressure exerted by other participating States such as Malaysia and Singapore, which have near-zero applied tariff rates.[22] Liberalization of services trade is also a sensitive issue. Although services liberalization is expected to bring huge efficiency gains, the participating countries tend to be more cautious and protective as the services sector involve much domestic concern.

Many new and overlapping economic cooperation arrangements in the Asia-Pacific region are also posing a major challenge to the private sector as well as policy implementers. The "noodle bowl" phenomenon has already reached an alarming

TABLE 6.1

Comparison of the combined economic size, populations and imports of the Regional Comprehensive Economic Partnership and Trans-Pacific Partnership

	GDP (Trillions of dollars; percentage in world)	Population (Millions; percentage in world)	Imports Billions of dollars; percentage in world)
Regional Comprehensive Economic Partnership	21.2 (29.6%)	3 400 (49.0%)	5 070 (27.7%)
Trans-Pacific Partnership	27.6 (38.5%)	790 (11.4%)	5 090 (30.6%)
Memo item: Asia Pacific Trade Agreement[a]	11.4 (15.8%)	2 816 (40.5%)	2 746 (14.8%)

Source: ESCAP calculation, based on IMF World Economic Outlook Database (accessed July 2014).

[a] including six current Participating States and Mongolia.

level in the region, making trade costlier rather than cheaper – thus opposing the basic objective of a PTA – and business difficult for small and medium-sized firms.

It was also pointed out earlier by the ESCAP (2012) that, once it is implemented, RCEP should consolidate all existing ASEAN+1 framework. If, however, the other bilateral and ASEAN+1 agreements remain in force it would add to the complexities rather than easing trade and trade disputes. Consolidation of existing agreements into one overall agreement would allow manufacturers in the RCEP region to cumulate with 15 other countries and enhance opportunities for regional supply chains, rather than undertake trading on a bilateral basis. The ultimate goal should be one integrated Asia; however, this may challenge the central role of ASEAN in the region.

2. Trans-Pacific Partnership

TPP is another comprehensive regional trade agreement currently being negotiated by 12 countries: Australia, Brunei Darussalam, Canada, Chile, Japan, Malaysia, Mexico, New Zealand, Peru, Singapore, the United States and Viet Nam (see figure 6.5).[24] TPP is seen as a vehicle for Pacific Rim-wide economic integration which can lay the foundation for a free trade agreement among the APEC members and promote the multilateralization of existing bilateral and other preferential trade agreements among the members. In 2012, TPP market accounted for more than 38% of world GDP, and more than 11% of the world's population (table 6.1). TPP intends to enhance trade and investment among the partner countries, promote innovation, economic growth and development, and support the creation and retention of jobs. With its vision of serving as a vehicle for Asia-Pacific economic integration, TPP seeks to forge stronger economic links among the economies in the region, based on common rules for trading.

The TPP market accounts for around 39% of GDP, 11% of population and 31% of imports globally.

TPP looks beyond the traditional liberalization of trade in goods and services, and negotiations are being held also on investor-state arbitration, intellectual-property protection, environmental and labour standards, the privileges of state-owned enterprises as well as government-procurement practices. These issues are usually at the discretion of domestic policymakers, and are not commonly tackled in bilateral trade negotiations. The participating countries of TPP, therefore, have had difficulties reaching an agreement on these issues.

On the last day of the 2010 APEC summit, nine of then-negotiating countries endorsed the proposal to set a target for the settlement of the TPP negotiations by the next APEC summit in November 2011. However, negotiations were joined by new parties and have continued into 2014. Several reasons have contributed to the delay, including sharp differences in negotiating positions in areas such as intellectual property rights as well as problems with alleged lack of transparency being sought by various national stakeholders.

Political difficulties, such as that related to the passage of a Trade Promotion Authority by the United States Congress, are also having an impact on the negotiation progress. At their latest meeting in Ottawa (July 2014), the participating countries reached a broad agreement on labour issues, and on sanitary and phytosanitary standards. However, the members still have gaps in issues regarding intellectual property, state-owned enterprises and the environment, while disagreements regarding market access are delaying the bilateral negotiations particularly between the United States and Japan over the automotive and agricultural sectors. For the United States, protecting its tobacco industry has been an important concern, while Japan has been keen to protect its rice sector.[25]

The biggest controversy actually lies in two main issues: a lack of transparency and the intellectual property chapter. The TPP negotiation process is viewed as closed to the public, allowing neither access to the draft texts nor an opportunity for input. TPP is gaining harsh criticisms for its secrecy, especially on parts such as intellectual property rights where public interest is particularly sensitive.[26] As per information available, the draft of TPP intellectual property rights chapter[27] indicates that American negotiators are pushing for (a) the adoption of copyright measures for music and film as well as (b) broader and longer-lasting applicability of patents that would be far more restrictive than currently required by international treaties, including the controversial Anti-Counterfeiting Trade Agreement. The document also shows that TPP would also make the approval process more difficult for generic drug makers and would extend protection for biological medicines, which has concerned several members of the United States Congress.[28]

A question also remains on the entry of China into TPP. In May 2013, the Ministry of Commerce of China announced the country's interest in joining TPP; the United States said that it would welcome China as long as the latter would be willing to respect the terms already being negotiated. The Republic of Korea, another potential member of TPP, made it clear that its bilateral FTA negotiation with China would have priority over its joining TPP. China is also deeply involved in issues regarding rules of origin, as several members of TPP import materials for their domestic products mainly from China. Considering the important role of China as a major trade partner for almost all countries in Asia and the Pacific, some are even questioning the effectiveness of TPP without the membership of China.[29]

CONCLUSION

The proliferation of PTAs still continues, however, it seems that at the time of preparing this report a plateau is being reached, especially from the perspective of the involved Asia-Pacific economies. The jury is still out on determining whether this is due to the positive movement in the WTO Bali Ministerial Conference or the fact that most of the countries have already concluded PTAs with their most important trading partners. However, as it has been observed above that the new engagements in PTAs go beyond the multilateral obligations and include issues such as competition, government procurement and investments – which were dropped from the Doha agenda. Thus, it can be expected that a number of agreements negotiated some time ago might be revisited with a view to deepening their current, relatively shallow liberalization content as well as expanding their coverage. There are already a number of examples of current members repeatedly expanding bilateral commitments (for example, China and Hong Kong, China and Macao, China, respectively; Australia and New Zealand; and the plurilateral agreements moving towards creating economic communities such as the AEC or Euro-Asian Economic Community). The ultimate game appears to be the generation, through the web of a critical mass of PTAs, of a consensus for including these WTO-plus areas in future multilateral agenda, following the building block approach.

The Asia-Pacific region appears to be the driver of PTAs with its 150 agreements, out of a total of 253 global physical trade agreements in force. The focus of the developing Asia-Pacific economies is on other developing economies, thus establishing a foundation for a stronger South-South trade through these PTAs. The economies in the North and Central Asian subregion were the major contributors to Asia-Pacific PTAs in 1990s. However, success in reformulating of some of the arrangements in that subregion into ambitious customs unions, such as the one between Belarus, Kazakhstan and the Russian Federation, and plans to move towards an economic community might re-energize the drive by those countries towards regional integration.[30] However, since the early 2000s South-East Asia, through ASEAN, has played a dynamic role in expanding the web of PTAs. Another feature of Asia-Pacific PTAs relate to its almost even distribution of intra-Asia-Pacific PTAs vis-à-vis outside the region; as 72 agreements out of 150 are with the countries which are outside the region. While through sheer numbers it appears that the agreements in the region are mostly bilateral in nature, it is also through the fact that all but the East and North-East Asian economies are involved in the regional trade initiatives.

The multiplicity of PTAs known as "noodle bowl" is already well-entrenched in the Asia-Pacific region and is an issue that needs to be addressed. It has been found that there is no correlation between the number of PTAs and the share of trade and its expansion under PTAs. Economies with a lesser number of agreements often have are greater share of intra-PTA trade than those that sign a large number of PTAs. It is therefore important that economies start reducing the complexity of negotiated terms and try to consolidate their multiple PTAs, which will ease the terms of trade transactions. A few such efforts in the Asia-Pacific region appear to be happening.[31] APTA is expanding its membership and is looking for providing an open-ended agreement which any developing member State of ESCAP can join. It remains to be seen if the agreement can be also opened to the three developed countries in the region and if, at the same time, it can convert itself to a high-standard free trade agreement. Other agreements that are emerging as strong alternatives are RCEP, which involves 16 economies of Asia-Pacific, and TPP with 12 economies of the Asia and Pacific Rim. It is important to note that there are seven economies opting for both mega-blocs (figure 6.5). It is not certain whether, after the implementation of RCEP and TPP, the ASEAN+1 agreements and other existing agreements (more than 50 in total) will be nullified or not. Only when RCEP and TPP become open-ended agreements and overtake all other bilateral agreements between its members, can a true consolidation be achieved that can truly address the "noodle bowl" problem.

ENDNOTES

1 For example, Mongolia is acceding (ratification is pending) to the Asia-Pacific Trade Agreement (APTA) and is expected to conclude an economic partnership agreement (EPA) with Japan by the end of 2014.

2 The WTO Doha Round negotiations saw some positive movement at the Ninth Ministerial Conference in Bali, Indonesia in December 2013, in terms of decisions on trade facilitation, agriculture and least developed country issues including duty-free quota-free, yet it is premature to conclude that the Doha Round will be completed any time soon and/or that a conclusion of the Doha Round will change the attitude towards PTAs.

3 This number refers only to the so-called "physical" agreements reported on the WTO website as of 14 August 2014 (http://rtais.wto.org/UI/publicsummarytable.aspx). Normally, WTO reports the number of trade agreements based on notification requirements, which means that if a trade agreement includes both goods and services, it will be counted as two notifications – one for goods and the other for services – even though it is physically one trade agreement. To prevent unnecessary inflation of the number of agreements, only the physical number of trade agreements is reported here, counting goods and services between the same partners as one.

4 In addition to the agreements notified to WTO, the Asia-Pacific Trade and Investment Agreements Database (APTIAD) records agreements that have not been notified to WTO, which has resulted in the increased number. The annex to this chapter lists the number of agreements per country.

5 For example, previous issues of the *Asia-Pacific Trade and Investment Report* (ESCAP, 2009, 2010, 2011a, 2011b, 2012a, 2012b and 2013) as well as other publications by the ESCAP Trade and Investment Division, including APTIAD Briefing Notes.

6 Classified as bilateral, plurilateral or bloc-to-bloc agreements.

7 Classified as "in force", "pending country ratification" or "under negotiation".

8 Classified as partial scope agreements (partial tariff reduction commitments), free trade agreements (FTAs), custom unions, economic integration agreements (EIAs) which are reserved only for services in the WTO taxonomy, and (comprehensive) economic partnership agreements (C/EPAs).

9 Under initiatives related to ESCAP's implementation of the Bangkok Resolution on Regional Economic Cooperation and Integration in Asia and the Pacific (see ESCAP document E/ESCAP/70/32).

10 A total of 150 are in force, 7 are pending ratification and 70 are being negotiated.

11 The numbers presented in figure 6.1 are based on the established WTO practice of self-classification by countries with regard to their development level. Following that practice, only three Asia-Pacific economies are "developed" and the remainder are "developing", including the special category of least developed countries, in spite of the fact that a number of them having a high rate of GDP per capita and a not insignificant share in world trade.

12 However, some of the countries from that subregion are involved in negotiating trade and/or investment agreements, such as the already mentioned bilateral free trade agreement between Japan and Mongolia. China, Japan and the Republic of Korea have signed an Agreement for Promotion, Facilitation and Protection of Investment in 2012 (enacted in 2014), and there are increasingly deepening Closer Economic Partnership

Agreements between China on one side and Hong Kong, China, and Macao, China on the other, just a few examples.

13 The Agreement on South Asian Free Trade Area (SAFTA) includes, in addition to Afghanistan, Bhutan and Nepal, Bangladesh and Maldives (which graduated from the least developed country group in 2012); ASEAN includes Cambodia and Myanmar (in addition to the Lao People's Democratic Republic); and the Pacific Island Countries Trade Agreement (PICTA) involves all least developed countries in the Pacific subregion.

14 There are 91 bilateral PTAs between developing countries, 26 between developing-developed, and 3 between developed countries.

15 Despite the official titles given to the agreed texts, WTO members are able to choose only among four different "types" when notifying their agreements. These four types are: free trade agreement and customs union (for goods); economic integration agreements (for services); and partial scope agreements (only for agreements between developing countries).

16 Furthermore three members are participating in another plurilateral free trade agreement known as P-4 (Brunei Darussalam, New Zealand and Singapore) that also includes a non-RCEP member (Chile) and is thus not included in the above number.

17 This is misleading because when EU-15 integration started, intra-bloc trade was already close to 50% (www.unescap.org/resources/asean-and-trade-integration) and intra-EU-15 trade, as a share in total trade, increased only by several percentage points. It was adding the new members to the European Union that really pushed up the share of intra-European Union trade, similar to the case of adding the "plus 6" members to ASEAN.

18 Given that many of these islands do not provide complete data in their exports/imports, these average percentages may be underestimated.

19 Another reason could be non-availability of complete data for 2008-2010, resulting in showing an inflated rise in imports.

20 More details available from www.asean.org/news/asean-statement-communiques/item/regional-comprehensive-economic-partnership-rcep-joint-statement-the-first-meeting-of-trade-negotiating-committee.

21 The Economic Ministers from the 16 RCEP participating countries attended the Second RCEP Ministerial Meeting on 27 August 2014 in Nay Pyi Taw, Myanmar. The Ministers reiterated their commitment to conclude the RCEP negotiations in line with the vision endorsed by the Leaders in the Guiding Principles for a modern, comprehensive, high-quality and mutually-beneficial economic partnership agreement that would support the achievement of the ASEAN Economic Community and deeper regional economic integration (statement taken from www.asean.org/news/asean-statement-communiques/item/the-second-regional-comprehensive-economic-partnership-rcep).

22 See http://thediplomat.com/2013/07/regional-comprehensive-economic-partnership-rcep-issues-and-way-forward/ .

23 Economist Intelligence Unit, 2014.

24 Japan joined last in 2013. China and the Republic of Korea have indicated interest.

25 www.forbes.com/sites/emmawoollacott/2013/12/10/us-fails-to-close-tpp-deal-as-wikileaks-exposes-discord/ .

26 https://www.eff.org/issues/tpp .

27 http://keionline.org/sites/default/files/tpp-10feb2011-us-text-ipr-chapter.pdf .

28 www.nippon.com/en/currents/d00124/ .

29 See http://thediplomat.com/2013/08/tpp-talks-show-promise-for-us-asia-strategy-with-or-without-china/.

30 This process might be complicated in the near future due to political problems in the parts of the subregion that deepened during 2014.

31 The most recent example is the one among those members of the ASEAN-Australia-New Zealand FTA (AANZFTA) that signed the First Protocol to Amend the Agreement Establishing the AANZFTA on 27 August 2014. The Protocol will provide for improved administrative efficiency by customs authorities and encourage enhanced business utilization of AANZFTA.

REFERENCES

Economist Intelligence Unit (2014). FTAs: fantastic, fine or futile? Business views on trade agreements in Asia. Available from https://globalconnections.hsbc.com/hong-kong/en/special-features/fta?utm_source=EIU%20channels&utm_medium=Banner&utm_campaign=FTA.

Economic and Social Commission for Asia and the Pacific (2009). *Asia-Pacific Trade and Investment Report 2009: Trade-led Recovery and Beyond*. Sales No. E.09.II.F.19. Available from www.unescap.org/resources/asia-pacific-trade-and-investment-report-2009-trade-led-recovery-and-beyond .

______ (2010). *Asia-Pacific Trade and Investment Report 2010: Recent Trends and Developments*. Bangkok. Available from www.unescap.org/resources/asia-pacific-trade-and-investment-report-2010-recent-trends-and-developments.

______ (2011a). *Asia-Pacific Trade and Investment Report 2011: Post-crisis Trade and Investment Opportunities*. Sales No. E.11.II.F.8. Available from http://www.unescap.org/resources/asia-pacific-trade-and-investment-report-2011-post-crisis-trade-and-investment .

_____ (2011b). *Statistical Yearbook for Asia and the Pacific 2011*. Sales No. E.11.II.F.1. Available from www.unescap.org/stat/data/syb2011/escap-syb2011.pdf .

_____ (2012a). *Asia-Pacific Trade and Pacific Report 2011: Update March 2012*. Bangkok. Available from www.unescap.org/resources/asia-pacific-trade-and-investment-report-2011-update-march-2012.

_____ (2012b). *Asia-Pacific Trade and Investment Report 2012: Recent Trends and Developments*. Bangkok. Available from http://www.unescap.org/resources/asia-pacific-trade-and-investment-report-2012-recent-trends-and-developments .

_____ (2013). *Asia-Pacific Trade and Investment Report 2013 – Turning the Tide: Towards Inclusive Trade and Investment*. Sales No. E.14.II.F.2 Available from http://www.unescap.org/resources/asia-pacific-trade-and-investment-report-2013-turning-tide-towards-inclusive-trade-and .

Online databases

Economic and Social Commission for Asia and the Pacific. Asia-Pacific Trade and Investment Agreements Database (APTIAD). Available from http://artnet.unescap.org/databases.html#second .

International Monetary Fund. World Economic Outlook Databases. Available from www.imf.org/external/pubs/ft/weo/2014/01/weodata/index.aspx.

United Nations, Statistics Division, Department of Economic and Social Affairs. United Nations Comtrade database. Available from www.comtrade.un.org.

Annex
Number of agreements in force and under negotiations per Asia-Pacific economy[a]

Economy	Total number of agreements	Agreements in force	Agreements under negotiation	Pending country ratification
Afghanistan	3	3	0	0
Armenia	10	9	1	0
Australia	18	9	8	1
Azerbaijan	9	9	0	0
Bangladesh	8	5	3	0
Bhutan	3	2	1	0
Brunei Darussalam	12	8	4	0
Cambodia	9	6	3	0
China	21	12	7	2
Cook Islands	3	2	1	0
Democratic People's Republic of Korea	1	1	0	0
Fiji	4	4	0	0
Georgia	10	9	1	0
Hong Kong, China	3	3	0	0
India	27	14	13	0
Indonesia	18	10	8	0
Iran (Islamic Republic of)	6	5	1	0
Japan	22	13	9	0
Kazakhstan	15	12	3	0
Kiribati	3	2	1	0
Kyrgyzstan	11	10	1	0
Lao People's Democratic Republic	12	9	3	0
Macao, China	1	1	0	0
Malaysia	23	14	8	1
Maldives	2	1	1	0
Marshall Islands	2	1	1	0
Micronesia (Federated States of)	3	2	1	0
Myanmar	10	7	3	0
Nauru	3	2	1	0
Nepal	3	2	1	0
New Zealand	17	10	7	0
Niue	3	2	1	0
Pakistan	19	11	8	0
Palau	1		1	0
Papua New Guinea	6	5	1	0
Philippines	13	9	4	0
Republic of Korea	25	12	11	2
Russian Federation	18	16	2	0
Samoa	3	2	1	0
Singapore	32	22	10	0
Solomon Islands	4	3	1	0
Sri Lanka	8	6	2	0
Tajikistan	10	9	1	0
Thailand	21	11	9	1
Tonga	3	2	1	0
Turkey	25	21	2	2
Turkmenistan	7	6	1	0
Tuvalu	3	2	1	0
Uzbekistan	11	10	1	0
Vanuatu	4	3	1	0
Viet Nam	17	9	8	0
Average	**10.3**	**7.2**	**3.1**	**0.2**

[a] The number of agreements in force and in total includes the Agreement on the Global System of Trade Preferences among Developing Countries (GSTP – a global agreement). American Samoa, French Polynesia, Guam, New Caledonia, Northern Mariana Islands and Timor-Leste do not report any trade agreements. Total number of agreements also includes pending agreements when they exist. Average calculated only for economies with one or more agreements.